THE MAKING OF A WRITER

RANDOM HOUSE

NEW YORK

THE
MAKING
OF A
WRITER

Journals, 1961–1963

GAIL GODWIN

EDITED BY ROB NEUFELD

Published in the United States by Random House,
an imprint of The Random House Publishing Group,
a division of Random House, Inc., New York.

RANDOM HOUSE and colophon are registered
trademarks of Random House, Inc.

Grateful acknowledgment is made to the following for permission to reprint
previously published material:
Hal Leonard Corporation: Excerpt from "Bobby's Girl," words and music by Gary Klein
and Henry Hoffman, copyright © 1962 (renewed 1990) by Emi Blackwood Music, Inc.;
excerpt from "That Was Yesterday" from MILK AND HONEY, music and lyric by
Jerry Herman, copyright © 1961 (renewed) by Jerry Herman. All rights controlled by
Jerryco Music Company, exclusive agent: Edwin H. Morris & Company, a division of
MPL Music Publishing, Inc. All rights reserved. International copyright secured.
Reprinted by permission of Hal Leonard Corporation.
Harcourt, Inc.: Excerpt from "Burnt Norton" from *Four Quartets* by T. S. Eliot, copyright
© 1936 by Harcourt, Inc., and renewed by T. S. Eliot; excerpt from "East Coker" from
Four Quartets by T. S. Eliot, copyright © 1940 by T. S. Eliot and copyright renewed 1968
by Esme Valerie Eliot. Reprinted by permission of Harcourt, Inc.
Tom Lehrer: Excerpt from "I Hold Your Hand In Mine" by Tom Lehrer, copyright
© 1953 by Tom Lehrer. Reprinted by permission of Tom Lehrer.
Harcourt, Inc., and Faber and Faber Limited: Excerpt from "Burnt Norton" from
Four Quartets by T. S. Eliot, copyright © 1936 by Harcourt, Inc., and renewed by
T. S. Eliot; excerpt from "East Coker" from *Four Quartets* by T. S. Eliot, copyright © 1940
by T. S. Eliot and copyright renewed 1968 by Esme Valerie Eliot. Rights outside of the
United States are administered by Faber and Faber Limited. Reprinted by permission of
Harcourt, Inc., and Faber and Faber Limited.

LIBRARY OF CONGRESS CATALOGING-IN-PUBLICATION DATA
Godwin, Gail.
The making of a writer : journals, 1961–1963 /
Gail Godwin ; edited by Rob Neufeld.
p. cm.
Includes index.
ISBN 1-4000-6432-5 (hard)
1. Godwin, Gail—Diaries.   2. Novelists, American—20th century—Diaries.
3. Fiction—Authorship.   I. Neufeld, Rob.   II. Title.
PS3557.O315Z468 2006
813'.54—dc22   2005044929

Printed in the United States of America on acid-free paper

www.atrandom.com

2   4   6   8   9   7   5   3   1

FIRST EDITION

Book design by Gretchen Achilles

To JCO
begetter

PREFACE

$\mathcal{T}$he impetus for this project came as a suggestion in a 2001 letter from a friend and fellow writer, Joyce Carol Oates. "Maybe someday you could edit your journal," she wrote to me, "and present it to the world in the way that Leonard Woolf shaped the wonderful book titled *A Writer's Diary*, an extreme distillation of Virginia's immense journal."

I reread Virginia Woolf's *A Writer's Diary*, which I've owned, in one edition after another, ever since college days. Its immediacy and charm were still fresh for me. Like any apprentice writer, I have been—and continue to be—avid for information about how others became writers, what they tried, what worked, what didn't, what they read, what music they listened to, the people and scenes that served as raw material for later works.

That same year, someone sent me a copy of a new book, Alexandra Johnson's *Leaving a Trace: On Keeping a Journal; The Art of Transforming a Life into Stories* (Little, Brown, 2001). To my surprise and pleasure, I found that the author began her first chapter with an excerpt from my essay "A Diarist on Diaries" (*Antaeus*, Autumn 1988). Quotes from this essay were sprinkled generously throughout the book, and another excerpt was used at the beginning of the final chapter.

Soon after this, I found a Woodstock poet and college teacher of Italian, Jane Toby, who agreed to transcribe the journals. I would go through each handwritten journal and mark in blue ink the passages to be typed. I also abbreviated names or used initials when appropriate. There was no rush; she could do it at her leisure. When Jane and I embarked on this project, I had no immediate plans for publication. But it seemed a sensible idea to have the selections stored away on disks.

The decision to prepare the journals of my apprentice years as a writer (1961–1970) for publication came when Rob Neufeld agreed to work with me to shape these selections into something useful in the field of writers' journals. A professional librarian and a book reviewer for the *Asheville Citizen-Times*, Rob has been reviewing, appreciating, and explicating my work since the mid-1980s. During our conversations for the interviews and questions for the Ballantine Reader's Circle editions of *Evenings at Five* and *The Finishing School*, I realized he was the ideal collaborator for this project, if he would take it on. I sent him some selections from the earlier journals and he e-mailed back:

> *I know with what kind of hunger certain people go to writers' accounts of their development. From your first selection, I can see that you offer a number of things—first, an opportunity to identify with an emerging writer . . . and then there are the life choices, also critical and dramatic ("Must take a gamble in less than twenty days"). There's so much more—commentary on other authors; examples of ways to sketch character portraits; good writing clues; witticisms; concerns about fleeting time, self-traps, and the writing market; insights into themes and motifs in your work; and connections to projects that might bear fruit in various forms in future works.*

This, the first volume of *The Making of a Writer*, contains entries from eleven notebooks dating from August 10, 1961, in Blowing Rock, North Carolina, to July 19, 1963, in London.

Gail Godwin

CONTENTS

THE PREPARATION

Blowing Rock and Asheville, North Carolina;
Washington, D.C.; and New York

AUGUST 12–OCTOBER 4, 1961

On August 8, 1961, with a firm plan very much in mind, a restless twenty-four-year-old Gail Godwin had settled in her dormitory at Mayview Manor, a once-elegant resort in the mountains of western North Carolina. She had taken a job as a waitress at the resort to earn money for the European trip that would inaugurate her creative writing career.

"My room was on the top floor," Gail now recalls, "and my bed looked out into the trees. The night was clear and spicy with wood smells. It was after the dinner shift and I had bathed and was drinking Hennessey eight-year-old cognac."

She took out her eight-by-five-inch "Record Book"—which she has said was her "savings account and safety deposit box"—and wrote in a heartfelt way about her father getting drunk in his little brick house and falling asleep on the sofa. Mose W. Godwin was divorced from Gail's mother, Kathleen, and Gail had spent some time nourishing his sense of hope as he supported her in her first year of college.

The memory would eventually find its best expression in Gail's story "Old Lovegood Girls."[1] Presently, she penned herself some literary encouragement: "Stand by me oh noble holy inspiration. Let . . . me . . . do . . . it."

Gail knew she was standing at one of the great turning points in her life. Studies at the University of North Carolina at Chapel Hill had left her hungry for knowledge and opportunity, and the loss of her job as a reporter at the Miami Herald *had added both fear and fuel to her resolve. During this period, she had also been married to* Herald *photographer Douglas Kennedy and divorced five months later, and she was conscious that she hadn't published anything except for a story in a Chapel Hill literary magazine and her newspaper stories.*

The surest proof of her calling to a writer's life was this persistent

---

1. Reprinted in the 2004 Reader's Circle edition of *Evenings at Five.*

sentiment, expressed on August 20: "I want to be everyone who is great; I want to create everything that has ever been created."[2]

She wished, in addition to encompassing the world, to be one of its masterful explainers. This is the first revelation encountered in her journals: the extent of her aspirations. It characterizes everything she creates. In this light, her books are revealed as attempts to explore, through dialogue and drama, territory both uncharted and vital. Success in such a journey involves negotiating doubts and embracing risks.

The Gail Godwin encountered in 1961 is both urgently confident and relatively inexperienced. She has begun to survey her universe and to accumulate and organize her impressions. Reading is a key experience in this process, for by knowing what she likes and studying what impresses her, she is able to get a picture of what she, in her unique way, wants to fulfill. We join Gail as she is about to embark upon a remarkable journey.

2. Godwin shared this Faustian urge with Thomas Wolfe, with whom she also shared a hometown—Asheville, North Carolina. In an introduction she wrote in 1990 for a Book-of-the-Month Club reissue of Wolfe's *You Can't Go Home Again*, Godwin described her enchantment with his writing and her desire "to capture the whole history of the human heart," as Wolfe had phrased it. It is also worth noting that when Godwin's mother, Kathleen, had worked as a reporter for the *Asheville Citizen-Times* during World War II, she had been dispatched to the dead novelist's home "whenever Mrs. Wolfe called up the paper to announce, 'I have just remembered something else about Tom' " (quoted from "Becoming a Writer," in *The Writer on Her Work*, volume 1 [W. W. Norton, 1980], a collection of essays edited by Janet Sternburg).

AUGUST 12, 1961

MAYVIEW MANOR[3]

Tonight I think I worked physically harder than ever before in my life. Letter from steamship company. Will I really make it to Europe? God, I am going to have trouble sleeping tonight. I will be setting tables all night long. When I left the dining room—limp as a reed, physically exhausted to the point of sheer exhilaration—as soon as the wind cooled my sweat and I had heard a few notes of music from the dance band playing upstairs, I felt free and whole again, completely at ease with myself and confident that I could make it down the hill and just about anywhere else I want to go.

AUGUST 14

Write *Glamour* magazine. Retype "Lazarus"[4] and "I Always Will."[5] Be independent, do your job, be involved in your duty.

Rewrote eleven pages of "Lazarus," existed through two meals, and swam across the pool four times. I have saved $200. I have made about $400. Should be able to get another $200 before September 10 IF I REALLY WORK.

AUGUST 15

The bovines will attend Montaldo's annual fashion show and the models will priss and primp—including [the owner's] niece with the kinky

---

3. Mayview Manor, a 138-room hotel built of native chestnut wood and fieldstone, made Blowing Rock, North Carolina, a mecca for the rich when it was established in 1921. The hotel was closed in 1966 and demolished in 1978.

4. "The Raising of Lazarus," an unpublished story, imagines a turning point in the life of a playboy. Godwin had begun it in 1959. Although it moves overdescriptively toward a safe ending, it exhibits a number of outstanding features, including the detailed imagining of another person's intimate life and the integral inclusion of music in a character's mood and routine. Godwin has appropriated one aspect of Lazarus's story—his management of a Miami hotel—for her new novel, *Queen of the Underworld.*

5. "I Always Will," an early story, no longer survives as a manuscript.

hair and the giggle. I will be clad in dirty pink uniform, running my tail off to get the pretty ladies fed their cold fruit plates in the hot, hot sun. The ice will melt in the tea. Marva will do something asinine. My legs will twitch and my makeup will disintegrate. Little L. the chipmunk[6] will grin out of the window and slouch against the door watching the fashion show, chompingly confident of his right to be there.

Mail "Lazarus" and "I Always Will" to Littauer's.[7] No matter how much you don't feel like it.

AUGUST 20

"Lazarus" could be an epic. I think I shall send it first to *Esquire*. Why not? I have a disease. I am trying to think of a word to describe it. It is that I want to be everybody who is great; I want to create everything that has ever been created. I want to own everything that everybody owns. In short, I have a desire for universal acquisition. Just looking at an issue of *Esquire* arouses a hundred different hungers. I want to have written all the good stories, said all the clever things. I want to buy all the clothes, try all the gourmet suggestions, and travel to all the countries.

As the summer season at Mayview Manor comes to a noisy close, Gail's journal dwells on the contrast between the ideal world of her imagination and the real world of resort society. Gail needed to be in both places—the ideal and the practical—but the call of the former was more seductive. The quality that bridges the two realms is refinement.

Refinement relates to how one engages with society. In this regard, Gail absorbs the advice of B., her friend and serious beau, about reticence and inner strength. Refinement also bears bitingly upon the affectations

6. L. was the young assistant manager at Mayview Manor.

7. Kenneth Littauer, a New York literary agent, in response to a query from Godwin, had said he'd look at her work. Godwin had turned to him after having sent another agent, Lurton Blassingame, a novel that she had adapted from one of her mother's works—only to discover that Blassingame had previously represented the original manuscript for her mother. As it turned out, Godwin never sent Littauer anything.

and habits of the upper class, to which Gail, as a kind of Cinderella, has to cater at Mayview Manor.

In her life, Gail experienced being part of many classes. Her search for refinement sometimes leaves both the barbarians and the bourgeoisie behind.

The last aspect of refinement has to do with art and, namely, Gail's writing. Magically, writing takes the other two types of refinement in hand. In society, Gail was training herself to observe, describe, and ultimately care for anyone and everyone.

Gail had to avoid falling into the observer's trap—dispassion and, in extreme cases, vampirism ("draining" people of their secrets).[8] A writer must find a way to take notes on his or her experiences while remaining a vital participant.

AUGUST 26

The girls are dropping out one by one . . . Seven left . . . We started with thirty-five. As soon as they clear out, their faces and voices fade from my memory as quickly as the little light which dwindles into nothing after you turn the TV off.

B. & I had a talk on reticence. I love the way he talks in outline. He doesn't ramble and he doesn't forget what he was saying.

"Each year I learn to say less and less."

I came back to the room and scrubbed myself clean of all those people. It is good to be exposed to troglodytes and their truisms and their bad manners. It makes one aware of the many layers which must be piled one on top of the other to make a sensitive, self-respecting, and aware individual.

In one of B.'s letters he explained that women can't accomplish security by marrying well and men can't find it by settling down to a steady job.

---

8. At the time, Gail was writing a story titled "Bentley's Girl," which depicted a man named Bentley who drained people of their secrets while passively listening and nodding. His victims referred to him as a "terrific conversationalist."

You get it through a long series of personal accomplishments. For some it is easier than for others. Others have to work harder, and yet the harder workers often outdistance the greatly talented ones, and then one day you realize you're carrying your own security in your own being. "If you can do it once, you can do it again, and so rises the indestructible pyramid."[9]

It is too early to go to sleep (10:30) and there is a full moon and there is music coming from downstairs and flooding the trees outside my window. And tonight is one of those clear, mystic, confident nights when the words flow. The Rachmaninoff Third[10] was coming through from New Orleans as I was driving back from work. I sat in the car and listened and stared at a light and thought, "I will do it, I *will* do it," then this suddenly emerged as "I am doing it." I am there. This summer has been a major achievement in my life. It has been an agony (which started off to mean "contest").

SEPTEMBER 3
SUNDAY

Marya Mannes[11] says to look around a man's apartment to determine what he is.

> *If he has* Exodus & Advise & Consent *on his shelves,* Reader's Digest *on his coffee table, the usual ducks flying over the marsh at dawn on his wall, and Andre Kostelanetz in his album stack, you are going to hit bottom pretty quick.*

On my many unaccompanied prowls around B.'s lair, I have found that he lives for comfort, for B., and does not surround himself with ar-

---

9. B.'s phrase "the indestructible pyramid" became such a key one in Godwin's concept of independence and of a patient accumulation of experience and confidence that she used it as the conclusion of her first complete novel "Gull Key" (unpublished).

10. Sergey Rachmaninoff's Piano Concerto no. 3 has a Romantic, Peer Gynt kind of melody that, in Rachmaninoff's hands, ends up sounding like a brave voice in a raging storm.

11. Marya Mannes, whose 1958 book *More in Anger* electrified the country with its satire, was a helpful guide. Mannes shared Godwin's tendency to replace abstract character traits with the habits and possessions of individuals, judiciously observed.

ticles he does not use just because he thinks he ought to have them. His living room—good solid, heavy furniture, a magnificent desk, uncluttered and organized, a large color photograph of some beautiful golf course in California, pipes with leather bowls, white crème de menthe, vodka, Johnnie Walker. Milk, cheese, and month-old chicken salad in the refrigerator. Well-supplied kitchen. On his reading table (by his bed, not in the living room where everyone can see what he is reading):

the latest *Sports Illustrated*

Golf Is My Game

Goren's point count

The Rise and Fall, etc. (which he is reading—"It makes me realize how uneducated I am compared to Shirer and Adolf.")

Justine (which a girl gave him to read and he has not touched it yet)

the August issue of the *North Carolina Diaries of Supreme Court Cases*

He has no clock and wakes at will every morning at eight, cooks his own breakfast, goes leisurely uptown to work.

In his closet are several very respectably used sports jackets of tweed & corduroy (he has nothing ostentatiously new), a thick gray cardigan, a slew of good suits—tweed, Oxford gray, navy, etc. And, of course, his white navy shoes with the oil from the decks of the *Coral Sea* still on the soles.

And the three-foot shoehorn ("If a man bends down every day to put his shoes on, he is more likely to have a heart attack").

And . . . his duck clothes brush.

SEPTEMBER 5

Anyone reading this would think I had absolutely nothing to do besides be by this window and read and sleep and think and write in this book.

Well, they would be right. I have never before had this much privacy coupled with security. For the next five days I have absolutely no worries. I have enough money, I am young, healthier than I have ever been in my entire life (I can tell from the way my blood throbs in my face), and I feel excellent when I wake up, I am clean inside and out. And tonight I stood outside on the de-awninged terrace and watched the after-rain clouds snuggle down between the ranges and thanked God for just letting me live. People like me, with antennae, sensitive, alert, and forever feeling, feeling—if they get through a certain period of life (thirteen to twenty-three) when everything hurts, then they embark upon a strange, magnificent epoch when everything is enjoyed—even pain.

And I must think of last September, about this time. How far I was from here! In spirit, in confidence, in every way, I came back from that navy reconnaissance flight into Donna.[12] I was worn and haggard and dry mouthed and gritty eyed.

GAIL ON GETTING FIRED

During my months in Miami, from June through September of 1959, I was the bright young journalist-in-training. Even after I was sent to the *Miami Herald* office in Hollywood, Florida, *Herald* assistant managing editor Al Neuharth, who later in his career founded *USA TODAY*, phoned me one day to say, "You're turning into a real newspaper gal. I hope your relationship with us continues for a long time."

A few months later, I was "promoted" to the *Herald*'s Fort Lauderdale office. The bureau chief, Keith, told me I had a flair for leads.

One of my masterpieces was: "A pair of flaming

---

12. On September 7, 1960, Godwin went out with the U.S. Navy's Hurricane Hunter Squadron to study Hurricane Donna, a landmark weather event with gusts of up to 175 mph. The next day, her article, "I Looked Donna in the Eye—She's Tough," was the top story on the front page of the *Miami Herald*.

undershorts saved the life of Richard Dolan, who was lost in the Everglades for three days and three nights." But as time went on, I pleased Keith and his assistant, the Broward women's page editor, less and less. They certainly had their justifications. I let my boredom show. There wasn't enough to do. After I had completed my one or two assignments for the day, I actually took frequent trips to the hairdresser down the block, and came back freshly coiffed, and even with different shades of hair. I acted out the role of the flighty starlet who was headed back to Miami as soon as her trial period in the bureaus was over.

The following spring, Neuharth sent me and a few others from the Miami office to start the Pompano office. This was a heady time. We were all young and ambitious, and we had lovely expense accounts. We had a hand in every aspect of newspaper production, including page makeup, and still had energy left over for late-night drinking and midnight ocean swims.

Then in June I was returned to Fort Lauderdale. I didn't know it, but this was my last chance. If Keith gave the okay, I could stay in the Broward bureau. One day in August of 1960, I found Keith's note in my typewriter.

I have spent more time working and worrying over your future than I have spent on the entire rest of the staff combined. I must confess I've been a failure. I apologize for my mistakes. But the fact remains that I cannot see any further benefit from my efforts or yours and I am convinced it would be to your benefit to find someplace to "start over." This has been harsher than I intended it to be. I really feel badly that I have failed to make a good reporter out of obviously promising material. I hope you can use this experience somewhere but I'm afraid you won't do it successfully until you look facts in the face and at the same time quit expecting to get to the moon in one day.

KLB

After Keith told Miami that he had given up on me, the powers there called me back to Miami to fill in for several people who were on vacation. My goose was cooked, but somehow I managed to withhold this knowledge from myself. I was going to show them!

I performed brilliantly during that respite period back in Miami, sometimes having six bylines a day. They sent me into Hurricane Donna with the Navy. My story had the banner headline and a photo of me. "This has been a real Gail Godwin day," said Marie Anderson, the Miami women's editor, passing me in the hall.

Several days later, Neuharth called me into a meeting in the boardroom with a few other solemn editors and said they were going to "help me find another job." Neuharth said the deciding factor had been my impatience to come back to Miami when others, more seasoned, had been waiting their turn for years. He said, naming a worthy bureau person in Fort Lauderdale, "Why, X wakes up every morning praying this will be the day he's called back to Miami."

Though Neuharth suggested I might try writing fiction, he said he was not suggesting I switch careers: he was going to help me find another newspaper job and give me good references. But I went to pieces and the gents left me in the boardroom, weeping in my upright chair. Neuharth had tucked the envelope with my generous severance pay under my thigh since I had refused to take it from his hand.

SEPTEMBER 6

Drove to the Ranch House Restaurant (across a little bridge, pine paneled, pine tables, Swiss-looking curtains, voluptuous marigolds bursting from tiny glass vases, a look of regimented pomp). Had breakfast with poor W, who insisted on coming along. He is so sad. Prefaces every remark with "I'm the type of person that"—and I'm the type of person that can't stand that. Bought Errol Flynn's *My Wicked, Wicked Ways*,[13] which I shall read in the dining room. The Doctors come tomorrow night: dinner/breakfast/lunch/dinner/breakfast/lunch/dinner/breakfast. Eight meals—and then freedom.

And the boys downstairs have Nina Simone[14] crooning away in her husky, equatorial passion. This screen is patched and rusty, my linen is dirty because Mrs. Young[15] won't give us any more now. But where else can I lie almost ON TOP of the trees and look to a future, enjoy the past, and relish the present?

A hot bath in L'Heure Bleu,[16] a half-quart of Budweiser, and *voici moi* under the blue blanket out of it again.

Saint Genevieve's[17] in the midafternoon, sitting by a window in the early spring, trying to do algebra, listening instead to Mozart by some advanced piano student on the third floor—the student pausing to think—then fingers rippling again over the keyboard.

Sitting in Howard Johnson's on the hill between Durham & Chapel Hill, watching the cars, talking—talking with Bill Hamilton, Martin, Uncle Wm, Ronnie, Shelley.[18]

Walking across campus that last year, knowing it was my last, savor-

13. Flynn's autobiography, released soon after his death in 1959, had stirred up controversy because of its blurring of fable and fact, objectionable portraits, and candidness about the author's convictions and obsessions.

14. The African-American pianist and jazz singer grew up poor in Tryon, North Carolina, about thirty miles from Asheville.

15. Mrs. Young, housemother to waiters and waitresses in Gail's dorm, "monitored our linens and our morals," Gail says.

16. Jacques Guerlain created the fragrance L'Heure Bleu (the name means "the blue hour") in 1912.

17. In 1908, a French order of nuns known as the Religious of Christian Education established St. Genevieve-of-the-Pines, a Catholic private school with a nondenominational educational mission, in Asheville. Gail Godwin attended from the second grade through the ninth.

18. Gail's recollection of her Chapel Hill confidants includes Bill Hamilton, an admired friend; Ronnie, a "playmate," who boarded Gail's boxer when the dog had been kicked out of Gail's dorm; Shelley, a doctor, with whom Gail had had a stormy relationship (for a fictional treatment, see "The Angry Year," in *Mr. Bedford and the Muses*); Martin, a Miami Beach hotel director and a mentor; and Uncle William, Gail's father's older brother, a Selma, North Carolina, judge who had looked after her following her father's suicide in 1958.

ing every minute of it. Looking out of the *Tar Heel*[19] office windows
from the vantage point of F.'s lap. What kept us writing each other so
faithfully all these months, '59, '60, '61? I never loved him. But I lent
him money, took him to dinner, bought him books, called him, mailed
him letters, did his errands. I think he is the example in my life of true
friendship. I never betrayed him (even when the CIA man came to Key
Biscayne and asked me what I knew) and he would never betray me. I
remember when he and I drove to Durham in the rain to see Hemingway's *A Farewell to Arms*. He had a Coke and popcorn and he conde-
scended to let me hold on to his thickly sweatered arm.

Tonight Sande & I formed a "team" to wait on the internal mediciners
(most people are so uncouth—it looks as if doctors could honor their
title by wearing coats and ties to dinner, by being polite to their wives
and to the waitress, and eat their soup correctly, tipping the spoon away
from them). I don't think I would marry a doctor. All they know is
the science they practice. I think I would prefer a lawyer, a writer (a
good one), a newspaperman (in an executive position), or a competent,
serious-minded playboy who just played well.

SEPTEMBER 7

10:30 P.M.

Fatigue is the very opposite of buoyancy. When I am in a state of
fatigue, everything about me wants to go down instead of up. It is a
sinking, dull, heavy, gray-black, dirty ache. It makes me do things hap-
hazardly, dangerously, cutting corners, surly and undeliberate. It wipes
out all other thoughts: sex, art, ambition, love, hate.

Tonight—I have the worst case of fatigue I have ever experienced
in my life.

This afternoon there was a note in my car. (They always get so attentive right at the end, like Bill H. handing me my diploma at Chapel
Hill and kissing me.) I followed the directions of the note and went to

19. The *Daily Tar Heel* was and is the official newspaper of the University of North
Carolina.

his family's chalet and took a shower with some of his mother's spice soap.[20] Then we sat on the porch watching the golfers below us zigzagging around in their electric carts. He read the financial section of the *New York Times* and told me about some bad stocks he'd bought. Then we read the sailing dates together and licked our chops over names like *Leonardo da Vinci*,[21] Tangiers, Honduras, Marseilles, Macao, Gibraltar, Napoli, Brazil, Alexandria, Antwerp. He told me about the little Italian man who invented the double-entry bookkeeping method while he was auditing the books for the building of a new cathedral. I ate honeydew melon and curled my toes in his lap, and decided it would be a long time before I got this close to such pure, healthy handsomeness again. Later, I sat alone in my "sidewalk café,"[22] drinking muddy coffee, eating a greasy hamburger, watching the clock, and playing "Raindrops" and "I Apologize" on the jukebox over and over again.

"I just might come to Asheville to see you," he said. And then: "Let's make a clean pact. No tears, okay?"

"You're just saying that to make sure you say it first and to hide your own feelings," I said.

"I have to keep one step ahead of you," he said.

He's not ripe yet, but he's all right.

God, I am so tired.

SEPTEMBER 11

ASHEVILLE, NORTH CAROLINA

The summer cares are over and I am setting about preparing for a trip—happy occupation! Tonight: Ask B. if I can spend a whole day

20. "He" was "L.," the young assistant manager at Mayview Manor ("the chipmunk"— see August 15). Gail had spurned him at first because he was four years her junior and rich. "He went home every night to his family's chalet," Gail recalls, "while the other young employees had to put up with the limited amenities of the dorm." But he persisted, and at the end of the summer she began to "appreciate his fresh good looks, his hunger to take his place in the big world," and his intensive campaign to win her approval.

21. The Italian ocean liner *Leonardo da Vinci* was put into service in 1960 as a replacement for the *Andrea Doria*, sunk in 1956. Financially unsuccessful, the *Leonardo* was removed from service in 1978 and destroyed by fire in 1980.

22. Gail is referring to a coffee shop in downtown Blowing Rock, where she often had a snack before going on evening duty at Mayview Manor.

writing at his house. Want to finish "Halcyone and the Lighthouse,"[23] "Lazarus" & "I Always Will." I think I could do it in one or two complete days.

Bought a fine book, Malcolm Lowry, *Hear Us O Lord from Heaven Thy Dwelling Place*.[24] Fantastic, multileveled feel of life conveyed. I am now reading about the sea voyage from Canada around the Gulf of Mexico to Rotterdam.

The margins are filled with passages from the "Ancient Mariner."

I want to go to St. Genevieve's and talk to Mother Winters[25] before long.

SEPTEMBER 13

There is no place—absolutely no place—like Asheville in the fall. Even the expressway isn't so bad. It affords visions one could see no other way. And the white chunks of houses nudging against the pockets of the mountains. And the country women stepping out of trucks in front of the *Citizen-Times,* their weathered faces hopeful, this week's "Coinword" entry clutched in their pocketbook hand. And Mosleys is still on College Street. And I love it all. The people are kind of a humorous appendage. Not all the people. Just the silly country-club set and the asses I grew up with.

Now, this afternoon—the essence. And I escaped again. What I am trying to say is that there are two poles warring inside: the one when I sit in libraries on sunny afternoons and read about people like Salinger[26] and wish . . . the other when I am inside of someone I love just for a minute and would sell the libraries of the world not to go outside again.

. . .

23. Godwin's "Halcyone" story had been inspired by a shipping incident that she had covered as a *Miami Herald* reporter. It came to encompass her interest in a sea captain and her soon-to-come transatlantic crossing.

24. *Hear Us O Lord from Heaven Thy Dwelling Place*, published in 1961 after Lowry's death, is a collection of his stories. It includes "Through the Panama," in which a writer voyages to Europe on a freighter, bearing the albatross of literary self-consciousness. *Under the Volcano* is Lowry's most celebrated work.

25. Sister Kathleen Winters, or Mother Winters, from Ireland, served as principal of the grammar school at St. Genevieve's, which Godwin attended from 1944 through 1952.

26. Gail had just bought and read *Franny and Zooey*, J. D. Salinger's novel about alienation from and compassion toward human society.

As noted by the above passages, I got out of hand and bought another book. Read in *Fielding's* about politeness in Denmark. Never never refuse a *skål*,[27] even though your belly bursts, and keep your eyes riveted.

And when you meet someone on the street you have spent previous time with you say, first of all, not "Hello" but "Thank you for the wonderful time we had together the last time I saw you."

SEPTEMBER 23

Night before last, when I chose between leaving my family and losing my sanity, I went uptown and parked down in front of the courthouse under a tree in the park. I watched the policemen's "changing of the guard" (riding off two by two in squatty little green & white patrol cars, looking ever so self-satisfied). And listened, smelled, and watched the sounds of Asheville as I had never done before. What struck me was the peculiar charm of the clash of architectural types and periods. The Jackson Building, with its elongated spire, reminding one of a king's crown seen in a mirror which distorts things so they look long and thin; the pink & bronze city hall; the gray ugly courthouse whose lighted barred windows, where human forms sway during the night, fascinated me as a child; the dirty little buildings where the bondsmen collect their money with smug, red faces; the squarish-jutting irregularity of Pack Square; the *click-click* (hollow sound) of billiard balls from an upstairs window painted green; the ex-bakery which now sells cheap clothing; Finkelstein's pawnshop, almost turned respectable with the accumulation of years; the Library, which saved my life in May.[28]

SEPTEMBER 25

Now Calmness. Confidence. Tomorrow will be an interesting day. Anyway, tomorrow morning I get all dolled up and drive to the airport, and

27. *Skål*, or "skoal," is a Scandinavian drinking greeting—a toast—and is derived from the Old Norse word for "bowl."

28. In the stagnant period in her life, between her divorce and her Mayview Manor stint, Gail took refuge in Pack Memorial Library, then located in an old, Renaissance-style building on Asheville's historic square. "I haunted the library," Gail says, "read all the magazines, took out the maximum of books, prowled the ill-lit shelves."

when Voit Gilmore[29] steps off the plane, *no matter how many ominous-looking people are waiting*, I will approach him first and say: "Mr. Gilmore? Welcome to Asheville."

Acceptable topics:

The *SR*[30] article on him.

How excited everyone is over the new U.S. Travel Service.

Home of Miss America.[31]

Know something about the Forestry Celebration Act. Weeks Act.[32]

Let him know that if there is nothing open in Europe, I would love to work in Washington.

Traveled a lot.

And my *Miami Herald* clippings will just happen to be resting expectantly in the Bank of Asheville briefcase in the back seat.

OCTOBER 2

WASHINGTON, D.C.

Aside from my constant companion (the headache in my left temple), I feel perfect and am lying here after a hot bath uncoiling. I guess the thing that makes me happiest about the entire morning is that I got through an ordeal all on my own and got past the personnel office on my own steam. Besides that, I have an assignment for the *Post*. I was actually asked to write something—a profile on Bill Blair's new wife. I can use Voit Gilmore's name to get in there: "Tell them you know me, and tell them you are going to be with the Travel Service." (He looked tired today.)

29. Voit Gilmore, a Winston-Salem native and Chapel Hill graduate, was appointed by President John F. Kennedy to head the U.S. Travel Service in 1961. Gail was hoping to be hired by him.

30. *Saturday Review.*

31. Maria Beale Fletcher of Asheville had just been selected as Miss America 1962.

32. The U.S. Forest Service celebrated the fiftieth anniversary of the Weeks Law in 1961. The Weeks Law enabled the government to purchase land for national forests.

OCTOBER 3

NEW YORK CITY

Bev Miller—who will head the Travel Service in London, I liked very much. Big, straightforward, no pretense, just a man with a good grip on things, none of this "nifty" business. I went up to a new office still in the process of being constructed. He was very cordial to me and I must say that I was struck by the naturalness of his approach. He was the first one to detail this business for me, instead of making it sound like a fairy tale. I told him what he could expect from me; he told me what I could expect from the Travel Service. He asked me about my job at the *Herald*, my public-speaking ability (said my Southern accent would be an "attraction," which he liked), my capacity for dealing with people, working with women, researching; he asked me how long I wanted to stay in Europe, where in the U.S. I had been, if I had any money of my own, if I thought I could make it on the small pay. This point, he stressed, was what concerned him most.

Frankly, what I see in this is a job with a future. I can even see myself as a young executive. I have grown up ten years in the last year. I can tell the difference in the way I react during stress. Oh yes, he said he didn't want any brash young teenagers in a conservative place like Britain. I don't blame him. So anyway, I am going to get in touch with him "by November tenth at latest."

"Well, it looks to me that you have the qualifications and we might work something out," he said.

The train ride early in the day, bumbling around Penn Station in the rain, getting bled by porters, having all these calamities, all of this, was worth this timely meeting with him. I think these men realize that I have not failed once to be at the right place at the right time. Gilmore at the airport, at his office between interviews, meeting Bev Miller just before he went to meet Gilmore. I think I have passed the entrance exam; now we must wait and see. There is no use to get frantic. And so I'm not going to.

Had dinner with a lady lawyer who is also a lieutenant colonel in the Army. Tried to commission me on the spot. But at least I didn't eat alone and pick up a man or something.

Bought volume 1 of Kierkegaard's *Either/Or*[33]—a Danish philosopher and something to bury myself in until Friday when my ship sails (I hope).

Also—visit the consul of Denmark.

OCTOBER 4

Alone, alone in a large large city. Tried my new "life on $5 a day"—breakfast: coffee and danish, 40¢—then felt so proud of myself I went into Macy's and bought a lipstick which cost $3.11. "Cellular Bronze." What I dislike most about NYC is its *nasal* sound.

I have discovered that courtesy goes far anywhere, *especially* with waiters, policemen, agents, desk clerks, etc. A sympathetic smile saying "I just know what you're having to put up with and I certainly don't want to inconvenience you any more than necessary." A nice little hairdresser from Barcelona who grew up with Garcia Lorca did my hair and gave me some addresses. Tonight I go out with Stu's cousin. Just hope he's suitable and not one of these "bright young men" with tight tight pants who smirk at the universe. If he's just as nice as McKee,[34] it'll be fine. Just the fact that I'll be having dinner with someone is fine, and if I don't like him, I can just come home early. God, have I changed since June 1959, when I last embarked on a strange new experience.[35]

---

33. *Either/Or*, one of the truly readable great works of philosophy in Western literature, speaks directly to Godwin. Wanting to depict how the person who commits himself to making honest choices achieves a kind of freedom and happiness that the intellectual and the pleasure seeker can only graze, Søren Kierkegaard invents memorable, representative characters. A few of them anticipate kindred souls in Godwin's fiction: the seducer, for whom every girl is woman in general; the despairer, who either learns to cherish himself or gives up; and the good husband, who performs acts of love every day, sometimes through simple tasks, which, nonetheless, assume great significance in context.

34. McKee was Voit Gilmore's assistant director in the U.S. Travel Service. Gail enjoyed her dinner with him on her last night in D.C.

35. Godwin, having graduated from UNC Chapel Hill in June 1959, boarded a train and embarked on her *Miami Herald* adventure. Bruised, over the next two years, by breakups in marriage and career, she came around to summoning a second confidence-charged leap of faith, one that also involved booking passage.

TAKING LEAVE

Aboard SS Oklahoma,

Hoboken, New Jersey, to Copenhagen, Denmark

OCTOBER 6–30, 1961

Aboard the SS Oklahoma, *Gail launches the first major character of her newly christened career: Halcyone Harper, whose ocean passage follows by one year her breakup with a sea captain. The tale combines unabashed romance with a deft handling of the theme of land- and sea-consciousness.*

The sky was black and I worshiped romance and wanted you to kiss me.

In such a manner, Gail Godwin, writing in her journal on October 9, addresses Captain C., the American sea captain whom she'd once loved. Whereas she will yield to romance on occasion throughout her trip, she dedicates herself to writing about it and to discovering what shape its story might take.

By invoking Captain C., she prepares herself to enter the mind of her protagonist, and thus compose her story. "What I need to do is just start— and not mind the ending," she tells herself. "The beginning—the way it really happened—will prophesy the end."

On her fourth day aboard the ship, Gail went to work, inspired by a remembered kiss. Half an hour later, she had profited several pages of writing by her frenzy. She then stopped to give herself advice: "Leave out parts which you found boring, don't worry about other stories and how they are written. The idea is here."

A story dictates its own design. A writer can know the design in advance without knowing the ending.

Speaking about her sixth novel, The Finishing School, *for instance, Gail has said that she had known that the teenage protagonist, Justin, was going to be the agent of another character's death, but she didn't know until the end which character would die and she didn't know how Justin would cause the event. Working out the plot is a process of discovery.*

In 1961, writing about romance, Gail was coming to terms with a num-

ber of animating spirits in her life. Her mother, Kathleen Cole, was a writer of romances, whose literary and professional career had not been granted full flowering. Also, young Gail imagined that a man's love might carry her to a heightened sense of being.

Gail Godwin has said: "In my earlier books, I was working out how independent women can be independent and still manage to love and be loved. The Odd Woman, Glass People, The Perfectionists. That was my initial concern. I've solved it to my satisfaction."

As her Halcyone story develops, Gail's diary reveals a young writer learning to navigate the fictional universe. She depends upon her instincts for drama and honest self-appraisal.

And Richard Cory, one calm summer night,
Went home and put a bullet through his head.[1]

OCTOBER 6, 1961

2:00 P.M.

One of the biggest mysteries is the vast difference between how we imagine something and how it really is. The way I had imagined it is already fading away and the reality replacing it. I thought only in terms of generalities and fanciful swatches from novels and secondhand experiences. Not until I stood on deck watching the stevedores going on with their loading, seeing the cables moving up and down and studying a large red hose turned on full force washing the boards on which I stood did I really claim the new experience for my own. What a way to be thrown out into the world! And I fancied myself a cosmopolitan. Now I can't even read the sign on my own door:

PASSAGERERNE FRA DETTE KAMMER

HØRER VED BAADMAN ØVRE

TIL REDNINGSBAAD NR. 2.

And outside some people are managing to have fun. There are more Danish passengers than American ones. The only ones anywhere near my age are a young eccentric couple named Walsh, both twenty-three, who have separate cabins. One Danish man smiled at me and I was indescribably grateful. The stewardess has lines on her forehead and when

---

1. Godwin begins Part 2 with an inscription that connects to her father, who—like Richard Cory, the subject of Edwin Arlington Robinson's poem—had been a dreamer and a suicide. Robinson, too, had seen himself as a failed dreamer, despite having won three Pulitzer Prizes. He shunned fame and wrote out of a need to express the conflict between his ideals and his perceptions. "This itch for authorship," he once confessed, "is worse than the devil and spoils a man for anything else."

I asked her what to do for the next five hours she looked very dense and asked, "You vant a drink? A drink?" The steward is blond. My only friend was a stevedore who I wouldn't have spoken to on shore. He just mailed a letter for me. Loneliness attracts and welcomes strange company. I have inspected the lounge and the map to København (might as well get in the swing here). The lounge has a price list (*prisliste*) of wines, whiskeys, Cherry Heering & kajafa, and chocolate, two packs of playing cards, and several records—Dylan Thomas's *Under Milk Wood,* a popular German singer, and lots of Danish stuff.

I am happy with my room—large, sunny (three portholes), modern sofa & chair (Danish modern, of course) in navy and turquoise, a chest of drawers, a coffee table & bunk in matching wood. The sheets are coarse & the toilet paper very much resembles post office wrapping paper. I looked on my bathroom door and in a little slot was written "Fri." How nice, I thought, they let you keep track of what day it is. But then I turned the latch and another word appeared in red: "Optage." I think that means "occupied." Thus *fri* doesn't mean "Friday" at all. It means "free." I am *FRI.*

The couple in the next cabin invited me in for champagne. They are restaurant people going around the world on Arthur Frommer & Norman Ford.

Thoughts that occur while leaving port:

If it is true that the more you share with someone else, the greater your variety of experiences together, the closer you become, then doesn't it follow that if you do many things alone, you should like yourself better?

Every person must find his own tune in the beat of the engine. For one it may be "Frère Jacques," for another "Co-ben-havn, Co-ben-havn," for another the "Mexican Hat Dance." For me it is the two-beat, iambic pentameter:

TO STRIVE

TO SEEK

TO FIND

AND NOT

TO YIELD[2]

Oh, those lights, those beacons, those strings of watt-pearls. The black ocean beckons and I remember Pompano and A. and Captain C. standing on the bridge giving orders through a megaphone. This captain wears a dark uniform with braid and stars, but then he couldn't possibly have the legs Captain C. did when he put on those Indian sandals and khaki shorts.

Fifteen knots, forty thousand tons into the night. With Captain Johanson at the helm, the sad frantic world behind us, and before us . . .

OCTOBER 7

What is the engine saying this morning as I sit here on the brown bench reflecting over the calm nine o'clock sea, feeling the wind, wondering. The engine song is a very soothing sound. It has all the virtues of people we like to know. It is constant—whether we wake at three in the morning or at four, whether we simply come outside blinking the next morning, it is always there. It is multilingual. Every nationality can find his song in the heartbeat of the vessel on which he travels. It is definitely masculine. I wonder if men think so?

How very calm the sea is. Hazy in the distance. We are traveling with the sun. Is the Director out there too? Surely of all the places he made, the sea must be his secret favorite.

This atmosphere is excellent for authors. If one can't write now, one never will. Must have a schedule. Wonder if the stewardess has a typewriter I might borrow.

Two of the older passengers have laid out their deck chairs with the cobalt & white striped pads. They are bundling down with blankets and snuggling up to the sea.

One passenger (the port manager from Copenhagen) fell asleep in

2. These words form the last line of Alfred, Lord Tennyson's poem "Ulysses," about the legendary sea voyager.

his deck chair while reading. He lay peacefully for about an hour, breathing evenly, his face turning pink from the sun. Then his wife tip-toed over and covered him up to his chin with a heavy red blanket. She did it with such a tender loving gesture, but he awoke at once.

Finished Kierkegaard's "Diary of a Seducer." It should be required reading for all girls before they reach their eighteenth year. If I have a daughter, which seems unlikely now, I will make her read every sentence and memorize the ending.

Sleeping and dredging up dreams. After a lunch of salmon, spiced herring, herring in wine, smoked eel with jellied eggs, sardines in oil accompanied by "snaps" (a liqueur with a licorice taste that makes your stomach come alive and burns your tongue) and Carlsberg beer, followed by salami, liver paste, meatballs, and a salad sort of thing creamy with corn & peas, followed by hot potato salad & frankfurter followed by cheese & crackers followed by (I had thrown in the towel long before now) tea & coffee.

Remind me after dinner to do a sketch of W.s,[3] the restaurant people, at table. Maybe then I will have something more to add.

The gong! My God. Time to eat again! *This* hasn't even digested yet.

"Danish is a hard language," explained Esther, "because we eat half our words." She sold yard goods in Akron, Ohio. Now she goes home to Copenhagen to sell yard goods. This is an interesting woman. She has been beautiful and loved. Yet she wears no ring. She has the middle-age grace of Bergman and Signoret. What is the story here? I can get it, but I must be careful and proceed slowly.

The Walshes, from Ann Arbor, Michigan. He is working on his math doctorate and will study a year in Germany under his math professor. They have been married two years. He is the typical lean and hungry

---

3. The restaurant people—the W.s—are to be distinguished from the young couple the Walshes, whose name is spelled out.

student with myopia, and holes in the elbows of his sweater. We four, Esther, I & the Walshes, sat around after dinner in the lounge & drank coffee (how bitter Danish coffee is) and Cherry Heering[4] (after I found out that 1.15 per glass meant only 15¢ of my money). But Esther warned not to go overboard on this attitude.

"My God! Is that all? I think I'll have some more."

Mrs. W. did not come to dinner. I think she is sick. I get embarrassed when she bills and coos at the table. "Oh! I just love this Danish food! Oh, aren't you Danes wonderful! Y'know, this is just like *Fielding's* said it would be!" Mr. W. talks fast and in his throat and is real nice to everybody and kept eating his venison while the whole table was waiting to *skål* with Esther's wine. The only time you must drain your glass is when you drink to the King.

Tomorrow I must write. I think the best place is on deck—if it's not too cold. Oh, this is a marvelous tonic. What idiot would take a plane when this way you can acclimate yourself slowly and not be thrown into anything?

Now the whole ship is breathing. It is getting rougher.

OCTOBER 8
Mal de mer from dawn to dusk. But they say you can get used to it. In a soft pensive mood. I have read five hours. Till the rims of my eyes ache. May tomorrow be calmer.

That big bowl of fruit saved my life.

OCTOBER 9
There was a young boy on the lower deck. I could only see him from the top. He was sitting on the deck, drinking a mug of coffee. His skin was pink and unlined. He must have been all of seventeen. But his arms

4. Cherry Heering, a brandy made from cherries and crushed cherry pits, was the invention of the eighteenth-century Danish shipowner Peter Heering.

writhed with snakes and naked belly dancers and flags and names of girls and places. Yes, he is young, but he has already made his commitment to the sea.

Tonight I buckle down and borrow the Walshes' typewriter. My weakness is the ear for our American idiom. I am always so busy correcting people's English that I do not listen to the natural music.

Captain C., now I understand you. The reason I stopped loving you was because I dragged you off your ship and into my world of newspapers and traffic and motels. If only you were master of this ship. What a love affair we would be having. Still remember that night while the SS *Gloria Dunaif* was docked at Everglades.[5] We stood outside on this same deck and looked at the lights from other ships and from the storage docks & power plants. The sky was black and I worshiped romance and wanted you to kiss me. And you did and it was perfect. I shouldn't have come to New Orleans that third time. It was all wrong. We ate too much and you told me too much about yourself and you became just another man. And then you mispronounced "taciturn," making the *c* hard (just as Esther pronounced "muscle" ["muskel"] at tea today) and it was over. We never should have left the ship. And now you are in Michigan, sitting it out, waiting for another ship. And I am where you belong and suddenly only the good memories are revived.

"Wednesday was a bad day for Captain C. of the SS *Gloria Dunaif.*" Another good story right there. What I need to do is just start—and not mind the ending. Do as Pursewarden says.[6] This may all resolve itself to a noble end. I am, so to speak, still in the note-taking stage. This story, we'll call it "Captain Courage" or some such, will bring out the sad the-

---

5. Gail and a photographer had been assigned by the *Miami Herald* to cover the running aground of a freighter, the SS *Gloria Dunaif.* It was through such an accident that she had met the ship's captain and formed a relationship.

6. Pursewarden is the accomplished author whom the narrator in Lawrence Durrell's novel *Justine* envies. Among his occasional pronouncements is this one: "The narrative momentum forward is counter-sprung by reference backwards in time, giving the impression of a book which is not traveling from a to b but standing above time and turning slowly on its own axis to comprehend the whole pattern. Things do not all lead forward to other things: some lead backwards to things which have passed. A marriage of past and present with the flying multiplicity of the future racing toward one. Anyway, that was my idea . . ."

sis of people's lives never touching at the right time. The beginning THE WAY IT REALLY HAPPENED will prophesy the end. This could be done well. I must develop an inner ear for what must be written at the right time. "Be Sure and Look Up Ben" was definitely a story to be written in a New York hotel room while the horns still honked and the humiliation was still fresh. If I can only recapture the formal wordiness of Captain C.'s letters. Tonight.

We are to see Newfoundland at eight tomorrow. I am becoming accustomed to the constant rock and shift. It stands to reason that if we are 90 percent water, our bodies should be very much affected by the tides. The trouble with my writing—I am impatient and not willing to *wait* for the right word.

> By eight o'clock, the morning of July 6 in Fort Lauderdale promised to be unbearable. In the bureau office of the *Star*, Keith Landridge swirled about in his chair and began typing out the assignment sheet. He knew that most of the stories stacked on the spindle that afternoon would have to be done as vicariously as possible. Reporters became very attached to their telephones since the bureau had gotten air conditioning, he reflected wryly.
>
> He pecked out the usuals first, habitually, without having to think.
>
> CITY HALL—REDFERN
>
> POLICE COURT—HANGER
>
> COMMISSION MEETING—SMITH
>
> PORT AUTHORITY—GRAY
>
> No, Gray was on vacation, he'd have to send Halcyone. Halcyone, the young problem, headache of the bureau, fresh from journalism school, full of delusions of Hemingway, blond and naive. Oh God, deliver one,

muttered Landridge, and pecked out HALCYONE[7] next to PORT AU-
THORITY. Well, we'll try her. Do her good to get buried in with those
dullards one afternoon a week till Gray got back. When she started trying to verbally decorate subjects like cargo and tonnage and ILA[8] grievances, she'd lose her illusions fast.[9]

Each sentence is torture. I stood up wretched and answered the
gong for tea. Esther was there and we were unimpeded by the loud W.s,
who simply spoil all real communication by talking so much. I could
sense that she was exactly tuned in to my mood and she started off ad-
vising me not to take it so hard. She said that once a person begins traveling and seeing the world, they can never never stay home again. The
people there don't understand and they "listen to your talk only with a
quarter of an ear. They do not care. But the way you feel tonight is good,
because then you are more sensitive to the impressions around you."

OCTOBER 13

Jonah has emerged from the whale three days after the onslaught of a
severe North Atlantic storm said to be characteristic of the months of
October and November. The ship is a small one, 330 feet, forty thousand
tons (not counting cargo), crew of only thirty-six. It rocked and racked
and shuddered and reeled. The waves yesterday came up over the captain's cabin. The W.s have not been out of their room since Wednesday,
and when I saw her peering out the door tonight, she was the color of asparagus soup and he had a three-day stubble. Their room reeked of oranges, said to be the worst thing you can possibly eat during an attack of
mal de mer. I found fruit, such as plums and grapes, and a simple roast
beef sandwich and tea to stay down quite well. But I, too, entertained

7. The name that Gail invents for her character refers, first, to sentiments about her
halcyon days, or days of calm. It is a nautical term denoting the placid weather that comes
amid winter storms to allow the kingfisher to hatch and rear her young on the water. In
Greek mythology, Halcyone, or Alcyone, was the daughter of Aeolus, god of the winds.
She tried to persuade her mortal husband, Ceyx, not to go to sea to question Apollo about
his bad fortune. Ceyx went anyway and died in a storm. Halcyone found his corpse in the
tide and transformed herself and him into water birds.

8. The International Longshoremen's Association.

9. See Appendix 1 for a fuller version of Gail's drafts for "Halcyone and the Lighthouse."

black thoughts about Danish food during my onslaught. The crew has developed a special storm walk. They look like characters out of a trick movie walking lopsidedly along, their bodies turned to a 45-degree angle. Tonight one of the mess-men spent ten minutes washing out my wastebasket and there was much teasing and carrying on in Danish.

I don't know whether to continue my story of Esther or get the W.s down first in a sketch of all-American ludicrousness (ludicry?). Ah well, it will be a long night and I am certainly not going to sleep. Let me mention just that we are off the coast of Greenland, will pass the northernmost tip of Scotland on Monday, stop eight hours in Oslo Tuesday, and twenty-three hours later arrive in Copenhagen.

Ah yes, the W.s.

Mr. and Mrs. Joe W. run a restaurant in New Jersey. Here is what they brought, besides their wardrobes, haunted by wash 'n' wear labels:

a case of American beer

4 bottles of Champale, 1 bottle of Scotch, 1 bottle of bourbon

1 box of Nabisco bacon thins, 1 large bag of potato chips

tinfoil packages of Sanka and Woolite—the Sanka he would
    happily shake into his cup, add hot water, and murmur gaily,
    "All the comforts of home, eh, dear?"

a box, a *box*, of magazines, consisting of:

    four issues of *Holiday*, with of course the issue on Scandinavia

    Around the World by Freighter, by Norman Ford

    Freighter Days, by Norman Ford

    Europe on $5 a Day, by Arthur Frommer

    1961 edition of *Fielding's Selective Shopping Guide to Europe*

    How to Get Along in French, Berlitz

How to Get Along in Spanish, Berlitz

How to Get Along in German, Berlitz

6 *Reader's Digests*

a novel by Isak Dinesen

the *Either* part of *Either/Or* by Kierkegaard

the fairy tales of Hans Christian Andersen

These last three as a sort of "cultural preparation" for when they land in Copenhagen, Joe explains, his apple cheeks lighting up like Christmas lights at his own ingenuity. The Kierkegaard fellow, Joe added, was certainly kind of unclear about things, but he got Esther to teach him to say "Suuren Keer-gart" and went around happily mumbling the Danish philosopher's name for days.

Fielding's Europe, 1959 (a friend had annotated it for them)

a Scrabble board, with blocks

2 decks of cards

2 large bottles of Dramamine

plus 2 huge empty spiral notebooks—for the W.s' immemorial logs

At table, they consider it their bounden duty to show the Danish that America is a friendly country. Who is to say why the Captain was flinching at Irene W.'s shrill giggle as she said, "Oh you Danes! How can you *eat* so much and not get *fat.*" Now the Danes, Esther tells me, eat their lunch, their *koldbord,* this way. They select *one thing at a time,* say like a sardine, put it on a piece of buttered bread, cut it with their knife and fork, and eat it. Then they butter another piece of bread, look around the table and decide what to make their next open-face sandwich out of.

"But this Mr. W.," Esther said. "He is forever *passing* things."

I could see him perfectly, even though I skipped lunch most days.

Poor Esther and the old couple would just be nibbling their first open-face, when rosy-cheeked Joe would start passing platters.

"Woncha have some fish, my this looks good, have some fish. Captain think it's gonna be rough today? Oh, there'll be a lot of seasickness tomorrow! A storm's comin'—have some salmon. Esther? Boy is this good. You Danes really put it away, dontcha. Ha."

For some reason known to God and his strange selective methods alone, the W.s were the only two Americans who didn't get seasick. Oh, ho! They were up at dawn to drink their Champale and eat their bacon thins and read Mr. Fielding and watch the storm. They never missed a meal. Mrs. W.'s shrill laughter, as she stumbled down the hall—"Oh, Joe! Isn't this *fun!*"—reached all the cabins where the near-dying lay. And this hardy pair again considered it their American duty to go around knocking on all doors, charging in, and "cheering the sick." The formula was the same for all passengers. First the knock; then the door bursts wide open and flame-haired Irene grins a hideous witch-grin.

"Whatsa matter with you, honey! Under covers? On an exciting trip like this? You're missing all the local color." (Ah yes, local color, that was her forte.)

And then hubby's cheery cheeks appear in the background.

"Miteaswellcomeonangetupandhavadrink," he booms. "Capnsaysthisisgonnalasteightmoredays." Not noticing you are swallowing hard now, like a person on the verge of throwing up.

Mariner Joe W. then proceeds to regale you with tales about how good the lunch was until you see the sardines, eyes open wide, floating in oil; the flat pink slabs of bologna; the goo of the liver paste; the hard, scaly exterior of the smoked eel; the thick mayonnaise base of the cold salad.

"Let us know if we can do anything for you" chime the friendly W.s as you stumble to the bathroom . . . again.

·   ·   ·

I'm sorry, but it had to be written.

This could very well be made into an *Atlantic*-type story.[10]

OCTOBER 14

I just read Henry James's *The Turn of the Screw*[11] and now, of course, am far from being lulled to a peaceful, childlike sleep by the creak of the walls and the other strange noises a ship makes in the night.

The events of the day are as follows: We passed two ships, both going the other way; I slept till teatime, had a mathematical discussion of God with the Walshes, played gin rummy with the W.s, which was an excursion into laughter. Mr. W. gins right off, spreads his cards happily on the table. "You've got a great big fat nothing!" his wife shrieks, exposing an ace of spades, a deuce of hearts, and a three of hearts. Of what was the poor man thinking?

OCTOBER 15

Quel dommage. Si yo no he habido tanto Scotch, pues entonces podia escribir la verdad.[12] Mr. W. and I almost came to blows, he started counting as I dealt. It is one o'clock & Esther & the Walshes & I have been talking. The Captain came in for a while and did us the honor. And the *Jungfrau* let me steal some chicken from the icebox.

I believe more each day that the more we talk to people, the less we understand them.

There was a rainbow late this afternoon that made an arc for us to pass through.

Will we ever find ourselves?

And would it be so good if we did?

10. A famous example of an *Atlantic*-type story is Katherine Anne Porter's "Holiday," published in the magazine in December 1960. "Holiday" is the story of a woman who stays with a German-American family in Texas for a month in order to get some distance on her troubles. She comes to empathize with the family's handicapped servant, who, it turns out, is the hosts' eldest daughter.

11. In James's psychological novel, a governess's perception of former servants' malicious ghosts leads to the death of one of her young charges.

12. "What a pity. If I had not had so much Scotch, perhaps I could write the truth."

My trouble is that I disillusion people.

I must learn to keep silent and let them think what a lovely person I am!

Why spoil their fun?

OCTOBER 16

Back to Irene & Joe.

If I could only reproduce the exact (monotonous) rhythm of his voice, the rhythm that makes all sentences sound the same.

- "Still there? The lighthouse still there?"

- "Play any way ya wanna."

I think the most maddening thing about him is the way he appropriates all ideas, all information, all scenery as his own by mouthing about it in his incomparable way. Thus, one cannot enjoy the thought of

the lighthouse of Scotland

the rainbow

the wonderful pancakes and jelly

the game of rummy

without mentally connecting the thought with Joe's descriptions:

- "See it. See it. See? Right there. Gee, lookathere."

- "Wunner how far apart the ends are. Say, Captain . . ."

- "Better not eat any of these, you gals. Fattening. Lotsa calories. Ha."

- "That's six . . . seven. Won't bend the cards. They have to go around the world."

- "Better get with it."

- "Man o chevitz!"

- "That's for the birds."

- "Six of one and half a dozen of the other."

- "I won't touch anything unner a hunnert dollars."

- "We cater to all kindsa banquets."

- "I'm a tough boss. But my crew's been with me for years."

- "Be reasonable bout thissing."

- "Gotta play the las card."

- "See Scotland t'morra."

Jesus! He knows everything.

On his face, pink from drink, there is trapped forever the look of a small boy, astounded and wounded to discover that time has caught up with him in spite of his teenage mentality.

I can just hear his Rotary Club speech.

Fielding is a huge snob & he depresses me. There are two ways of looking at this thing and I have chosen my way (I had no choice). If I can't bundle up my youth, my looks, my talent & my personality to get what I want, then I'd better just give up. When I get to Copenhagen I'll have $900—stash away $400 to go home on if worse comes to worst and that's *still* $500. If I can't go to Copenhagen, Berlin, Vienna, Florence, Rome, Paris & London for twenty-one days on $500, then something is wrong.

The biggest thing I have to contend with is my own recoiling, insecure, "Excuse me" alter ego. Get rid of that.

The Walshes are a reflection of my own pessimistic self. They are regarding their European trip as a chore to be endured, they cast skeptical glances at any offered pleasure, they weigh down any conversation with their humorlessness, they are stuck in the gray muck of facts instead of beauty. They sort of shuffle, from activity to activity, with shoulders hunched, clinging to one another.

I must start right now even when I doubt, even when my heart is heavy, even when I am SCARED to death before an interview or an experience, TO OUTWARDLY PRESERVE ALL VESTIGES OF A SMOOTH, CHARMING, CAREFREE, SLIGHTLY RETICENT EXTERIOR.

Soon, and with experience with the intercourse of the world, the outward will simply reflect the inward; the exterior will *be* the interior.

Met the steward in the corridor during my nocturnal ramblings. He looked rather attractive in a maroon brocade bathrobe—or is it just that I am becoming preoccupied with men due to the very lack of them? Not at all sleepy, and here it is one or two o'clock.

The breakfast thing depresses me most. The Danes (an EATING race of people) pick breakfast as their one meal to skimp on: one soft-boiled egg sitting perched up there in that minute eggcup (and one morning she even *forgot* the eggs); thin slabs of raw pink bologna, dry toast, marmalade, tea or that unbearable *kaffe*.

OCTOBER 17

Someone explained to me why my sleeping habits are all fouled up: they've been setting the clock up thirty minutes a day. I'm still sacking out on New York time. After breakfast, I went up on deck and saw a beautiful square-looking island, rather anvil-shaped, jutting up, halved by the rising sun. I went back to the room to read Kierkegaard while waiting for Esther to wash my hair & fell into a dead sleep where dreams became almost lifelike. (Lately, I have noticed, my dreams are peopled with men—the men I don't have. I wake up and feel so happy and then remember with a bang that I'm all alone and I have to search my mind to see if there's anyone anywhere that I have any claim on.) I woke to the tea gong and went stumbling into the dining room only to find them all sitting down to dinner. Much laughter, etc. Rummy & tea. Some verbal stumbling with the Walshes, then I retired to my room (which, incidentally, is the best, being situated on the prow, therefore wider and angular instead of cell-like) and emptied my thoughts to B., wrote Uncle Bill, and went up for a breath of air. It is suddenly more temperate—warm & moist. The ship was broken down for four hours. We are due into Oslo tomorrow night late. All day Thursday in Oslo. Arrive Saturday in Denmark. *Shake* the W.s.

OCTOBER 18

Norway for breakfast—

Talked to Mrs. Engineer today at tea. She told an anecdote about a women's group in Baltimore "with hats like THAT" that had a forum on all kinds of serious problems. ("And now, tell us, what is the criminality situation in Denmark?")

She plays tennis almost every day, outside in good weather, indoors in bad. In the summer, she and her husband go camping in Lapland, land of the midnight sun. She described the experience in glowing sensuous terms, and I felt I could see the strange flowers nourished by extra sun-hours, feel myself sleeping at night, under the sunshine.

They are a couple of the "First Rank," which means, from what I can gather, that they get to go to the King's Christmas party.

Danish women love to "go shopping."

The Queen herself never misses a sale.

The sea is rough tonight. We have started up the fiord, should dock in Oslo around daylight. Ah, won't it be fun to get off a ship and browse around town ALONE? I am going to see the Viking ships—that is my only museum "must"—and just look in the shops, mail my letters & write a few postcards.

—2:00 a.m. I wonder what sleeplessness is like at fifty! If, at twenty-four, I can be kept awake hour after hour by whirling dervishes of past incidents, tumbling one upon the other, no one an end in itself, *always* attached to a new chapter, a cross-reference, a footnote. And being starved does not help. I am mad for a tomato & cheese sandwich like the ones I use to put away by the dozen on Key Biscayne. Or a peanut butter sandwich & a glass of milk. Ah! When we get to Oslo, I shall have some milk. Oh, isn't this silly? I've never been hungry and unable to quell it.

Reason for coffee & croissants in Europe: They think stuffing oneself in the morning is barbaric. I have a feeling I'll love London with its big breakfasts, love of words, snobbery.

OCTOBER 19

OSLO

I have so many impressions to record that it makes me happy to know the next few hours will be occupied writing them down. Today was important, mostly because it was a dress rehearsal for the rest of Europe. By this I mean I was thrown out on my own in the rain in a large city where I spoke only one useful word of the language (*tak*)[13] and where I had to use my brain making a purchase as simple as a tube of Pepsodent. I learned one thing first: A lot of smiling, gesturing, and enunciating will get you one hell of a long way. I found out my "talent" while walking with the Walshes tonight. What the essence of it is, really, is letting yourself go, opening up, showing all whom you meet that you like their country, you are in it to have fun and you want nothing more than to learn to mingle with them and practice their customs. The aloof wariness one must assume in New York or Washington has no place in a land where you are the guest, the noncommunicant sampler. I don't really know how the W.s will manage. Everywhere my smile was returned. (Ah, the men are restless tonight. I can hear them talking, breaking into laughter, talking low again.) Not only are most of the Nordic people on the streets strikingly attractive (strawberries under their cheeks, glossy, unbelievably golden hair, profiles clean & rugged as the word Skagerrak),[14] but very well dressed. Short skirts, Bally shoes with walking heels, belted raincoats with fur collars, duffel coats with wooden fasteners. Well-fitting cuffless trousers for the men, short raincoats, duffel coats. Ah! Tomorrow if it's nice I shall dress to kill and hunt bear. Also,

13. *"Tak,"* with a short vowel, often spelled *"takk,"* means "thank you."
14. Skagerrak is the name of the part of the North Sea between Norway and Denmark.

what is the history of the troll? I love the carvings of them you find in every window, along with the daringly colorful enamelware, the pewter, the silver.

We had the Captain's Dinner in port—sherry, two white wines (a very good Rhine which means "reach for heaven"), two red wines (a bitter & a sweet), and the Captain's own brandy, beef soup, lobster, duck, flaming ice cream with fruit, much coffee. Johanson really tried tonight—especially after he got a few drinks in him. Joe W. was unbearable, sticking a lobster leg behind his ear, handing Esther a lemon in his fingers, putting his dirty knife on Fra Norwegian's plate. Esther had a bad day. Her ship-broker friends, seven years ago lighthearted, drinking buddies, proud of her, today took her for a drink but didn't drink themselves, looked left & right in fear of ostracism, said apologetically: "We'll do it *right* in Copenhagen, when we don't have to preserve face. Ya?" She was almost in tears at dinner.

OCTOBER 20

Almost to Copenhagen. The day we leave Oslo is beautiful. The gray comes alive. The fantastic shoreline with the castle on the hill. Kamma Rode has invited me to spend a day with her. "I love to show visitors these—uh—because I am so proud of my country." She told me the story of the Little Mermaid (and if you climb up and kiss her you will never drown). I have the rhythm of the Danish language in my mind all day. The pungent Ø sound, not duplicated in English, but strangely enough almost in French.

The navy town of Horden is unbelievably lovely, fairy lights twinkling all along the hill, a steeple, a lighted bridge, colored lights, all rising out of the water against a pink & black sky.

For an exchange of three kisses (one rather ardent one), the second mate Jacobsen, wiry, red-haired, from the Faroe Islands, gave me a few hours of Scandinavian lore and let me come up on the bridge and see what went. I found out, while we were drinking (TERRIBLE rum) in his cabin with the second cook, the reason for my lack of popularity. I would have had a man knocking on my door every night had it not been for the damned purser. The idiot, looking at the passenger list and seeing "Kennedy: Occupation—None" immediately thought I was a *none* (Danish for "nun"). He spread the word and all smiles stopped. Only, they couldn't understand. They had never seen a nun in slacks.

This slays me. I am still chuckling. The American nun in cabin 8 who drank Scotch, wore slacks, and smiled at men—who respectfully nodded their heads & covered their eyes.

OCTOBER 22

COPENHAGEN

Arrived under the worst conditions and still survived. Wet, rainy, Saturday. American Express closed. Kiosk P closed. The W.s on my tail, and the looks of them makes prices soar anyway. Went to the Tourist Office. Then tried hotel after hotel. All full. Finally, the Kansas. Comfortable bed, centrally located. Eighteen kroner a day—$2.75. As soon as possible I move to Mission Hotellet, $1.75. Dinner last night at ABC Cafeteria— 3.50 Kr. Today 7.25 Kr ($1.03) at Tokanten, the intellectual haunt, weird, macabre, never a dull moment. (Baby carriage hanging upside down on wall. Puppets hanging with nooses around their wooden necks, a merry-go-round horse, an old gramophone, students of all nations, sparkling with exciting talk, switching languages by the instant.) Last night I picked up (very delicately, "Could you please tell me where the cutlery is?") an Australian engineer who lives in Guernsey, invents tractor & tank runners, about forty-five, interesting, well-traveled. We went strolling on Vesterbrogade. The Bond Street of Copenhagen. Drank Tuborg at festival at Tokanten and at least five men tried to lure me away. A boy played soulfully at the piano. Sight to remember: ruddy blond boy riding a horse along Tietgensgade Bridge (a white horse); at his side his pale-haired sweetheart pedals her bike, placidly holding his hand. My companion of last p.m. (Neville) then took me to the Ambassador. The bathroom there is the only place I encountered a Dane with his hand out. The bathroom attendant literally stopped me and demanded a krone for peeing. After that, the Palladium, where couples danced wildly until 1:00 a.m. and Neville and I became extremely intoxicated. I had a headache this morning. My God. Today for my companions I had "four Arab monkeys" as they called themselves, chattering in French, Danish, English, and Arabic, at my table. (They simply sat down.) From Algeria & Morocco. Very amusing. Then, the more articulate one took me to the beautiful modern Royal Hotel, where we coveted Swiss watches, Jensen silver bowls & magnificent, sleek mobile furniture.

OCTOBER 23

GODNAT—GOOD NIGHT

The Embassy is behind me. The ambassador invited me to his party for Marian Anderson[15] Friday night. A Danish couple—brother & sister—sat with us tonight at Tokanten and the sister gave me a bunch of fresh violets.

B. loves me.

The way always to be loved is always to be just leaving!

—GODWIN

OCTOBER 24

Oh Christ, am I tired. *Mal de tête.* Curse. Budget worries. Took two aspirins. I cannot possibly go to Malmö tomorrow. I don't trust McCullum anyway. The day was memorable. Sights to remember: the man plowing his field by the sea, the gulls flying behind him digging worms from the new furrow. Also, the sea from the rampart at Elsinore, the boy sitting in a cove, reading poetry while the wind whistled by him. Fredensborg, Frederiksborg. The *Ocean Pearl.*[16]

· · ·

15. Contralto Marian Anderson was at the apex of her career in 1961. That year, she had sung the National Anthem at President John F. Kennedy's inauguration.

16. Fredensborg was a fishing village (it's now a suburb) near Copenhagen on the island of Zealand, or Sjaelland. The island was named for the seals that populated it as well as for the word "soul," which, for the natives, was closely related to their totemic animal. Gail was trying to soak in as much culture as possible on her journey. She was willing to use her charms to do so, but not without reserve, as she had declined going to Malmö, the Swedish city across the Ore Sound (Øresund), with the untrustworthy McCullum. Frederiksborg is a county of Denmark. The *Ocean Pearl* is a cruise ship.

The Rode home is cozy, full of paintings of ancestors hundreds of years old. Dinner of salmon, asparagus in a frozen gelatin topped with horse-radish whipped cream, pork, fruit & nuts, Tuborg, Tuborg & Tuborg. I didn't even recognize the martini Kamma had made in our honor. She had made it with sweet vermouth. Fell in love with Erik, whose father says of him, "It amuses him to be correct." All I can say is, he must have been amused tonight. What polish for a seventeen-year-old, clicking heels, perfect grace, a medal for his jujitsu. I ate fifteen walnuts just so he could crack them for me. Also Kamma had invited a young woman medical student who had been to England. She was charming, too.

Dammit. I may have to buy a dress for the ambassador's party—or maybe not. Tomorrow I will try on things and see. Otherwise I will go shopping, to the Damefrisor, splurge on the taxi, unless I can meet someone with a car between now & Friday.

OCTOBER 26

I went over to the *Berlingske Tidende* and got a guided tour first.[17] Then an "audience" with Knud Meister, the daily columnist who took about ten pictures of me and jotted down some notes for his daily column. So I will be in the column one day soon—maybe tomorrow. Meister is ac-robatic in both English & Danish. "Don't want to fight windmills . . . Gushy . . ." He has been through the U.S., is an ardent advocate of jour-nalism, writing a book; I gave him Dean Luxon's address. Says trend is only upper-class, university men go into paper now, wants to avoid this & get the best talent. He got Lis & me front-row seats at Marian Ander-son and also arranged for us to dine out tomorrow evening . . . I am sure he will mention me to Peter Heller, the cultural attaché, who I learned is a language whiz. (Everybody around here is!) I just may do that inter-view on DB. "Deeda" is her name.[18] Saw an article on her in the Octo-

17. The *Berlingske Tidende* was one of the two major daily newspapers in Denmark, the other being the more socially progressive *Politiken*, whose offices Gail had seen on her itinerary four days earlier.

18. Deeda Blair's husband, William McCormick Blair Jr., was the U.S. ambassador to Denmark from 1961 to 1964. Deeda was one of the heroes of public health education in the twentieth century.

ber *Madame.* She is tight-lipped, looks like she has been through a little bit of hell . . . or has put somebody else through it.

Granted: I have spent more than planned in Denmark (both in time & money). But it has been a good investment. I will train to Berlin—stay one–two days, then over to Paris to see what Miller is going to do. Might try *Tribune* (Meister knows the editor). It will be *bon* to have the clipping enclosed so he can see I am a woman to be reckoned with.

Will put my hair up tonight and really look the part tomorrow.

Courtesy—that is the magic word. Will write a complete text tomorrow. I have the secret now. It is up to me to use it, to keep it.

OCTOBER 30

Stayed up all night with N. and helped him shine shoes.[19] Went to the flower exhibition at Glypotek and will never forget the fragrance, the violins playing, the fountain guarded by Rodin's shadow.[20] And the sculpture that brought tears to my eyes. Dubois's *The Prodigal Son.*[21] Niels, Niels, Niels, Niels, Niels. If only I could kidnap him and take him to America. But no, he is a typical European and would be unhappy without *Fidelio* and Spain and sailings through Gibraltar. When I came in last night, I went straight to him and still nothing was said. Will I ever feel again what I felt when he suddenly stood up from his chair and came over and kissed me? He was in a concentration camp and still bears the tattoo on his arm. They killed his father.

19. N. is Niels, a major character in Gail's Danish experience. He was her love interest—in some ways an ideal Dane, in other ways a troubled exception.

20. The Ny Carlsberg Glypotek is a museum that houses a large and important collection of ancient sculpture as well as a modern collection specializing in works by Auguste Rodin.

21. Paul Dubois (1829–1905) was a French sculptor who twice won the Medal of Honor from the French Academy.

Part three

WALK, DON'T RUN

Klampenborg by the Sea, Denmark

OCTOBER 31–DECEMBER 17, 1961

Before receiving any assurance about her upcoming Travel Service job in London, Gail spent two months in Denmark, securely housed but overly guarded, admired by men but ruled by a need to write, in possession of money but running out of it quickly. To complicate things, there was the season: late fall and Christmas in a country where morbid joking disguises the loneliness brought on by winter darkness.

On a few occasions during this period, Gail fell ill with colds and flu. "All you can do is count them," commented her friend Gaert. Yet amid all this turmoil and uncertainty, the seeds of stories were planted.

Gail's experience of her overbearing landlord, Mr. Høiaas, culmi-nated, seventeen years later, in the story "A Cultural Exchange," published in Atlantic Monthly. (*She later included it in her collection* Mr. Bedford and the Muses.) *The story's conception can be traced to the journals. On December 21, 1961, Godwin wrote down the tale's original title, "A Dollar's Worth of Hygge." Witnessing here the development of "A Cultural Ex-change" provides us with an illuminating look at Godwin's writing tech-nique: her use of personal experience and journals, the creation of organic stories, and the development of ghostlike presences.*

Reading the works of Isak Dinesen enabled Godwin to absorb the Danish ethos. Gail also found Hans Christian Andersen's tale of the Little Mermaid, whose statue on the Copenhagen coast she visited, especially evocative. It speaks of the cultural exchange between a voyager and a sea denizen, and of their crossing of worlds. The mermaid, in order to cross, painfully transforms her fins into feet. The ordeal relates to Gail's per-ceived need to change her hurried mode of existence—running—to the Danes' philosophical gait.

It is a conflict worthy of a novel, Godwin thought, and she titled her work-in-progress about her Denmark months "Walk, Don't Run." But Gail did not stop running. She was no mermaid. She'd stick with her own nature and not marry herself to Denmark.

OCTOBER 31, 1961

Calm down, self. Buy paper, go to Embassy library, read everything, and then come home and write, write. After hacking a considerable chunk from my budget I will leave for Berlin.

Sight to remember: the windmill from the train en route to Hellerup. Niels boarding the trolley . . . the parrot shop.

NOVEMBER 1

I am happy. And I am going to see about staying in Copenhagen for the winter. I could write and learn Danish & German. Lorraine[1] & I spent the day together and I like her so much. Niels & I met at Drop-In and then went on to a small bar with carpets and soft sofas, and—MOST IMPORTANT OF ALL,—no people. There we planned to build another boat and sail to Mexico this summer in June. He built one before & sailed it to Calais, where he sold it.

NOVEMBER 2

Niels: "Whenever I wonder whether I can do it I think of the Vikings and I know if they can do it, so can I."

I am coming down with a cold. Mailed the story on Mrs. Blair[2] to the *Washington Post*—and got a letter off to Bev Miller. I feel awful.

---

1. Lorraine O'Grady became a longtime friend of Gail's. They first met at Ambassador William Blair's reception for Marian Anderson in Denmark, October 1961. An anecdote drawn from that first meeting appears in Godwin's story "Some Side Effects of Time Travel," published in *Dream Children* (1976). Gail and her friend, seated on either side of Copenhagen's prison warden, heard his mournful opinion about the possible extinction of the Danish language and his meek revelation about Denmark's most prevalent crime: bicycle theft. Later in the journals, Gail muses about her color blindness regarding Lorraine, a light-skinned African-American, and registers the contrast with the race consciousness of the South.

2. Gail interviewed Deeda Blair, wife of the ambassador, for a freelance spec assignment for the *Post*. The interview never ran.

NOVEMBER 4

What will happen now with the U.S. Travel Service?

NOVEMBER 6

Now to describe yesterday briefly. What a wonderful way Mr. Rolf Høi-aas[3] had of deciding for himself whether or not Miss Godwin would be suitable to live with him and his motherless twenty-seven-year-old son, whom he affectionately calls "Frowsy" because of the boy's general un-tidiness and bristly beard. First he met me at the station, looking much more like the Cook's travel rep at a London station than a Norwegian migrated to Denmark. He suggested we first have lunch at the Rytter-garten (part of the riding academy at Klampenborg), during which we were joined by a Mr. Munk, from a Danish noble family dating back to King Gorm almost.[4] He lives alone over Ryttergarten; his wife & daugh-ter both, as Mr. H. put it, "have bats in the belfry."

Mr. H. then took me for a lovely ride in a horse-drawn carriage through the woods, all yellow and bittersweet with cold, looking down over Øresund over to Sweden, finally coming to the King's hunting lodge, where deer swarmed on the golf course and a few albinos plucked at the weeds at the base of trees.

And then Mr. H. & I drank hot lemon rum at the Bellevue, and fi-nally he let me know I'd passed the test and said: "Well now, shall we go across the street and have a look?"

It is a warm, cozy house, badly in need of paint in the kitchen (which I shall do) and flowers in all the lovely vases. The Russian samovars need to be polished to brassy perfection and Frowsy needs to be encouraged to leave his Gillette razors and biological specimens somewhere besides the dining room table.

Funny thing: The only thing I fear is that Mr. H. will begin loving

---

3. Rolf Høiaas is transformed into Rolf Engelgard in Godwin's story "A Cultural Exchange," published in *Mr. Bedford and the Muses* (1976). His role as host becomes a spooky interplay of charm and manipulation. Gail notes that the pronunciation of Høiaas "sounds like someone saying, 'HI-yos?' with an emphasis on the 'Hi,' as in 'Hi-yo Silver!'— very musical, with a little upbeat question mark at the end."

4. King Gorm unified the warring clans of Vikings on Jutland, the mainland part of Denmark, in the early 900s. Old Danish families like tracing their genealogies back to him.

me too much. I will not forget how he raised his glass for a *skål* and said, This has been a very happy day for me indeed. And indeed it had. But a tear slid unabashedly down his lined face and I almost got in on it myself.[5]

NOVEMBER 7

> *To what purpose all this everlasting thinking and worrying, when life is so fleeting and goes like wind through the grass?*
>
> *So now I stick to the wisdom of nature and simple things and the freedom they give as I stand and marvel over them. The hunger in the twilight, as the first migrating wild duck comes flying in, feels himself free, released and uplifted. Or watch the rye grass swaying in the wind, see only that and you are free. Or take some soil in your hand, a handful of the timeless earth, a handful of peace. You are free one precious instant.*
>
> —MARTIN HANSEN, *The Liar*[6]
> (Denmark's Albert Camus)[7]

The thoughts here express the essence of what I love about Copenhagen and Denmark—and Niels. Although I must bear in mind that in many, many ways Niels is not a true Dane because he is happy, even during what they call "the depression month of November," he is not loud, and he does not like parties.

The bells! They are always ringing here. Again today I am full of so much to say and I have learned new things. Got up very late, 1:00 p.m., or thirteen o'clock, as they say here, because I was up until four this

---

5. A tear also falls down the face of Mr. Engelgard in Gail's story "A Cultural Exchange." Godwin places the fictionalized tear-shedding at the Deer Park in Klampenborg as newly arrived Amanda, overwhelmed by the vision of deer bathed in sunset rays, grabs her guide and says, "You certainly do know how to give things a lovely beginning."

6. Martin Hansen is considered one of the leading post–World War II writers in Denmark. He turned from social realism to fables during the German occupation. His 1950 novel *The Liar* portrayed the plight of a modern idealist.

7. The French existentialist Albert Camus, like the Dane Kierkegaard, was an early influence on Godwin, reflecting the intellectual climate of the day as well as Gail's affinity for a state of mind preferred by Danes in general.

morning. Met Lorraine at the Embassy library and must again marvel at the warmth and understanding shared. She has accepted me as a friend. I am sure, because over egg rolls and ginger in the Chinese restaurant at Øesterport, she told me she was twenty-seven instead of twenty-five, had been married, had an eight-year-old child. She went into detail, describing her feelings before, during, and after the marriage, and I understand. Her husband went to Tufts, while she went to Wellesley. Enough said. Lorraine, I understand. We discussed sex and pregnancy and such things and how wonderful it is to have a friend. Not since Eleanor Stem[8] have I had a *woman* friend with whom I could really say what was on my mind. So she took the train home to her rather restricted life with a Polish family and I will begin such a life tomorrow with Papa Høiaas.

NOVEMBER 9

KLAMPENBORG BY THE SEA[9]

It is always difficult for me to relocate. But here I am bedded down comfortably in my new room. It needs so much cleaning, but other than that, it's all right. Tomorrow I go to Berlin with Klaus & another friend.[10] This was the life I wanted, wasn't it? This is the life I have chosen. I will never forget how I felt last February, sitting in my very comfortable house in Key Biscayne with all my belongings. I was terrified that I would never see the world, never travel, never have romance.

Tonight I am a little ill at ease, but it *will* pass. It will pass. I love the sound of Danish in the next room.

Lars[11] and his girl sleep together here and it is all right. There are so many things I want to know about the Danes.

---

8. Eleanor Stem was Gail's best friend at Peace College in 1958.

9. Klampenborg is a seaside resort town six miles north of Copenhagen. It is most famous for its Deer Park and forest of beech trees.

10. Godwin will chronicle her journey to Berlin, including her interrogation by the East German police, and write an article that will appear in the *Asheville Citizen-Times* in November 1961.

11. Lars is Frowsy's given name.

NOVEMBER 13

I am very happy. The wind howls, and if I turn around I can see the ocean (which is very wild today). I am listening to a symphony, cuddled deep within a chair. I am preparing dinner, received just the letter I wanted from Bev Miller in London. It said, in effect, I would be in the Travel Service soon—but not yet. Perfect.

Let me describe my comfort. I picked the last white and bittersweet flowers from Mr. Høiaas's garden and put them in a crude round bowl—blue ceramic—they bloom their last under a fluttering hanging lamp-light. I have put Papa H.'s pipe and things in order and opened a small bright enameled teakwood container of matches. The wind howls. The radio is playing "Yesterday."[12] This is one of the few times it is *today*. Lorraine's love affair popped (he came into the cafeteria with another girl and said to Lorraine, "Oh. What are you reading?") and I gave her directions over the phone from my *Europe on $5 a Day* on how to get to Spain. She wants to try her luck in Salamanca.

Lars has put a sign on the bathroom door: "Ladies and Gentlemen." Mr. H. & I went to see *Sanctuary*.[13] How well I remember the last time I saw it. This was the third time. And finally I saw that when Candy Man says "everything is going to be all right," he is doing it to reassure himself.

NOVEMBER 14

For dinner we had a very snobbish hors d'oeuvre: mock oysters—a thin slice of bread, spread with butter; center, a raw egg yolk, sprinkled with onions, capers, and circled with a slab of herring. Followed by a very heavy golden pea soup and sausage and potato—and much leg-pulling from Lars.

---

12. "That Was Yesterday," a song from *Milk and Honey*, the Jerry Herman musical about an American man and woman who meet in Israel, became a hit in 1961. "And there's not a chance of a backward glance / Over all the bridges that I've burned. / For I was someone else in another time" was a refrain heard repeatedly on the radio.

13. *Sanctuary* is Tony Richardson's 1961 movie based on William Faulkner's novel of the same name. Lee Remick played Temple Drake, who, the movie poster proclaimed, "sank into degradation and rose to seek redemption," and Yves Montand played Candy, "the Creole lover who taught her the ways of evil."

"We have a very strict Danish custom, little sister. When we *skål* each other we must *always* use the same *liquid.*" And raising his glass of that (to me) detestable schnapps, he said sweetly, *"Skål."*

"Just wait till Gail starts pulling *your* leg, Frowsy. You'll have as much chance as a celluloid cat in hell," said Papa H.

This has been a rather frustrating day for me: (1) I spent money, (2) I forgot to mail my letter to London, and (3) I couldn't find a typewriter to write my article. And it is still inside me, weighing me down. I bought the Jaeger suit Niels saw in the window—but I am not sorry. It cost enough to last a lifetime. And Niels will like it on me. But I shouldn't have bought the sweater and *two* cashmere scarves. The girl was most charming after I had bought everything. She invited me to a fashion show next August. Ha. Tomorrow Lorraine comes in the morning, Niels calls between four and five, and I can enjoy another day. I am going to do exercises tonight so I won't get fat.

We borrowed a phonograph and listened to the Red Army Choir.[14] They are marvelous. "Ka . . . lin . . . ka, my love."

Mr. H. just finished my articles and said quietly, against the background of Volga music and pipe smoke and reading lamps: "I like your writing very much . . . you go straight to the point . . . You'll be a big shot someday . . . if you want to."

NOVEMBER 16

The honeymoon with this country is over. I have begun to find in the people certain careless qualities I do not like. And I begin to see the weaknesses in a socialistic form of government. I am very satisfied that I am an American, and when I go home, I might go back to the university and take a master's degree in American history. Yesterday was hell on earth. Niels didn't call. It was so unlike him, I was shattered. Poor Mr. H. ordered a dozen oysters and a bottle of liebfraumilch and offered cin-

14. The Red Army Choir was formed in 1928 with an initial company of twelve performers. Subsequently it grew to a body of over two hundred performers, drawn from amateur art circles within the military. It gained an international reputation for its presentation of folk songs.

emas, walks & talks. The more he offered, the more uneasy I became. Finally I worked myself up into a frenzy and was actually afraid to stay alone with him in the house. Ah, why must there be complications in what seemed to be such a pleasant situation? If I can just stick it out until Bev Miller notifies me.

I took the train uptown late at night and waited for N. on the corner of Helgolandsgade. At least five men thought I was a ———. At last he came tramping across the street with that walk of his that looks always as if he is embarking on a foot trip around the globe.

HE WAS SICK AT HEART BECAUSE MY ADDRESS WAS NOT IN HIS WALLET WHEN HE WENT TO CALL AND THOUGHT THAT I HAD STOLEN IT BECAUSE I DIDN'T WANT HIM BOTH-ERING ME ANYMORE. THAT GODDAMN VIRAGO OF A MOTHER TOOK IT. SHE DIDN'T EVEN COME TO SEE HER SON IN PRI-SON . . . But I'm ahead of my story.

We sat in the lobby of the Hotel Kansas until five talking. And we talked of many things. I understand him better now. I must get this down in order. It is very important.

First he told me what he had seen after each bombing in Berlin. ("A man in a horse-drawn cart came around with a shovel.")

When he was nineteen, the army called him. He told them he had rather go to prison for two years. They took him anyway. So, one night, he stole a jeep and tried to run down a sergeant whom he particularly hated. He ran him down (all this he drew for me in diagrams) and then got out and picked him up and drove him to the hospital. The sergeant recovered and today waves at him in the street.

His mother found out we went walking that morning. She doesn't like me one bit and I'm sure I'd hate her because I think she is a queer kind of mother. She wants for him only what *she* wants. She wants him to marry that blond acrobat Ina and invites her over and pushes them together every minute. She tells him he "doesn't *know* the American girl." Oh, I hate her. Anyway, on May 20, the deed is erased from Niels's record, he is free to go. He promised to come to London and work with the theater. He has a friend who will get him a job.

The radio is playing the theme song from Glenn Miller.[15] Oh, naturally, I miss the U.S. This is a self-imposed exile. It is only me that says, You can't go home. And yet, I miss my car. And B. And all the little habitual things. I miss being a master of my language. But enough of this. If I sell some articles maybe Lorraine and I can go to Spain for a few weeks in the spring. That damn typewriter has not arrived yet. If—when—it comes, I will type a letter to Bev Miller and go downtown and mail it. Will see Niels tonight at eight. Hope he took my record back. He has to tell his mother when he will be home for dinner.

Got home and had tea with the H.s. Frowsy really puts on a show. I think he is about the most cuddly looking Dane I have ever met. He sits there with that mop of wild, undisciplined hair springing in all directions from his head, his long underwear peeking from beneath his trousers, and gives animated discourse on Danish humor, dinosaurs, and anything else I happen to mention. He makes these long-dead animals, the crackly little crustaceans, the wiggly fish, come alive with his amiable language. It is as if he loved them.

"Can't you see the mother dinosaur coming home and finding that little devil about to make off with one of her eggs? She smashed him so hard, he was recently discovered fossilized in the rock where she left him."

His description of the "enthusiastic Danes on skis" almost broke me up.

"Ah, yes, when we have two inches of snow on the ground, they pack up their skis and hurry to break their legs on the little mounds of Deerhaven.

"Thousands of Danes go down those little hills until there is no snow left—and then they still go down.

"Beer sledges, with no provisions for steering—oh, no, they can't think ahead, come down at about fifty kilometers and smash into the

15. Glenn Miller's big band's theme song was "Moonlight Serenade." During World War II, it was called America's second national anthem.

people going up the hill. Everybody breaks his neck or his leg or at least his nose and they all sit about afterwards with their parts in casts, drinking beer, impatient to get back and try to kill themselves again."

The Danish humor is rather sick, bizarre. The Danes love Thurber, Charles Addams, and lyrics like these by Tom Lehrer

> *I hold your hand in mine, dear,*
> *I press it to my lips . . .*
> *My joy would be complete, dear,*
> *If you were only here.*

And the Danish hobo standing reverently in front of a good liquor store, saying, "How can people *sell* liquor."

If all this doesn't make a good book, nothing will.

NOVEMBER 17

After one! And still I procrastinate on this idyllic afternoon in Bella Vista. There are days—and times—and periods of time when life flows smoothly and we are very much in tune with all around us. This is one of those times. So what does it matter if I drowse. It can be done tomorrow—when Niels and his memory are out of the way for a while.

What a glorious morning! It will be remembered long after I leave this place. Niels came at eight, Frowsy overslept, and so we all started breakfast. Frowsy went for the eggs and met Lorraine coming back from the stables, so she came, too.

EGGS & my too-weak coffee and fresh bread & marmalade—and the macabre songs of Tom Lehrer. Niels didn't like them. Lorraine thought N. was beautiful and I caught her looking at him more than once.

I walked with him to the train and watched it till it was out of vision. I was alone in the clear, crisp, yellow & blue morning and only a moment ago, he was here. Now it was only a matter of intellect whether or not he existed at all.

We walked hand in hand through the village and picked a small window where we decided we would like to be living. As we crossed over to the station and passed the old crone on horseback and the flock of children returning from a walk in Deerhaven, I thought: *Now* here it is. I've *got* it.

> *Now she began to think of what she had read about deep-water fish,*
> *which have been so much used to bear the weight of many thousands*
> *fathoms of water, that if they are raised to the surface they will burst.*
> *Was she, herself, she wondered, such a deep-water fish that felt at home*
> *only under the pressure of existence? What was a deep-water fish to*
> *do, if married to one of those salmon which here she had seen spring-*
> *ing in the waterfalls? Or to a flying fish?*
>
> —ISAK DINESEN, *WINTER'S TALES,* "THE PEARLS"[16]

NOVEMBER 19

The old men scrubbing down the white tile walls of Norregade Station with long-handled brushes. At 12:30, as I'm waiting for the last train home, they look like misty, gray souls damned eternally to the underground.

Gudrun's father came last night. First he called and said he couldn't come. He told Gudrun he didn't think he should be around such nice people. But Susan, Gudrun's little girl, took the phone and said, "You have to come, *Mor-far,*[17] *I'm* here." And so he came, a big man, a welder in a shop, with big laborer's hands and elaborately polished round-toed shoes. I knew he had on his one suit. At first he was nervous, but soon he relaxed—and took off his coat—and held the child in his arms. After a wonderful dinner of boiled hen with soup and wine and asparagus sauce, I dressed and took the train to town to see Niels at the hotel. I was feeling no pain either way. Of course as soon as I saw him, all qualms & reservations melted and I was again his meek little girl. I am afraid of him, Lorraine was right. And yet, if something doesn't happen quickly, I am going to be free of him and once more in love only with myself. Why do I have to be so intelligent? I demand all the subtleties & nu-

16. Isak Dinesen (Karen Blixen) lived a few miles north of the Høiass family, also on Strandvej, the oceanfront.

17. *Morfar* is the Danish word for "maternal grandfather." Gudrun, a waitress, also lived with the Høiass family.

ances and vibrations of a superquick mind. I can only fool myself for so long that a man I love has them when he doesn't. Fink didn't have it, really. Paul did. B. did. Niels? Well, let me try a little longer. I am not absolutely slam-bang sure.

Lorraine is having trouble with her Polish woman. She accused L. of eating too much chutney. Today, I was irritated by my dear friend, even while liking her. First of all, she gets up early in the morning, rides horseback, writes her novel, and *then*, just when I am waking and getting sufficiently alive, she comes over to interrupt my work schedule. Today that happened. Plus she criticized my stories after I had been dishonest and told her I thought her work had great possibilities.

Tonight I went to Palle & Gaert's. Gaert likes me very much and I find him a cuddlesome way to spend the evening. He is an artist and knows art and a few other things to make him sufficiently interesting. I like his silver-blond tousled head ("Dammit, I had it cut in France a month ago"), and I like his silly, wistful grin. He is a strange, unusual, *nuzzling* kind of boy. He necks rather well, but makes no effort to seduce me.

I hope Niels doesn't come tomorrow morning. I have to: finish the story, tidy the house, pick up mail at American Express, and go by the office.[18]

My newspaper articles, Paris, starting the novel "Walk, Don't Run."[19] Gaert. Niels. Reading. This winter may be glorious, God willing.

Yes, you believe-nothing people, there *is* a Director.

I need a ream of paper & must write Mother, Frank Crowther, Aunt Sophie & Uncle William.

NOVEMBER 21

I have been in Denmark one month. Went to the Royal Hotel to the hairdresser; stopped by Feature Press & collected 75 Kr, had squid and

18. Godwin had acquired a freelance job with a local news agency. She rewrote articles to improve their use of English.

19. "I was completely engaged in living/writing," Gail recalls about her precious first weeks in Europe, "often not stopping to distinguish one from the other. 'Walk, Don't Run' was to be a collection of Copenhagen experiences that would add up to a novel. I know I typed furiously on that rented typewriter. I can see the single-spaced lines and feel the thin paper."

antipasto with Frowsy at an Italian restaurant with fine music & service. Afterwards we came home & made coffee and I slept in my special new boots from Italy. Niels called at 11:30 and Frowsy talked to him for a while. Then me. Niels got Kierkegaard out of the library instead of buying it. First steps toward rehabilitation? Then I lay on the sofa & Frowsy read me a bedtime story from a book called *Deals with the Devil*.[20] We then went out on the terrace and looked at the moon with a frost ring encircling it. A train rattled back to Copenhagen and I went in the bathroom. When I came back, Frowsy had made my bed and my new boots were tucked in, too, the toes resting on the pillow. I had told him I always wanted to sleep with new shoes when I was a child.

NOVEMBER 23

Tonight at 6:00 I simply sat down at the typewriter and wrote until 9:30. It was painless and I enjoyed it. I wanted to go on into the night but I had to go to town to see Niels. I did ten pages—about twenty with a bigger typeface. Twenty more and "Roxanne" should be finished.[21] Then comes the hard but happy part—the core of the book—NIELS. I want it to be about the size of a Sagan novel.[22] I can finish it in two more weeks if there are no interruptions. Then comes the polishing when I retype it. For the first time, I am not scared. I was trying too hard before. I am not Virginia Woolf, not Durrell. My forte is understatement and non sequiturs. I notice that I am catching the language well in the writing.

Helsingør[23] tomorrow. We are staying at the Prins Hamlet. I must pay close attention because this will be the center of the book.

---

20. *Deals with the Devil*, edited by Basil Davenport, was an anthology published in 1958 by Dodd, Mead.

21. "Roxanne" was a part of Godwin's novel-in-progress based on her new friend, Lorraine O'Grady.

22. Françoise Sagan's novels, such as *Bonjour Tristesse* (1954) and *A Certain Smile* (1956), were typically 128 pages long.

23. Gail took Niels to Kronborg Castle, immortalized by Shakespeare in *Hamlet*.

NOVEMBER 25

Niels tonight: "Do you love me?"

"Yes, of course. Why?"

"I didn't want to go to the trouble of meeting you tomorrow if you didn't."

NOVEMBER 27

Frowsy left a picture for me with my glasses on top. Hilarious. He just finished reading Sturgeon's "Fluffy"[24] to me aloud.

NOVEMBER 28

Today has been one of those days when no material comfort has been denied me—but at the same time a day in which I have actually suffered from self-doubt. I have recently become aware of the most unpleasant characteristic in myself. I allow myself to be dominated, stepped on, and made uncomfortable by people I really *do not* like. When they are doing it, I stand around looking restless and making all kinds of terrible faces so that they invariably ask, Are you sick?

Høiaas dominates me because I give in rather than risk criticism. Why? What does it matter?

I allow criticism to overwhelm me. For instance, worrying about the hotel desk clerks and grocers and landlords and selfish opportunists of the world.

I don't need them.

Don't I know by now the extent of my own assets? Why do I flinch when Lorraine tells me Palle thinks I am stupid? Don't I know after at least twenty years of adulation in school, at home, at work, that I *am* intelligent? Can't I keep up a memorable conversation with almost anyone I meet?

So I am not pretty—many people have, of course, told me I am, but I don't believe them. I *do* know I have some kind of appeal—have had it, have attracted all kinds of men for ten years.

24. "Fluffy," by Theodore Sturgeon, was published in the March 1947 issue of *Weird Tales*. It features Ransome, a self-absorbed, perennial houseguest who meets his deadly match in a talking, scheming cat, inappropriately named Fluffy.

· · ·

I am going to start keeping a list every day of

    1. the number of things I do that I don't want to do,

    2. the times I get "taken."

NOVEMBER 29

I am having mental troubles with the novel. Where is that plane where levity and soberness meet? What happens when I get to the "Christian" chapter?[25] Remember the "walk, don't run" episode.

"Don't *run*," he commanded, annoyed. "You're in Denmark. Not in America."

The Dud Avocado[26]—

Salinger[27]—

It occurred to me, as I watched his face just after I told him I loved him, that I must get him to go to a really good photographer—the Karsh[28] of Copenhagen—so that I could preserve that magnificent face, shadowed to its best advantage, in just the right frame on just the right piano in an apartment in America. I would be telling someone at home (Jackson perhaps) rather wistfully, "This is a boy I once loved in Denmark. He was the most beautiful man I ever knew."

This. This duplicity was the kind of thing I was capable of.

DECEMBER 1

Mailed Christmas cards . . . Hobbled along with the novel and met Niels after he finished at the theater. He is completely contrary to my image of man. I can't do a thing with him.

25. Christian was Godwin's fictional name for Niels. His chapter in her novel about Copenhagen corresponds to the novels that make up Lawrence Durrell's quartet about Alexandria.

26. *The Dud Avocado*, Elaine Dundy's sharp, comic novel about a fearless young woman's experiences among bohemians in Paris, was a best seller in 1958.

27. J. D. Salinger did not achieve publishing success until he was thirty, in 1949, when the *New Yorker* published his story "A Perfect Day for Bananafish." Two years later, *Catcher in the Rye* defined an innocent, hurt, postwar, psychoanalyzing American nation, and Salinger's consequent fame drove him into seclusion.

28. The Armenian photographer Yousuf Karsh, whose career spanned half a century, is famous for the portraits he made of such greats as Ernest Hemingway and Albert Einstein.

He bought me Durrell's *Dark Labyrinth.*[29]

It will either inspire me or undo me.

DECEMBER 2

He said: "I've begun a novel inside. It should take five years to experi-
ence and a year to write. It will be my only justification for taking
such a long holiday from myself."

—DURRELL, *DARK LABYRINTH*

I am gradually learning to accept those days during which I feel no
response to the love, questions, wishes, or intensities of others. I am
completely detached and look upon all forms of human intercourse as
somewhat of a nuisance. I don't love. I don't hate. Conversation trickles
right out of my ears and I only wish they would all leave me in peace to
read or to sleep, or simply to lie and think. I am beginning to like myself, and the number of hours during which I find myself acceptable is
increasing.

Niels wrote a poem to me in German which said he would kill me if I
left him. And yet, how relieved I was when he and Frowsy became occupied with the slingshot so I could read the very book in which he had
written that dramatic poem.

DECEMBER 5

Some things are a little bit hard to take. Of course I have been sick, but
I don't think that is it. Of course I have hypnotized myself with really
good science fiction for the last three days while I endured this cold. But
all the enchantment of my novel is gone and it reads like a silly school-
girl's English composition. "My Summer Vacation." It has no plot, no
central thread. Could it be that I am mediocre?

---

29. Lawrence Durrell had originally published *The Dark Labyrinth* under the title *Cefalù*
in 1947. "Cefalù" refers to a labyrinth of caves in which had dwelled the legendary
Minotaur. Durrell's characters go on an archaeological tour of the site and become trapped
by a cave-in.

Or do I just feel bad?

Or do I just need to keep groping without hope until I stumble upon it?

DECEMBER 7

Tonight I came in and found my bed occupied by a monkey wearing gloves and my brown shoes. I stifled a scream & giggled instead. Frowsy's been reading horror stories again.

Read an *excellent* article on DURRELL in the *Atlantic*. Must save it.

DECEMBER 11
MONDAY

Slowly something is hardening inside. Pretty soon I will be indomitable. This weekend, being my "first anniversary,"[30] was a horror to get through, but offered some pleasures, some enjoyments, and some enlightenment. Saturday morning Niels came. I went to meet him at the station but he got the wrong train so I was halfway to the market when I saw that camel-colored coat bobbing up and down beside a København-bound train. The ticket collector had told him that his "fiancée" had just passed, headed for the town train. If I had not seen Niels in time, he would have boarded the train and gone back to town.

"Didn't you *know* I wouldn't take the train *to* town when I am expecting you *from* town?"

"I never know," he said.

Such is that state of affairs. He—working day & night, not really trusting me; me—sleeping, eating, and playing day & night, not to be trusted.

We enjoyed a very proper breakfast with Høiaas & Gudrun, eating eggs bacon toast jam coffee milk & Tio Pepe dry. Niels wanted them to have it, I said no, fearing that it wasn't done; he recoiled faithfully, then in a spurt of renewed individuality poured it into their glasses. So they enjoyed it, he retained his masculinity, what the hell?

30. On December 10, 1960, Godwin had married Douglas Kennedy in Miami.

I then washed the dishes and we retired to my room for a little furtive passion which left me quite cold (what with listening to Høiaas's hacking cough in the next room and fearing he might walk in any minute).

Rode on the train to town with Niels, he piqued because I left early just to get a letter at American Express before it closed. We parted at Svanemollen amid much hand squeezing and I promised to call him. "Call me *every night*," he ordered. And so I didn't call him at all.

(Even the old bastard's cough is self-assertive. I will never feel sorry for him again, I feel sure.)

So I got my letter from B.[31]—saved and savored it—and browsed in Boghallen until it was too late to mail my letter. I found out that *Buddenbrooks* is now out of print and bought Sturgeon's *Some of Your Blood*[32] instead.

By the time I got back to Klampenborg it was growing dark and windy and the ocean was as bleak as dirty mop-water. I came inside 425 Strandvej to find myself quite alone with "Papa," who just could not see fit to leave me in peace. Making me coffee, bringing me old scarves which belonged to his wife. Finally I escaped in sleep at about 4:00 p.m. and he, discouraged, went off with Gudrun for beers in Toorbeck. I was awakened once more when Gudrun called and INSISTED I have beers with them, offering to send a TAXI for me. (What is this fatal charm of mine?) After ten minutes of saying no I finally went back to bed. The phone rang once and I knew it was either Gaert or Hartley so I did not answer. The next time I woke it was Mr. H., who was calling me to the phone. "Fellow calls himself Mr. Heinrichson," he said sourly. "I *wormed* his name out of him." By this time I was mad. Dear soft-voiced Gaert with his throaty "HOW *AH* YOU?" He said perhaps we could go out and I said no and he said well, maybe I could come Sunday at noon and I said "Okay." (Anything to *get them off!*) Then I hung up and saw the old tyrant dozing puckered up like an owl under his checked blanket and I knew I couldn't stay in that silent, dominated house with the wind

31. B. was Gail's friend, beau, and mentor in Asheville, an attorney who kept her library and had power of attorney over such matters as the sale of her car.

32. *Some of Your Blood*, Theodore Sturgeon's novel about a soldier's horrific obsession—revealed slowly by an army psychiatrist—was published in 1950.

howling and nothing but SF to read. So I called Gaert back and told him I'd be there in an hour.

Funny thing: I can remember the reluctance, resignation, and weltschmertz I felt as I kicked on my clothes and swept out into the wind. I felt very put-upon, one of nature's oppressed . . . Now I enjoy writing about it as a prelude to a very enjoyable weekend which got better by degrees, which started out BLAHHH and wound up fine.

Which always proves: When you least expect it . . .

DECEMBER 11

Saturday night was spent complaining to Gaert, socializing with two rather drab people, a middle-aged chess partner of Palle & one of his ex-girls. A pallid desperate blonde of about thirty with bad gums who teaches school. She hated me, all Palle's girls do, because I simply do not care. Gaert & I walked clear across town to buy sandwiches in great fervor, only no one was hungry when we got back. Palle blithely shut everyone out and read Russian and I tried to entertain the weary guests who'd invited themselves.

On Sunday, G. wrapped me up and forced me to go for a walk. "PLEASE," he said. "I never get to see daylight in the winter." I remember at the beginning of that walk I just gazed up at the gray skies and let my arms hang at my side like sticks. I was feeling sorry for myself, and very fashionable to be having my very own Danish depression. Of course, it helped to have a strong hand holding me by the scruff of the neck. After he had taken me down by the canal (where I teetered on the edge, wishing I could fall in and scared to death I *might*) and by the old stone fishwife. And in front of ABSALOM on his rearing horse. By the time I had heard the tinkling message of the NICKOLAI chimes and G. had bought me a chunk of NOUGAT I felt better.

We then returned (Palle had left) and played *Carnaval*[33] & Mozart and I was a real bitch. He finally said that my passivity irritated him and that made me mad, which was better than passivity.

33. Robert Schumann's virtuoso piano composition features several balletlike themes representing characters who elude and confound the tempo of a stately waltz.

Then we went to Det Lille Apotec[34] and sat at a big overturned barrel by the window and had fried chicken & beer. I unwound. And his shock of blond hair became endearing. Indeed his whole aspect became angelic, his overbite puckish, his huge, veiny hands complex towers of strength. He told me his favorite animals were the penguin & the turtle and I told him mine was the cat. He said he figured that. Then he said that he liked many aspects of me.

I LIKE TO LOOK AT YOU

TALK TO YOU

DISCUSS WITH YOU

WATCH YOU MOVE

DECEMBER 15

JINGLE BELLS—

Read TW's *The Web & the Rock* & Salinger's *Catcher in the Rye* and decided my forte is somewhere in the middle.[35] I am in a bad slump. Come January, plans have got to be made. I will write Bev Miller January 1. Meanwhile, look for job here.

Sore throat again. Cold. Said Gaert: "All you can do is count them."

Now into hibernation for a few days.

What's with Niels? He didn't call back the other night. Something ominous portends. There is something creepy about this still, quiet house. Høiaas is hacking away. I'm sorry, but I feel no sympathy anymore. Had a *glug* or *gluk* with the Fat Boy at Magasin du Nord.[36] Rum, sweet vermouth, gin, raisins & almonds SCALDING. Mmmmm. I can't help it. He looks so funny running for the train, coat buttoned tightly over fat belly, the homburg and the everlasting briefcase.

34. Det Lille Apotec (The Little Pharmacy), established in 1720, is the oldest restaurant in Copenhagen and had numbered among its regular guests Hans Christian Andersen. Among other things, it is famous for the prodigious amount of beer it serves.

35. Among young intellectuals, Thomas Wolfe and J. D. Salinger were gods, equally revered, representing different stances. In *The Web and the Rock* (1939), Wolfe re-created his personal mythology to make it more of a social commentary, whereas Salinger's *Catcher in the Rye* (1951) is antiheroic, its protagonist, Holden Caulfield, cast as an existentialist, beloved because of his irony and unself-conscious self-examination.

36. Magasin du Nord, built in 1893, is Denmark's oldest and most famous department store. The "Fat Boy" is Hartley, an acquaintance who sponged off other people.

. . .

Gaert called yesterday at twelve, woke me up & asked me over. We spent a small fortune (rather I did) and were rewarded with succulent beef béarnaise, the excellent service of the manager of the Café de Paris (who looks like an assistant professor of political science at UNC, or a young, alert, shy-clever *Miami Herald* recruit bound for stardom), and a lovely warm sad red wine drunk. We all got drunk. Palle & his chess partner—who knew only one tune on his guitar—got drunk. Gaert— got drunk. And of course . . . I.

Only last night was a little off-tune. I remember lying there watching the candle flicker and looking at that terrible aqua & orange painting where Gaert tried to copy Van Gogh and, of all the stupid things, I thought of my twenty-nine-year-old cousin Jeannie sitting at the table in the den of her little house and drinking coffee with me, saying, "And I want to get a marble table for the living room . . . We have this couple who belongs to the same group we do and we play bridge at their house on Saturday night . . ." And then I thought of that special walk my mother & I used to take in the woods behind the house in Weaverville and before I knew it I was crying and listening to *Carnaval* and staring at a streetlight through tears.

Gaert didn't say, What is it? What? What? *Tell* me. I want to *help* you.

He just touched me several times as if it were the most natural thing in the world to have a *wine-tantrum*. Then he carried me to bed and covered me up with the blue quilt.

Earlier, I asked him what he would wish if he only had one wish.

"But I usually get three."

"No, this time it's one."

"Well, then I . . . I would wish to have the secret of the blue color," he said. "And you?"

"I would simply wish to get it all down," I said.

He calls his diary his night book. I think, aside from the hair, I like him because he croons little nothings to me in Danish and not English.

• • •

I bought one small cake of Balmain soap and squandered it in the tub.

Tomorrow, if I write, it will be the ERIC & MARTIN[37] CHAPTER—complete with descriptions, etc.

DECEMBER 17

5:30 A.M.

Oh strange day, full of much anger and talk with Frowsy and continued battle with Niels. I won somehow and with Frowsy's help. I think that from now on I have a new tenderness for Niels.

When I saw Høiaas's olive green shirt, the one he wears under the plaid vest, day after day, hanging by the radiator in the bathroom, I suddenly felt all the badness drain out of my heart as if, somewhere deep down & far away, someone had pulled out the plug.

I have been reading *Of Time and the River*.[38] Tom, I too have the Faustian disease. And I thought I was alone. He thought the same things I thought.

And yet, people like Mr. Cole[39] can stand in the kitchen and say between whiskey swigs: Old Tom, he was a little touched in the head. Drunker'n hell all the time.

I will not return yet.

I can stay here until the spring.

The idea of being a maid at Bellevue appeals to me.

Why is it?

More than being a journalist, even. That is so damn safe.

37. Eric and Martin are fictional characters based on Palle and Gaert. The story has been lost.

38. Thomas Wolfe's *Of Time and the River*, published in 1935, is a gargantuan novel, in which the hero casts himself as "young Faustus," contends with the million faces of a city, pursues a love affair with a "Helen," and ends up at a drink-fest and fight in Munich. The book is subtitled "A Legend of Man's Hunger in His Youth."

39. Eugene Cole, father of Gail's stepfather, Frank Cole, had been a classmate of Thomas Wolfe's at Claxton Elementary School in Asheville.

THE FATEFUL CALL

Copenhagen by Bus and Train to Málaga

DECEMBER 20, 1961–JANUARY 30, 1962

Gail was living very much on the edge—obviously alone among men whom she had not known two months earlier—protected mainly by the shield that her writing intensity afforded her. To make matters worse, she had little money and no definite prospects. Her journal notes sometimes reflect on how she has eaten little or gotten through a day without any expenses.

In her dark and "companionable" Denmark months, Gail found herself in a rather remarkable and dangerous mise-en-scène, where individuals acted out their demons while claiming lovability. She was a part of it, yet she strove to treat it as a waking dream, analyzing and making fictional use of her initiation into a foreign existence.

In order to gain the kind of experience that would serve as meaningful material for many years, she had to allow herself to plumb the depths of the dramas she encountered. Whereas a normally functioning person shuns the irrational, Gail, as a writer, had to be keen to it, drawing the world out from behind its guises.

The subjective, risk-taking approach to a writer's education involves not only personal dangers but also literary traps. Imposing one's preconceptions and conceits upon experiences threatens to invalidate the journey. In her journals, Gail counsels herself to be honest, knowing that her own needs and tendencies alter reality and cloud understanding.

Gail's approach also depended upon faith in a reward—becoming a writer rather than a defeated person, fictionalizing drama rather than simply being dramatic, as her stepfather might have characterized her.

In the following pages, you will see how Gail's attempts to assure herself of a successful writing career become increasingly intense and various as the window of her opportunity begins to close. Despite the rough and exerting ride, Gail holds on. She does not go home, although she contem-

plates doing so. And when she finds her lifeline, it does not come from a publisher or a patron, but from an employer.

The office job in London comes through. It is more like a safe house than like a field of dreams. Yet a safe house can be an outpost with doorways to new truths.

DECEMBER 20, 1961

Copenhagen, Denmark . . . the season of interminable nights and unfathomable thoughts. And much good fun.

I have come here to hear myself.[1] The trouble is: I have no system. I want to get it all down, but fly in all directions at once. I am starting *The Alexandria Quartet* for the second time. It has been almost a year since I last began it and then I was primarily interested in the plot and driven crazy by his references to things that had not happened yet. This time, I shall savor it and, at the same time, study it. I think Thomas Wolfe is the best Southern American writer. Tolstoy, the most lasting. Durrell, the best writer in the English-speaking world *at present.* Who knows who may transcend him tomorrow or the next day? Brother, when one finally decides to write a book, how the branches stem, the crosscurrents flow & mingle, the memories fuse and then bear new memories. I can't get it down as fast as my thoughts go. THE THING I MUST WATCH, I have discovered in rereading myself, is KNOWING WHEN TO STOP. Eureka! I just devised a system to get down all the images and keep them organized. At the back of this journal I will keep pages on each character, plus several on my word-picture of this city. God only knows what I shall end up with. It will be either a book or a mess. First, dammit, before I do another thing, I have got to get down some things I don't want to forget. For the first time in my life I have had all the time in the world to read. I have read all the best sellers I never cared to read at home, *Advise & Consent, The Ugly American,* Steinbeck's new one, *The Winter of*

1. Godwin is echoing the opening movements of *Justine.* Durrell's narrator removes himself to a Greek island in order to reconstruct the romance of his Alexandria and "rebuild the city in [his] brain," whereas Godwin, having lived for a month in her most foreign city so far, is trying to "hear" it even as she is living it. Gail lived with the Høiaases from mid-November 1961 until January 20, 1962.

Our Discontent. I have discovered Steinbeck at his best in *The Wayward Bus* and *Cannery Row.*

I thought today: What I am building inside now I can take anywhere.

DECEMBER 21

A Dollar's Worth of "Hygge"[2]

Notes on the city: It is Christmastime in Copenhagen. On the corner at Øesterport—street of the embassies—a woman in wooden shoes sells straw reindeer and *jule* wreaths from her stall, and a blind man, wearing the yellow armband, which identifies him as one of Denmark's sightless, sits outside Øesterport station on a little wooden stool. He is playing Christmas carols on an old-fashioned phonograph that has to be wound. He stops grinding away to change records or to pocket some charity.

I wonder what would happen if someone gave him a 100 Kr note. Would he feel its value by running his fingers along the edges? Would he then pick up his stool and go home to some bare attic room and warm his hands?

I am sitting on the train, reading (it is no longer a novelty to look out the window at the scenery because I know it by heart). Vesterport, Norregade, Øesterport, Nordhaven, Svanemollen, Hellerup, Charlottenlund, Ordrup & Klampenborg, clackety clackety . . . screech . . . stop—a rush of cold air comes in with the new passengers. It seems only boring people sit in the cars marked "Til Ikke-Rygere."[3] It is only the old ladies and the very young who do not smoke.

Tonight I was caught in an act as shameful as picking one's nose. I was reading as the train sped along. It was a depressing story about a poor man in Paris and his affair with his haggish old janitress so the rent would come down. I grew bored and flipped through the pages to read the end, then sighed and closed the book. I looked up to see a man

2. *Hygge* means "companionability."

3. *Til ikke-rygere* means "No smoking."

sitting opposite me and chuckling silently. I looked at him and he looked at me and we both laughed out loud. All the old women turned to stare. He got off at the next stop, and I felt sad for a minute because I knew he understood me better than anyone else on that train.

For me, sooner or later, every city turns into a man. In this particular time, my city was Christian.

September 25, 1961, Regi Friedmann's controversial letter about Copenhagen from Tel Aviv. It appeared in *Life* magazine.

> *The apparent gaiety and hygge of Copenhagen cover an unspeakable self-torture which must be rooted in complete emptiness. There is an extraordinary loneliness about these people, a colossal misanthropy and every second Dane, when asked at the right moment, will tell you that he is fed up. When one describes Copenhagen, one should not refrain from representing this Kaleidoscopic truth: the Tivoli[4] versus the Mal de Vivre.*

The last train shuttles back to Copenhagen . . . the moon is full . . . and it's just me and Frowsy and our big blue pitcher of grapefruit juice. One must ever be warding off the scurvy.

THE OLDEST MONARCHY IN EUROPE
has the houses Christian IV built & the names of the streets.[5]

DECEMBER 23

Hark the *Herald Tribune*. Tomorrow & Monday I shall finish "Roxanne." I must, for my own good. I remember sitting in Bar-Dot with Niels drinking Hof and looking out at the wooly-capped shoppers on

4. Tivoli is a huge amusement park in the heart of Copenhagen. Established in 1843, it has grown to include Tivoli Gardens, rides, stage entertainments, and more.

5. Christian IV ruled Denmark and Norway from 1588 to 1648. He is known as the Builder King. Fires and wars have eradicated most of Christian IV's projects, but the Børsen (Stock Exchange), Rundetårn (Round Tower), and the Palace of Rosenborg survive, as do the medieval foundations of the streets.

Strøget.[6] I had a flash of insight. I knew I was in Denmark and knew why. I could, as Lorraine would say, place myself. Writing is a process of refining. It is also a painful process of introspection demanding complete honesty. Tonight I want to get down the two faces of Copenhagen.

On one side—the Paris of the North—playground of the grizzly trolls, blond blue-eyed descendants of the Vikings screaming with glee on the merry-go-round at Tivoli. A pale tall flaxen-haired goddess walking, arms linked, with a black man in an American sport jacket . . . A thousand ways of saying thank you.

DECEMBER 24

Funny, the way things suddenly come to you. I know exactly what I am going to do next and I have almost a whole God-given month.

1. The two stories. One "Roxanne," the other a sort of mood piece on Copenhagen with the Aarhus[7] home as the center.

2. Then inquire about Spain.[8] I must work without thinking ahead.

She gave me the Nothing look and disappeared into the entrails of the long silver car followed by a porter carrying her white leather luggage.

There goes Roxanne O'Day, down another set of shining rails, across continents, over mountains. Who knows, just over that next ridge, the other side of that ocean—or maybe just around the corner—she will find a stopping place.

I have done twenty-four pages and, in my heavy-headed ecstasy, I think I finally captured it. Interesting. The longer I write, the easier it becomes to say just what I mean. I am at the basement scene now and will save this for a clear head & a new day.

6. Strøget is a chain of five streets—a pedestrian mall—that emanates from the northern corner of the Tivoli and features shops, restaurants, and entertainments.

7. Aarhus was Godwin's fictional name, at this time, for the Høiaas family.

8. "I had always intended to go to Spain," Gail recalls, "to see the Goya at the Prado, to practice my advanced Spanish, which wasn't quite as good as I'd thought, and to GET WARM before going to England."

Then the retyping, the mailing off, and the horrible suspense.

At least I have had this winter to find out if I'm any good.

Last year I was under a heap of covers with my new husband. His skin was always smooth & warm and smelled freshly scrubbed. He was gentle and proud in Canada before I began tormenting him. I remember him saying huskily in the dark bedroom in his parents' home, "I'm doing all right by you, aren't I?"

The whole episode was so pointless. But am I really sorry?

Christmas 1961. I must say in all honesty that last year, smothered in Canada Kennedys, I could not even imagine being in Copenhagen a year from then. My imagination never stretched farther than Paris.

No, I'm not sorry. I only hope he's not lying alone tonight in that big bed in Windsor, reviewing the dreams that went up in smoke and remembering a sweet, gentle me that never existed.

DECEMBER 29

The three blasts of the foghorn are the loneliest sounds in the world. I am marking off the hours. I could even go to Barcelona and stay a week or two and *then* decide what to do next. I am sure of one thing. I am learning to write. I don't even know when or how it happened. And it is all that matters. I think Spain will be fun—if I can just do it *right* for once in my life. But to stay here any longer would be warming up cold soup. October 21 to January 21—funny, three months to the day. Don't think in extremes about the short story. It is neither good nor bad. It is an unborn child. Do *not* fret over imagined monstrosities.

Called Niels, not out of love but curiosity. There is nothing between us anymore. I only want to dissect him now and study him like a rare cold fish. Maybe I can learn something more. He is in trouble. His father [stepfather] was at the hotel at midnight when I called. "He has some problems with me," said my mad youth.[9]

9. The reference to Niels as the "mad youth" shows empathy and love as well as a distancing. Niels's attractiveness had to do not only with his manliness but also with his being troubled. After his father's death in a concentration camp, Niels had been left under the care and scrutiny of a stepfather.

DECEMBER 30

I love these Saturdays, but it is time to move on. The foghorn. A good breakfast. The short story half typed. *Balthazar* delivered to my door[10] & Bradbury's "Fog Horn"[11] to read. Tomorrow I must hem up the black dress, wash my hair. New Year's party at Sven's.[12] His sister just married an American & there will be friends from Paris. Sven came by this morning, all pink & fresh from a bath. I will miss the blondes.

Now that I know I am leaving, I relish each moment. Who knows, I may be doing this or that for the last time. Frowsy and his explosives![13]

Copenhagen—a certain sterility. The very thing that cleansed it of its slums also cleansed it of its extremes.

Isak Dinesen said antiseptic, antibiotic, cleansed her of her extremes like a mouthwash destroys bacteria. It never occurred to her that cleanness sometimes means sterility.[14]

Their king is tattooed and they love it; they don't love people lying on HCA's bed![15]

There ought to be some way, sufficiently descriptive, to get down on paper the sound of Høiaas skarking up his tons of phlegm. It is maddening, inconsiderate, unsanitary, sticky, and disgusting. And in between, he whistles "Wonderful, wonderful Copenhagen." Well. Poor old man. He is old, bitter, lonely, frightened. I will be hell at sixty.

---

10. The book, the second volume in Durrell's tetralogy, was delivered by the local bookshop in Klampenborg.

11. "The Fog Horn" is the first story in Ray Bradbury's collection *The Golden Apples of the Sun.*

12. Gail had met Sven, a young man from a well-established family, at a party that one of her shipmates, Kamma Rode, had thrown for her.

13. Two of Frowsy's "explosives"—expletives—were called "For Satan" and "Satan's Ass."

14. Copenhagen is famous for its cleanliness and its antipollution laws. Dinesen contracted syphilis from her husband in 1914, while she was in Africa. Doctors administered to her the then-current cures, which involved intake of mercury and arsenic. The effects of the cleansing medicines did her more harm than the disease.

15. Frowsy had told Gail how the Danes had hated it when Danny Kaye lay down on Hans Christian Andersen's bed.

JANUARY 1, 1962

Hartley took advantage of me tonight by inviting Frowsy and then *making* me pay—29 Kr![16] I wanted only to spend 6! With Høiaas, it is easier. I have only two rooms to keep out of trouble in: bathroom & living room. Tomorrow I shall *entirely* clean out the objects of mine in the bathroom. Then, all I have to worry about is washing out the tub and not dripping or tracking things. That leaves the kitchen. Wash up and empty my garbage. It will drive him batty. Then, all he can do is to start taking things out of this room. That should be interesting.

JANUARY 2

The feeling is mainly curiosity at this time. A small group of phantom people have completely vanished from me and it is interesting to speculate. There are Lorraine & Niels, Palle and Gaert, Sven, Klaus,[17] the people at the embassy, the Old Tyrant. All enveloped in a quiet, white silence. Lorraine has gone to Spain. Niels has fled like a mad hare. I might have asked him for something, and I was the kind of person who made him uneasy. He had other facets, too. Only I was so busy trying to squeeze all his traits into a chapter that I lost the third dimension. Palle and Gaert can be coupled into one. There was a twisting of the wills. The turning point came when G. called querulously from the studio-bedroom.[18] I'm twenty-four. Klaus? He owes me money.

JANUARY 3

I have read too much SF. Høiaas wouldn't answer the phone. Niels hasn't called. I am so unsure tonight. All I lack is money.

16. Hartley was the American whom Gail characterized as a "fat boy" as much for his spoiled behavior—he sponged on others despite having a good income—as for anything else.

17. Klaus had traveled with Gail to Berlin in November.

18. Gaert was lying down and he thought Gail was having too much fun with Palle and his friends in the next room. Gail was supposed to be his date, he had thought, and should have come and cheered him up.

JANUARY 4

I am really proud of my story. Tomorrow I shall buy twenty more sheets of paper, finish copying (it will run about twenty-six pages), and polish, polish, polish. I can send the story away with pride and the assurance that I have done my best. If it fails to be appreciated by others, it will not hurt too much because I have learned much from it.

I have worked on "Roxanne" so long that I can't think straight about it tonight. I decided it was awful. Things I must learn: Avoid the obvious. The intelligent reader looks forward to a little gambol with his mind.

The damn thing is over ten thousand words long. In other words, on a European typewriter a short story should be about thirteen pages! Niels has vanished into the earth.

IT WOULD BE CHILDISH, AFRAID, and unadventurous to go home now. I can always take a Spanish freighter home. It would be nice to get a Mediterranean *brown*. I need faith in myself, like the girl said. "After all, you can *always* get fifteen kroner an hour scrubbing the dead bodies in Sweden."

After "Roxanne" is finished, I start "Walk, Don't Run." A short story, mostly about Frowsy's capacity for enjoying life. "We will come a little salt in it" . . . "I will come on my clotheses" . . . his hat on the train . . . his love of animals . . . fine slides of his travels . . . the Bach prelude . . . the automobiles & oranges in Greenland . . . watching him cook a dinner. This cannot be written till I'm away. Must be warm & humorous . . . fireworks & Mrs. Kaufman's dog . . . the policemen on the beach . . . the feeling I derived from it . . . Gudrun makes a story all by herself . . . These journals are so important . . . stay away from the sophisticated stories for a while . . . make simple line drawings, clean astringent word-pictures.

> If I had contemplated any . . . (for, being a Southerner, this was, needless to say, the first time I had ever met a Negro on equal footing at a cocktail party) . . . After that night Roxanne dominated me.

Not only was I forced away from any overflow of Sisterhood, etc., but I was literally forced to hold on for dear life to any personality I had in the presence of this Creature of Assurance.

Roxanne had read more than I had, gone to a better college, spoke better English, dressed with more chic, and conversed with more freedom & greater choice of words.

JANUARY 8

This room[19]—the old chest 1783 from Bornholm with "L.O.S." & a parrot— Nefertiti's head on top with a bullet hole through her right cheek. The desk with explosives. The old laughing Buddha, the Norwegian land- scape, the art closet[20] with the orange, tan & black horizontal striped curtain, the leather wine pouch from Spain, the *thing* swimming in formaldehyde—the green bottle—a forgotten shrunken sea monster. Some ornery plant that stands over the radiator and has not been wa- tered during my entire time. And the books! A bibliophile's dream. "This is the room where you may ask stupid questions in," says Frowsy.

"The squid copulates more gentlemanly than any other animal. He makes a neat little package of his sperm and hands it over to his lady in a special tentacle. She, in turn, pockets it, to use whenever the mood strikes her."

JANUARY 10

Finished Roxanne's last nadir. Tomorrow it only remains to transcribe it [the story] mindlessly and emotionlessly.

I am rather disgusted with everyone tonight. I am more displeased with myself because I depend on people and perhaps expect them to act like saints.

Big news. Høiaas called through the stillness: Gail? Do you want to talk to me?

19. Gail's room at the Høiaases' was the former workroom of the late Mrs. Høiaas, a well- known Danish illustrator of magazine stories. Gail is noting down some of the contents of the room.
20. Mrs. Høiaas's art materials were behind this curtain.

1. He apologized for being a "stupid old fool."

2. He said he never wanted me to leave his house thinking he didn't like me.

3. He made no effort to defend himself except to say he was worried about Frowsy's exams.

Of course there followed a blubbery scene. I fell on his neck, he told me I shouldn't be so casual about my affairs, and then he said over & over again, "I wish I had a daughter" (about six times). "I need someone to console." Then he made me a pot of tea and we talked about the German occupation of Denmark.

This would make a good story, only I must know where to begin & where to end. This will be a process of sifting events. There is much flotsam & jetsam.

Funny. Yesterday, the sound of his coughing or flushing the toilet sent hostile quivers through me; now, they are simply reassuring sounds. And yet: Nobody has really changed. We are forever turning in our orbits, exposing new sides to one another, but we are still the same inside. Is my luck changing for the better?

(I think the thing that bothered him most was that I preferred Frowsy to him.)

JANUARY 12

Got through an entire day without spending money. Monday I must buy ticket to Barcelona. Should be interesting trip. I am going home on a freighter. Am retyping "Roxanne." Hemmed MOST of my raincoat.

I really shouldn't have such a defeatist attitude toward rejections. The only stories I have ever submitted were the following: "I Broke the Code" to a "Confessions" magazine (they said it was well written, but not enough action); "Exposition" (*Atlantic Monthly*, for God's sake); "New Year's Eve" to *Male* (they said it was sloppily written and it was); "The Raising of Lazarus." The ending was wrong; rejected by three magazines. The last man sent back a note: Well done, but not our kind of ending. Then I have sent two queries, one to *Glamour* & one to *McCall's*. *Glamour* said to submit the finished manuscript. So that wasn't a flat *no*. Of course there was "The Otherwise Virgins," but that was sent only to two agents. Actually, "Roxanne" is the first thing into which I put any effort. I am going to type it impeccably, shorten it as much as possible, and send it to *Mademoiselle* with a short introductory letter.

How Frowsy relishes each incident in his life.

- "Now I shall come on some clotheses and go and fetch some bread and milk mmmmm . . . We shall have a fine breakfast!"

- "I shall have my *smørbrød* and then we will listen to *one* Bach cantata."

- "Tonight I shall go to my fiancée. Mmm. She has a *lovely* ass."

- "Now, I shall go shit."

All in the same zesty tone.

I am always searching for a story. Until I find it, would it not be better to try little drills? Short, clean sketches of things that I understand.
Nautical terms.[21]
Written in GG's journal by Frowsy—at GG's invitation:

Cristmastraditions in Denmark

First of all in Denmark we celebrate the evening the 24/12 not the following day. The celebration actually starts with the preparations finish the night [evening] before 23/12. This evening is called *lillejuleaften* [Little Christmas Eve].

---

21. Gail had found a dictionary of nautical terms among Frowsy's books, which he kept in his late mother's room. She compiled a list of those terms that would be useful to her in writing her Halcyone story.

Lillejuleaften skal du barrke
pa min dor,
for lillejuleaften es leagen
aldrig Sor.

Little Christmas Eve you shall
knock on my door,
because little Christmas Eve
the cake is never dry.

Everyone coming the eve 23/12 shall have at least one cake or he will "carry out Christmas." We have a Christmas tree with candles on and besides it a bucket with water. It is of course decorated with lots of things in a more or less traditional way. I have personally things to put on that tree which are more than one hundred years old. Under that tree is placed gifts from our friends and the gifts among ourselves as soon as they arrive. In the afternoon we go to church and when we come home we dine. First we have rice porridge. In that is placed one almond, the one who gets that in his portion shows it before eating it and then receives an almond gift. MANDELGAVE. Then we have goose or duck filled with apples and such inside and after that baked apples with jam inside. To the goose we always have a good red wine, chianti or bordeaux. Then the dinner is over, we sit down to coffee and cognac, children get some too (only time in the year), and then the head of the family read letters and cards from absent friends. If there are children, gifts are given now, and then we dance around the lace hand in hand singing Christmas carols. If there are only big children, we dance first. Then we sit with our gifts having chocolate, nougat, almonds, marzipan, and homemade little dry cakes of different colors and tastes, drinking cognac and—whiskey.

Then the candles of the tree will begin to go out, if we wish when the last candle dies the wish will come true. We go to bed very very late, when we awake we have a gorgeous breakfast.

GLAEDELIG JUL,
Lasse.

SVIKMOLLEN
BLAEKSPRUTTEN[22]

This is an ADVENTSKRANS [Frowsy's drawing of an Advent wreath].

There are four Advents Sundays in December. The first Sunday and following week the first candle is lighted, next Sunday and following week two candles is lighted and so on.

JANUARY 16
TUESDAY
More Wisdom from the Satyr in Long Underwear:

- "Later on, you won't need so many words to say exactly what you mean."

- "I think it is all right to go for the extremes. However, know ahead that you may pay and pay dearly."

- "There can be no art without experience. Expression, yes, but no art."

- "Take a situation and examine it and write about it in the light of

  1. what you understand, or

  2. what you don't understand.

Images for Sometime:

NEW ORLEANS: What was it about that city?

Mother Winters's disillusionment syndrome.

---

22. Frowsy—aka Lars or Lasse—is wishing Gail a merry Christmas and naming two classic Danish works of humor. "Svikmollen" was a syndicated cartoon feature by the graphic artist and social commentator Haakon Hesselager, who was awarded Danish cartoonists' and journalists' highest honor in 1962. *Blaeksprutten* was an 1896 book of Danish wit, the cover of which featured a picture of dancing polar bears.

The whole story → from eighth-grade enthusiasm to the night in the rain.

Why did I keep up with her? It is interesting to speculate on the causes and durations of friendship. That was a delicate and intangible thing.

The diary—into which went painstaking care.

The hospital on the hill.[23] Grieg.

Da da da da da da da dum.

And slowly answered Arthur from the Barge
The Old Order changeth, yielding place to New
God fulfills himself in many ways
Lest one good custom does corrupt the world
Comfort thyself; what comfort is for me
For I have lived my life; may that which I have done
May God within himself make peace
For the whole round earth is in every way bound around
*   the feet of God.*[24]

23. When Gail's mother and stepfather moved to the Beverly Apartments (see page 90), Gail would walk up the hill to sit on the bank of Memorial Mission Hospital and look across the Biltmore Avenue cut to the tower of St. Genevieve's Preparatory School. She would hear the bell for prayers ring and feel connected to her teacher.

24. Gail is inscribing lines that have to do with the passing of Arthur (from Alfred, Lord Tennyson's *Idylls of the King*, "The Passing of Arthur," lines 407–417) from memory, evidently, for the actual poem reads:

And slowly answered Arthur from the barge:
"The old order changeth, yielding place to new,
And God fulfills himself in many ways,
Lest one good custom should corrupt the world.
Comfort thyself: what comfort is in me?
I have lived my life, and that which I have done
May He within himself make pure! but thou,
If thou shouldst never see my face again,
Pray for my soul. More things are wrought by prayer
Than this world dreams of. Wherefore, let thy voice
Rise like a fountain for me night and day."

... and I would kill my mother if she came into my room; even Wiggles was too earthy for my rhapsodic Grieg & Tennyson. Religion and Sacrifice Flights.[25]

To the tune of "Notre Dame": "She always has a sweet ready smile; she makes our classes all seem worthwhile—eighth-grade class stand up and cheer for our teacher very dear."

I went back every year at first, and then I went back whenever I came home. I always went expecting to find something and I always came away with a sense of having been deprived. GENTLE FAITH. HOW CRUEL IS TRUTH!

GAIL AND MOTHER WINTERS

In the autumn of 1950, Kathleen Winters, an idealist in her mid-thirties, came to Asheville. The Religious of Christian Education, a French Catholic order, had sent her to St. Genevieve's Preparatory School (grades 1-8) to serve as principal and eighth-grade teacher.

An Irishwoman from Galway, Winters had taken religious vows in her late teens. Her order then provided her with an education in Brussels and Boston, which she followed up with advanced degrees in English and science at the University of North Carolina at Chapel Hill.

For eighth-grade students at St. Genevieve's in 1950, this spirited woman, with her warm wit and steady heart, and her passion for music, literature, and mathematics, immediately became a favorite. They worked hard for her, imitated her sprightly walk and surprised, throaty laugh, and composed a "class song" in her honor to the tune of "Notre Dame." She was to become a central figure in Godwin's life.

At thirteen, Gail began her first diary, bound in black paper, which

25. The religious thought that Gail received from Mother Winters, her teacher and mentor at St. Genevieve's Preparatory School in Asheville, merged with Gail's literary and romantic thoughts.

she illustrated with drawings and cutouts. She wrote in it faithfully every day in order to get down as much as possible about each school day under the influence of her mesmerizing mentor. She began slanting her handwriting to resemble Winters's distinctive script more closely.

At this time, Gail was living with her mother and stepfather in the Beverly Apartments, which was within walking distance of St. Genevieve's. She regularly stayed after school and helped Winters straighten up the classroom. Or the two would take a walk around the grounds of the old Victorian building, or listen to classical records until it was time for the nuns to go to chapel.

Back home, in her room, Gail would write in her journal, listening to Grieg or Rachmaninoff on the record player. She would recite passages from Tennyson's Idylls of the King.

In the early evening she would walk up the hill to sit on the bank outside Mission Hospital and look across to the tower at St. Genevieve's. She'd wait for the bell for evening prayers to ring and feel balanced between the "Winters" world and the not-too-stable world of the Coles. Gail's mother had miscarried a baby and was trying to have another one; Gail's stepfather was growing unhappy in his job as a management trainee at S. H. Kress & Co.

The "disillusionment syndrome" Godwin writes about in the Copenhagen journal refers to less-than-satisfying visits with Winters in Asheville during the decade or so after their eighth-grade closeness. The Coles had moved away, and when Gail returned for visits to Asheville, there was never enough time to talk of real things.

In her teens and early twenties Gail had become secretive about certain areas of her life, and there was an awkward formality between herself and her old teacher. Also, Winters had stopped wearing the habit, an accommodation that was, at first, disconcerting to Godwin.

Nevertheless, the friendship and correspondence between Gail and Mother Winters continued and grew. In the final years, their relationship blossomed. The mentor-disciple dynamic evolved into an easier relationship between equals who enjoyed each other's company and conversation and were able to discuss their spiritual lives. After Gail's mother, Kathleen

Cole, died in 1989, Winters took to signing her letters "The Other Kath-leen."

Mother Winters died in her mid-eighties on Good Friday of 2001.

JANUARY 17

Frowsy routed me out this morning at an unprecedented hour with dire threats and many slaps on the bottom. I went to the Spanish Embassy, met a Spanish woman & experienced for the first time the thrill of speaking in another language. Bought my ticket for Sunday (320 Kr). It is interesting to speculate about other passengers. I don't think there will be many.

Anyway, several important things I want to get down. Dug out my old *Herald* clippings and Frowsy was reading the one about the old men at the Stranahan shuffleboard court.[26] I had forgotten that I could once write simply & humorously, but I could. "Flanked by two faithful incisors," etc.

JANUARY 18

Today it happened. Frowsy brought a letter to my bed and I saw the regular red, white & blue stripes of the airmail and *knew*. "This may be from the man in London," Frowsy said.

"Yes," I said. "But I'm not going to read it. It's a no. I can tell because it is thin."

But I was wrong.

JANUARY 19

One *hell* of a day, weather-wise, that is. Got two of Salinger's only four stories I haven't read out of the American Embassy library, even though it means getting up early in the morning. I am going to lie in the sun forever for one month, get a tan, get healthier.

---

26. Stranahan Park in Fort Lauderdale was one of many neighborhood parks in the city that featured a variety of recreational facilities.

. . .

I can't even remember what clothes I have at home to be sent. Probably end up buying new ones anyway. Well, I'm going to take the London job, devote myself to it (because, let's face it, I have to earn money in order to live) and to my writing. This won't be easy, because I know myself. I know my puttering tendencies and I admit that I love to sleep. Also, I will be tempted to get in the RAT RACE once more (clothes, parties, affairs, status symbols, etc.). Remember, Gail. Just remember. I know very well how many years I have yearned (however foolishly) for my chance to work abroad. Now I am getting that chance and I realize the pleasure of it all. I must try, once again, to establish certain rules to go by and try to stick to them *once again*. I have been luckier than most. Now, (1) Don't tell anything about yourself to anybody that you don't have to. Always be polite, cheerful & evasive. And (2) Do your very best on your job. Don't clock-watch. Don't come in late. And don't (as Keith said)[27] try to reach the moon in one day. I sincerely believe if I want to be a writer I can. It may take longer than I expected. That's all. My duty now is to faithfully keep journals.

Høiaas just tried to make a Bloody Mary with tomato juice & schnapps. He is coughing his brains out. Life is full of surprises for those of us who are inventive.

JANUARY 24
BARCELONA—OLÉ

I will probably die any minute now. I just drank two sips of Spanish water.

Things I want to remember re travel article "The Art of Blending In":

The lobster-bedbug joke.

The Pyrenees—I couldn't believe it. All that hot, ochre grass, the green powder puff–like eucalyptus trees & *then the snow.*

27. Keith was the bureau chief in Fort Lauderdale who had given up on Gail.

1. The two sisters in black. Toilet tissue, wine from tin cups, Elizabeth Arden facials in the reflection from the sun.

2. The seventy-year-old artist cum knapsack & five necessary sentences in any language. Eggs raw through a hole.

3. The Swedish couple.

4. The farmer-gardener from Ohio & Copenhagen. Horse-feathers. "Just 'supplement' them on their good wine or their beautiful scenery and they'll do anything for you!"

5. Berlitz session on the bus:

> *not one camera,*
>
> not one time did they ask for specialties from their own country,
>
> not once did they shout their own language with much arm-flailing, etc., expecting to be understood.

The travel bureau went overboard to help me and we didn't speak a word of English. I go to Madrid on the night train & spend mañana . . . El Prado (if I can see where I'm going). Then tomorrow night I take a sleeping car to Málaga.

Things are going too fast.

A priest in a motorcycle helmet.

The foxy taxi driver. "In a taxi, of course!"

First time in my life I've been ashamed of having too much money. The man in that ratlike cell of a *zapatería* fixed my shoes in ten minutes—*Cuanto cuesta?* I asked.

He said 12 pesetas.

I gave him 25 pesetas, murmuring something about *"por la bondad."* He accepted it with a graciousness I found touching.

ENERO 26

MADRID

Estoy muy cansada y me duelen los pies.[28]

I am sitting in the Goya room in El Prado after spending four hours here. I have five more hours to kill (it is two) before my train leaves [for Málaga]. I do not know what the difference is, but I do not like Madrid as I liked Barcelona. This place is a little like New York in public attitude.

. . . and there will always be an American . . . picking his nose in front of a Goya.

One bitch just passed the picture of the Giant eating the girl.[29] "Oh, my God! Ugh!" Classic.

MÁLAGA

How many people know what it is to be completely alone—languageless, companionless, with one hell of a cold, all your clothes wrinkled so you feel like a scarecrow whenever you emerge on the street? To beat that, you are in a town where there is *no* heat. Ever since I have been here, I have felt a thin veil between my senses & reality. I cannot *quite* seem to smell, or taste, or hear or see or feel as I used to.

This afternoon—have money changed (if possible) & pick up plane tickets. Will I *ever* be warm again

and secure

and with a man

and looking *nice?*

This morning I dried my hair in the sun under the Moorish ramparts. Bought a bathing suit for 390 pesetas—$6. A bikini—what the hell. If I can just survive until I get into a hotel in Canarias.

28. "I am very tired and my feet hurt."

29. From 1820 to 1824 Francisco Goya created a series of paintings that expressed his horror at the reign of terror perpetrated by Fernando VII, King of Spain. *Saturn Devouring His Son* is perhaps the most horrifying: placed against a purely black background, a naked giant, his eyes wide with maddened lust, engorges himself with a half-devoured human figure.

. . .

Went back to Wagons-Lits and found out they weren't *"seguro"* about the plane to Las Palmas. So I came home and had another nervous breakdown.

I have lived in Europe for four months. Whether or not I have learned enough to write I do not know, but I have learned many other things. The main one is how much I love the U.S.; the second, how to save money; the third, how to write better than before.

Perhaps I can find *something* in Torremolinos.[30]

Ah well. Canarias may still come through.

It did.

JANUARY 30

Sitting in the sun at the sidewalk café I laughed at myself. This is supposed to be *fun*, you idiot! I said.

Now, all I must do is:

pick up my shoes at 5:00 p.m.,

pay my bill after supper,

leave a call at the desk, and

write out the Spanish phrases.

B. will send me as much as I need & deduct it from my car sale.

Gibraltar was too cold (at least I will be practically in Africa in Canarias). Also I am going to have a bath.

---

30. Torremolinos was a sleepy fishing village in the early 1960s, when it had begun to be developed as the first of the Costa del Sol resorts.

ANDANTE

Málaga to London

JANUARY 30–APRIL 29, 1962

Before Gail arrived in London she secured for herself an extraordinary respite in the Canary Islands. "I have a prescience that this is going to be a happy month of tropical warmth & golden beaches & memories of strange freedom," she wrote on January 31, anticipating not only the next rhythm in her life but also the retrospective view of it that she would have years later.

Her month in the Canary Islands was a special time for Gail, one marked by an unequalled degree of luxury, idleness, and sunniness. For the islanders, it was historic, too—a period between the economic depression and population flight of the postwar years and the tourism-fed turnaround stimulated by Generalissimo Francisco Franco in 1960.

"I had never been to a place like the Canary Islands," Gail says today. "It was just beginning to become a tourist destination and was basically unspoiled—warm sun, beautiful banana plantations—like going to heaven and being able to bring my books."

Gail's paradise of literature-and-freedom was accompanied by a relationship that, despite some disturbing notes, tempted her to consider putting marriage before career. This conflict, along with the boardinghouse dramas that follow in her London entries, would make for some suspenseful moments—challenging situations that forced a young woman into difficult decisions about what was truly essential to her.

JANUARY 30, 1962

Málaga—the city is not so bad now that I have my ticket securely in my pocket to leave. Sat in the sun on Avenida Generalissimo Franco & drank cognac (6.50 pesetas) and squinted happily in the sun. Was joined by an assorted entourage (two Argentinians, one Scotswoman, one Canadian from Toronto). And the *lotería* women filed past, and the men with black bands sewn on their collars and left sleeves (every man seems to have lost someone here), and the jingling horse carriages and the fat priests taking afternoon strolls.

I like the way the Spanish bureau of tourism is set up. You know how much you're going to pay before you get there.

The little *zapatería* did an A1 job on my shoes. They can save anything in the way of leather here. Too bad I don't need shoes or suede or something. This time last year . . . the poison had set in. I had broken the first rule of marriage. The Slaters were due to arrive the next day.[1] I chose this life. (I remember the conversation with Bud Koster. "It was either Tahiti or my family."[2]) And I am not sorry. This way, I will not yearn. Most people write so they can get enough money to travel to other countries. I did the last first. Why do I need to write? We shall see. Slowly. Get to London. Get settled. Buy a typewriter. Write the stories that I have planned.

Walls of terra-cotta & cream & ochre. Green-tiled roofs topped with a thousand different minarets, vanes and decorations, terraces & balconies,

1. The Slaters, old friends of Doug Kennedy, were visiting him for the first time since he had married Gail. They may have sensed his and Gail's dissatisfaction with their marriage. The visit went so poorly, it precipitated Gail's departure from the house.

2. Bud Koster had been Gail's neighbor when she was married to Kennedy. Discussing personal and marital callings, Koster had confessed he'd once considered running away to Tahiti, as the artist Paul Gauguin had done.

broken-off top stories, wash hanging along Alhambra-like porticos—
the ruins of the Moorish palace almost in touching distance. And the
great purple hills to the north, orange trees in patios, a hundred families' lives observed at dusk from one fourth-floor vantage point. The
plash of the fountain, the chimes of the cathedral, a clang of a mop
bucket set wearily on a tile floor.

The hotel room in Málaga—blue walls, terrazzo floors of Indian red &
white squares, one chair, one table, one stained sink, both taps reading
"Frio." A huge brown wardrobe & an iron bed with a blue & white cot-
ton bedspread like the hospitals. One window under which all the
sounds of humanity blended together. "*Compro botellas!*" A child crying, a motorcycle resounding in the narrow alley.

Set the mood for isolation. No language, no heat, no way to get out of
the town.

A brief insight into the futility of plans & ambition.

No way to contact anyone. In a private chamber of retrospection.

the little cloth salesman from Barcelona

the huge ventana with the faded tapestry curtain in ochres &
greens & reds of forest paths & clumps of fern & red flowers

the bells (three of them, the last one always strikes three too
many)

This is *yours*. Don't try to spoil it by adding elaborations.
Don't forget the chamber pot [which she used furtively rather than
go out into the dark hall into an unlighted WC].

JANUARY 31

ENERO 31—LAS PALMAS, CANARY ISLANDS[3]

> Hostal Concha
>
> Dr. Grau Bassas, 7
>
> Las Palmas
>
> Gran Canarias

I have a prescience that this is going to be a happy month of tropical warmth & golden beaches & memories of strange freedom. A taxi driver drove me all over the place, running in & out, making phone calls, & found me an ideal spot—if only I can stay. At the moment I am in a room on the third floor more outdoors than in. I can hear the ocean (my old friend) & feel the salt breezes. I am in the middle of an island in the South Atlantic and I am free & *warm* & happy. *Que seré seré. La Giralda y Palacio del reyes* in *Seville* today.[4] Afterwards, a lunch in a glassed-in upstairs restaurant with a view of the city.

The little manager here is already enamored, so I shall have a native to show me the ropes. Ah . . . I am a born roamer. The sun, the sun, for twenty-eight days. Maybe more. I hope Miller takes his time.

FEBRUARY 1

I think I will be forced to draw some pictures of this island. The colorful houses, the schoolchildren (all dressed in brown), the houses nestled around the volcanoes (one of which let loose with a gentlemanly belch in 1949). The canaries are singing away and the sun is hot. Buy: bathing suit. Writing paper. Drawing tablet. Some sort of food. Sunday the l. m. is taking me to the island of golden sands.[5]

---

3. The Canary Islands, located in the Atlantic Ocean off the coast of Morocco, is composed of ten islands, which fall into two provinces, Santa Cruz de Tenerife and Las Palmas. Las Palmas is also the name of the capital of the Las Palmas province. It is located on the island Gran Canaria, and should not be confused with La Palma, an island in the Santa Cruz de Tenerife province.

4. Gail had stopped in Seville before going to the Canaries. It was a short hop. The next day, she reflects on her highlights tour while ensconced in Las Palmas. The Giralda and the Palacio del Reyes are famous landmarks in Seville, the Giralda tower being a twelfth-century Moorish minaret, and the Alcázar Palace, built in 913, the home of many kings.

5. The hotel manager—the "little manager"—was planning on taking Gail to the island of Fuerteventura, whose southern part forms the Peninsula de Jandia, known for its miles of golden sand. Fuerteventura lies fifty miles to the east of Gran Canaria.

This morning while walking on the beach I thought: I have been so many places, had so many experiences, when, *when* will I begin to write it all down? This climate is too marvelous to be believed. Naturally have been thinking about Florida this a.m.

Conquest. He is most obliging & bought me a bottle of perfume. ("Well, you were mad at me because I smelled so good, so what could I do?") And tonight we are going to see a Spanish film called *La Llegado un Ángel*[6] & starring a fourteen-year-old girl. I guess it's too much to hope for English titles. Afterwards we will have dinner (I keep forgetting these Spanish *eat* so late) & then come back here. During this month—get brown, get hair fixed like that girl I saw today, have my suit shortened, have everything cleaned. (This perfume is like everything else about this magic island, fruity, spicy, heady, exotic.) Why haven't the Americans discovered Canaria? Well, I'm glad they haven't ruined it here. Antonio & I went uptown to look for a bathing suit (the styles are about ten years behind)—the smell of fish, the trucks of bananas rattling by, the dirt everywhere. But this hotel is immaculate & smells of Lysol—the tiled steps, the mosaic walls, everything is scrubbed down to perfection. Of all my European travels, this was the end. A.'s suits are made by a loving tailor, he changes his shoes & socks fifty times a day. He has a satyr's face.

FEBRUARY 3

SATURDAY

Last night we went into Las Palmas & bought a bathing suit & walked up & down the promenade & went in a little sweet shop & drank Cuba libres (even if Cuba is no longer free) and ate sweets. Sweets, sweets. It's a wonder that boy has any teeth. I am getting a little disgusted with myself. London ought to be a change. I shall try to be a lady. Last night I dreamed about my first day at work—catastrophic. Everybody was always taking collections for coffee & going out to lunch & I couldn't get my work done. Then I threw a cognac at a fellow worker and called her nosey. Ah, it was a true "Godwin Nightmare."

6. *La Llegado un Ángel* (*An Angel Has Arrived*) was a new, feature-length Spanish musical comedy about an orphaned girl who moves in with her uncle's troubled family and lifts their spirits.

From eight to twelve, the bellman in Hotel Gran Canarias wears a uniform and serves the idle tourists. But from twelve to three, he is entitled, as are all Spaniards, to a princely three-hour lunch. Commerce literally stops for three hours, and if the visitor has to buy a bottle of perfume or a roll of toilet paper between twelve and three, it is just too damn bad. All in all, I think it is a lovely custom.

FEBRUARY 4

Overcast—dammit. Watch me lose the little tan I have. Last night we took a bumpy bus ride (the bus just starts when it decides it has enough people and leaves them hanging out the doors) to the new city on the hill where we ate squid & sea salmon and drank Cuba libres in a small glass-enclosed restaurant. There was a sweet clean little mongrel which we fed and he followed us the whole night. We visited the new church and A. made the sign of the cross on my forehead with holy water. I wish he hadn't done that. It made me feel odd. After all, I'm not impervious to religious symbolism.

What a beautiful day we had yesterday. Took a car to the mountain village of Teror (stair-step plowed fields, geraniums growing wild, white & ochre houses growing between mountains). The village itself sports balconies of canary-pine wood and a big church of which they are fanatically proud.[7] We had three or four kinds of meat—all fresh—with our various alcohols. Then we walked to the very top of the hill to the city of Arucas, the site of banana plantations,[8] stopping along the way to get rum & Coke from roadside bars where the countrymen gathered to play cards. We got progressively drunker along the way. Dear Tony outlined for me all the ways he would be a good husband and said he needed a wife to help him run his three businesses. I haven't the slightest doubt that he will be a huge success. I like him, he is attractive & knows how

7. Gran Canaria is a volcanic island and features mountainous terrain. Teror sits on a plateau a third of a mile above sea level. After the island had been colonized by Christopher Columbus, Teror developed as a cattle center. The big church, Our Lady of the Pine Basilica, is located on a site where locals had experienced a visitation by the Virgin Mary.

8. Arucas is on the northwest coast of Gran Canaria at the foot of the volcano.

to treat a woman, but talking in terms of a lifetime—that is a different thing. He has no desire to live anywhere except the Canaries (I must say I can't blame him). But it is nice to speculate on all my might-have-been lives.[9] If I don't quit being so selective I may wind up with nothing.

Old Mr. Wilmot, a long-term British guest at Las Conchas:[10]

- "I was looking at my list of relations to see who was going to die next and by damn I found I was the next on the list."

- "I give him ten of those peseta sort of things."

- "I get tired of living alone. In London, whenever I heard a funny story I wanted to share with someone I'd hop a train and go to my bookseller. It'd make his day."

- "I have a son sixteen, haven't seen him in almost seventeen years."

- "She does right well at it . . ."

- "Y'know, these kids don't mind letting you join in their games at all."

- "I got a job setting out the red lanterns for a construction crew— it was bloody good fun until I set my tent on fire & almost burned down the Piccadilly Hotel."

9. Gail says of that time that she was tempted to accept Antonio Ramirez-Suarez's offer. "He was upbeat," she acknowledges. "He had said to me, 'You're twenty-five years old— it's a good offer!' " Although her ambition to be a writer had drawn her away from Antonio, she admits, "If I hadn't had all that studying, he wouldn't have wanted me. There haven't been many people in my life who learned who I was quickly, as he had. Then we had to withdraw. It was hard." Years later, Gail would attach Antonio Ramirez-Suarez's name to the hotel manager in *The Perfectionists* and the courtly professor in *The Good Husband.*

10. Mr. Wilmot was staying at Hostal Concha for a while. Gail had in hand Aldous Huxley's novels *Chrome Yellow* and *Point Counter Point* (noted February 20), which drew their inspiration from the conversations and interaction of eccentric, seasonally migratory guests at boardinghouses.

FEBRUARY 9

Must take a gamble in less than twenty days. Once taken, once decided, I must never, never look back or second-guess myself. This island has a great & prosperous future. Tony has asked me to stay here & help him start his business and share his life. This is hard to put into words, but my choice will represent the selection of one way of life & the complete rejection of the other. I have thought of nothing lately but what certain other people think: B., Uncle Bill, Aunt Sophie, Dean Luxon, all those. But what do I really want? It is indeed a comforting feeling to have a man like this who so completely and warmly respects & loves women. If only that damn job in London would fall through . . . I'll never forget how mad Tony got when I spent 120 pestas on a *Vogue* & *Esquire.* "Write to your mother and ask her to send your old magazines & you can read them over."

But could I give up my books? My writing? Etc., etc. All I am speaking of is the very layer I have only recently acquired. Perhaps the very fact that I have read too much, studied myself too much, grown away from God is what is causing all this trouble.

What do I want out of this world? It is so wearying to be always thinking of oneself. What if one lived for another person, too? I've never tried it. It might be interesting.

FEBRUARY 11

The thing that is both frightening and rather wonderful about this island is that the people are still living with the basic Catholic precepts of the fifteenth century. They eat, sleep, marry, have as many children as God sends them, & die.

Well. 9:00 p.m. Antonio just returned & I won't see him anymore tonight. Some German people reported 2,000 pesetas plus shaving equipment gone. So Tony has to go to the police. Damned irresponsible people leaving money in their rooms. Actually, I'm relieved that I'll have a little time to myself. The man hasn't given me time to think. This room is not so bad. At least it's private & warm. Portrait of Tony to remember later on cold nights in London.

A very Spanish face, dark complexion, jagged bones in his forehead—which gives him a "rumpled" look. Fine small Roman nose & compact ears. His smile always starts with his nose. It wrinkles. His mouth, when closed, is pink & childish. When opened, rather like a rogue (bandito). His teeth are hard & big; one top front one was chipped when a friend tripped him in the cinema when he was eleven. He is very clean & has nice hands & feet (small also). One finger (his left index) was shattered by a firecracker at the top joint. So he looks like a scarred soldier when he motions a waiter or rests that hand on the table. His suits fit him like loving caresses. His legs are magnificent—the legs of a cyclist & swimmer. His hair is not quite black, and dry & curly. He uses no glop or goo. Only Colgate, Varon Dandy,[11] & Camay soap. His English is touching & original. He is going through the stage preceding the perfect mastery of a second language, and says "proyect" instead of "project," "fithful" instead of "faithful," "make a walk" instead of "take a walk," "for whole life," "recept" for "receipt" . . . and consistently refers to himself in the third person. "Tony will change you . . . You think you can be a block of ice with your Tony? Not for one minute." And "Ahff coorse!" (Of course) He will be a good businessman if I will get the hell out and let him concentrate.

FEBRUARY 14

El día de los queridos[12]

Heard from Lorraine yesterday. I am brown & have lost the dissipated look around my eyes which worries me so much. Am eager to rewrite the beginning of "Roxanne" from a better, less emotional perspective. Finished a book of Moravia's short stories.[13] Totally depressing. His

---

11. Varon Dandy is a fancy Spanish cologne for men.

12. *El día de los queridos* is "the day of the lovers," or Valentine's Day.

13. Alberto Moravia, the Italian fiction writer most famous for his 1957 novel *Two Women* (made into a movie starring Sophia Loren in 1961), published *The Wayward Wife and Other Stories* in 1960. In the short stories that Gail was reading, characters find themselves in two settings: the vestiges of aristocracy, in which the lowborn seek the luxury of the high, and all are soulless; and an industrialized, consumerist society, in which participants lose the ability to communicate.

women are all viragoes, his men lacking in resolution & character. Each story is only a segment of an affair. I could do as well, I am sure.

FEBRUARY 15

Hoy llove. "Rain is like god here. Be happy," said Antonio. Perhaps in five to ten years we can purify water from the sea, but it will cost twenty-five million pesetas. Life goes on. When the faucet has no water, someone must carry buckets upstairs & empty them into tanks. Such is day-to-day existence in L.P. Tony received word from Martinez in Madrid that his travel agency has been granted. He will be a huge success. He has such a "straight line" way with people. Joking, honest & stern. At night, the women & babies lean over windowsills & watch the people pass by. When women are not having babies or feeding families, they are hanging out clothes. One thing about a hotel—it completely isolates you from the local ways. You can be in New York, Las Palmas, Miami Beach, or the Côte d'Azur & it will be just the same: good plumbing, thick towels, soft beds & a bar.

"Tony, I think I *should* leave you for a while to make sure we love each other . . ."

"Okay. You go to Tenerife for two days. I will buy the ticket."

It is fatal to wear slacks around here at night. The men go *"hssst!"* and stab lighted cigarettes toward your face.

FEBRUARY 20

8:45 P.M.

In my room overlooking the roofs of Grau Bassas. The moon comes up full and quickly, almost sinister. Child's voice. Sound of a muffled radio. Some old song. Church bells. Motor scooter. Dog's bark; goat's maaa. Feel strange & dreamlike. Haunted by memories & fragments of I-don't-know-what.

All day I have felt drowsy & as if I am about to be launched—like a spaceship.

·   ·   ·

Eat, sleep . . . eat, sleep . . .

Finished *Point Counter Point*,[14] by Huxley. Wrote it when he was thirty-four.

Tony is becoming reconciled to the fact that I must go. But can *I* be strong and not wishy-washy? Can I keep from wavering, making new promises in a weak moment?

Standing on a curb, legs apart, briefcase in hand, bargaining for his first office building. Warm, dry hands, fragrant hair, the ever-burning *puro* between his teeth, even when he talks. The sure, confident, self-assured yet self-forgetful way he holds his head. A man at twenty-four. A little giant.

MARCH 6

A surfeit of sun, idleness, the taste of sweets on my tongue, the smell of suntan oil turned to vinegar.

I am so completely disgusted with my idleness, with the same clothes I've worn since October. I long for all the civilized niceties that aren't supposed to matter: a manicure, a fresh coiffure, clean new underclothes, polished shoes, a very unemotional, cold evening at a play or a good concert.

Mr. Wilmot gave me the first three chapters of his autobiography to read: "Selected Stills in Black and White from the Highly Colored."

Chapter 1 begins: "It has always seemed to me singularly unfortunate that ante-natal instruction is not made available to the forthcoming immigrant, as well as to the hostess."[15]

Antonio is in a rage because I shook hands with Rosenbaum.[16]

14. *Point Counter Point*, published in 1928, represents Huxley's attempt to place his characters' preoccupations and ideas into a musical design.

15. Gail describes Mr. Wilmot as a crazy old man. One day, she recalls, he went wild and threw pots down from his balcony, smashing them. The "forth-coming immigrant" to whom he alludes is himself as a newborn; he had evidently not done so well by his "hostess," that is, his mother.

16. Rosenbaum was another guest at Hostal Concha. Gail describes him as having been a cynical, saturnine Englishman of her age. He took walks with Gail and offered constructive criticism.

• • •

"De acuerdo . . . hasta luego . . ." Tony is jabbering on the phone.

I'm sure his cigar is between his teeth.

MARCH 7

Tomorrow I was supposed to leave. Each day my endurance stretches to endure still another postmanless day. Everything has changed. The tides, the sun angle, the visitors. There are new flocks of lily-white tourists on the beach. The Mullingers & the white-haired lady & the sick man leave tomorrow. Tony is engrossed in his business. I think he secretly knows it is all over. Oscar Wilde said: Only the faithless can understand the real sorrows of love.[17] I'm bored with my tan. Am as brown as I want to be. Thinking of Anderson this morning[18]—exactly ten years ago this June. Where is the old gang now? Married & at home. Do I envy or flout them? The thing here is, there is absolutely nothing to do. I am sick of reading & eating & escape-sleeping. Only 11:30—one more hour & then I'll either pack or go into a depression. Manuelo finishes the suit today. It will probably be all wrong but I must smile & say how much I like it.

MARCH 11

Things are silver & gray-green cool today with a breath of moisture over everything. Although it is cool & almost sunset, the water has never been more tempting. Not to fight it, as I did the other day when I was crying for a good fight & no human was available.

But to go in slowly & definitely & let it slosh over my thighs, stomach, chest, neck—soothing, healing. I know it would be warm.

17. The exact quote is, "Those who are faithful know only the trivial side of love: it is the faithless who know love's tragedies."

18. For one year, 1952–1953, Gail had lived in Anderson, South Carolina, where her stepfather, Frank Cole, had taken a job. She attended a girls' public high school and made many friends. Thinking back to that time, she recalls how she had passed as one of the girls, and she wonders where her peers' life choices have taken them. "It was the first time I had gone to public high school," Gail reflects again in 2004, "and I was elected vice president of the class and was extremely popular. I spent the last two months living with the Calhouns, as Frank had gotten transferred again to Norfolk. Mary Calhoun had been my best friend." Despite their friendliness, the Calhouns' social status—they had a butler and maids who helped Mrs. Calhoun manage her mansion—caused Gail to feel self-conscious about her limited economic background.

Two seventy-five-year-old queers in no. 3. An American & an Englishman. The American went out for a walk & the Englishman almost died of jealousy. "Have you *seen* McNabb?" he screamed. "You see he hasn't been well. He was supposed to meet me for lunch & he *didn't* and I'm *worried.* He hasn't been *well,* you know."

He clawed a flaccid face, his milky blue eyes looking over my right shoulder, lisping a little. " 'I *pay* for water & I *want* water.' That's what Mr. McNabb said to me only this morning. He wanted his *bath,* you know. He has a frightful amount of money, and then, of course, he's American, and you know he's sick. These Americans are different, you know."

A pleading look at me for agreement, thinking I was Spanish.

"Yes," I said.

There goes a couple who gives me the courage to get old. A man & his wife walking along the Canteras.[19] About fifty-five or sixty, each of them. No freakish beauty preserved through endless ritual & no frantic evidence of trying to look younger. She was wearing a full-length brown coat—the kind that could have been advertised in this month's *Vogue* for Mrs. Exeter[20] or could equally be fifteen years old. He had on a tailored suit—I think. Their faces I couldn't see because they were directly below me & walking in the northerly direction. Both had good posture, without being stiff. They walked in step (unconsciously). I am somehow sure they are happy and are not afraid of getting to be seventy-five.

MARCH 14

—Four more days.

Tony took me to Pueblo Canario & we drank tea & ate biscuits and I got my family some presents. Wine flasks for Tommy & Rebel, castanets for Franchelle, a Toledo brooch & inlaid case for Kathleen. Also: a pair of Toledo cufflinks for B., & Tony bought me a pin just like my mother's.

19. Las Canteras is an attractive beach in Las Palmas along which runs a promenade.

20. "Mrs. Exeter" referred to the icon for "outfits for the more mature woman, with a blue-haired lady modeling the fashion," as *Vogue* photographer Helmut Newton put it.

· · ·

I am excited about my story. Decided now to just do December to April & see what happens.

Note: Philip Roth's treatment of Libby in "Very Happy Poems"[21] as contrasted to the what-she-ate what-she-wore slickness of a Marcia Davenport heroine.[22]

The difference is hard to describe, but oh, can you feel it when you're reading. Roth's Libby is human & has human frailties: (1) her conversation is not a series of thought masterpieces; (2) she is not always right—always adhering to the moral code of *Good Housekeeping* & *Ladies' Home Journal;* (3) she thinks in disjointed spurts, not montages; (4) everything doesn't fit together so damn neatly like a five-and-ten jig-saw puzzle.

If "Roxanne" was any indication, this new project will take a year to finish. I cannot write down to people—even if I were desperate for money. This is why I must wait.

Heroine's name? I don't know.

She must have a little of Lisa's temperament (of course, I'll call her Lisa) & a little of Madame Bovary.[23]

Publishers will go on publishing novels about discontented wives.

Anyway, she is constantly looking at herself & no gruesome details must be spared. Pick it up anywhere, waking on Sunday morning, & go from there.

---

21. Roth's "Very Happy Poems" was published in the January 1962 issue of *Esquire*. It tells the story of a woman who falls apart when questioned by a Jewish Children's League representative investigating her and her husband's application to adopt a child. Her inability to know herself apart from what she imagines people's opinions of her are is her downfall.

22. Marcia Davenport, daughter of opera singer Alma Gluck, inaugurated her writing career in 1932, at age twenty-nine, with a biography of Mozart. She subsequently wrote five novels, including her best known, *Of Lena Geyer. The Constant Image,* published in 1960, enfolds a love story with many pages of observations about Milan.

23. Lisa was an early choice for the name of the heroine of Godwin's unpublished novel "Gull Key." Gail eventually named the heroine Bentley.

STRESS her sense of uselessness. She tries to paint, write a history of Gull Key (send for that manuscript, and quote verbatim), make collages; she accepts her husband's advice about the futility of the lighthouse history ("Besides, who'd buy it?") and writes a women's magazine a query about an article.

Some of Moravia's sullen narrative is good to keep in mind.[24]

Only, my heroine gets free at the end by creating & shaping a perfect excuse for divorce. Describe *everything* (even the deputy serving the papers) & try to put across the fact that she is so honest with herself she forces herself to take her affair seriously.

"Pick it up anywhere," Gail advises herself as she starts her new novel, "Gull Key," "waking on Sunday morning," for example, "& go from there."[25] Anticipating a year of work, she already knows certain things about the book, partly from her reading. Stories about tragically married women by writers such as Philip Roth and Alberto Moravia enable her to declare, "My heroine gets free at the end."

The spirit of the times places Gail's generation at a key point in the history of male-female relationships, which were undergoing perhaps their first major shift since the medieval invention of courtly love. In responding to this, Gail is not only answering to a calling, she is responding to the marketplace. The market, at its best, is a good indicator of pertinence: "Publishers will go on publishing novels about discontented wives," as Gail notes. Women needed mirrors that reflected more than just their bodies, and they found greater context in books.

"I was one of those people who have the misfortune to grow up with one foot in one era and the other foot in the next . . ." said Kitty.

24. Moravia's novella "The Wayward Wife," which Gail had just read, provides one of the variations on the unhappy-wife story. The story has gothic, class-conscious, fairy-tale similarities to Isak Dinesen's "The Caryatids."

25. The manuscript for the unpublished novel "Gull Key" is part of the Gail Godwin Papers, held by the Manuscripts Department of the Library of the University of North Carolina at Chapel Hill.

"Sometimes I think those persons raised in the interstices of Zeit-geists are the ones most punished," said Jane.

—JANE, THE HEROINE OF GODWIN'S 1974 NOVEL,

THE ODD WOMAN, CONVERSING WITH HER MOTHER, KITTY

Using her living experience, Godwin enables herself to freely play with her material and attain a method of storytelling toward which her previous journal entries have been building; that is, the representation of drama through design rather than progression. Design reveals how the mind works and how fate operates.

"Everything doesn't fit together so damn neatly," she writes in admiration of Roth's "Very Happy Poems." Roth's heroine "thinks in disjointed spurts, not montages." Reality is an organic thing; it has an accidental brilliance.

MARCH 17

NIGHT—

New worries. How much income tax will the British gov't take out? Ah, these last days kill me. Tony is getting a little nervous, too. *"There ought to be a law against goodbyes."* Good title for a song.

Ah, hell. I prefer oblivion tonight . . . I'll be glad when it's over. Feelings hurt too much.

MARCH 23

LONDON

Where to begin: with the *where*—I am settled in South Kensington in a comfortable room (except for these Britishers' damn antiquated heating methods).[26] I am situated so that I don't have to pay any bills or cook any meals, which is fine with me. I think now—the next two years—will be the test. The thing is to keep my head & try to unwind a little bit. Think & Act.

---

26. Gail's lodgings at 31 Tregunter Road were at what she called a "good" address in a letter to her mother. "Douglas Fairbanks Jr. lives across the street," she noted.

In a place like London, one could go crazy with indecision. There are so many things to want. I must make my plans & stick to them. Once I get started it will be easy. The room will be okay for the summer. I'm going to ask for Eugenio's room in June. I shall make it livable for my occasional "ventures" and for myself by putting up a few pictures, maps etc. & decorating it, so to speak. Or I may keep this for the summer. It would be nicer. Tomorrow I must see about renting a typewriter, getting a hairdresser, another pair of shoes. I can work, go to plays & to dinner & write my book. This time I have to. I need to hear myself thinking.

MARCH 25

Yesterday I went to see *Luther*,[27] had an Italian lunch in Soho & bought *A Long & Happy Life*,[28] by Reynolds Price, which I read & admired.

There is something not quite comforting about Sunday afternoons. It has to do with a feeling of suspension, of waiting, of wanting to be outside when you're in and inside when you're out. This house is full of people who are coping with this Sunday afternoon. The Handel from above is Michel's way of dreaming with his girl in the attic room where you can't stand up but have to lie about on pillows. The first few times, I thought the black ladder leaning against the wall was due to the carelessness of a painter or workman who had finished & gone away.

Michel teaches convicts to read & write Monday through Fridays. This house is full of these people. Some keep cats or a hamster for company, rather than music. The Yoga teacher sits in his room below me and breathes. Eugenio, the millionaire's son from Mexico, is spending the weekend with friends. I think it's a shame to vacate that room of his next door even for a weekend. The fireplace, the bookcase stocked with shiny hardcovers of Ayn Rand & Mary Renault, the Mexican wrought-

27. *Luther*, John Osborne's play about Martin Luther and the glories and failures of the Catholic Church, premiered at the Royal Court Theatre in London, July 27, 1961, with Albert Finney playing the lead.

28. *A Long and Happy Life* was twenty-nine-year-old Reynolds Price's debut novel. Price shared Godwin's North Carolina home soil (although his was in the piedmont, not the mountains). *A Long and Happy Life* portrays a country girl trapped in a marriage to an unsuitable mate, who had impregnated her.

iron candelabra with no two candles reaching upward from the same level. The other night I had a headache & went to borrow an aspirin.

"Yes, I can see you need a treatment," Eugenio said in his perfect, slightly American, English. "I have a few things here in my bag . . ." And he pulled out a TWA canvas travel kit and unzipped a small pharmacy. His manicured hands hovered and plucked.

"Here. Try a Bufferin. Then you look a little white, you know. I believe you shall have a vitamin C. Just chew it up. Now is anything else wrong?" (Hopefully.)

Last night I sat in the lounge and a fattish, pink young adult with baggy trousers began playing the out-of-tune piano with complete unself-consciousness. He smiled the whole time. I did not recognize the tune. It sounded a little like circus music on that tinny piano. Later, when he left the room, I went over and looked at the book he had played from. It was Bach's *Preludes & Fugues for Major & Minor Keys.*

At the table I began drawing out an interesting young man with graying hair & a ring on his little finger. His name is Neil & he has a history degree from Oxford and those perfect, almost effeminate graces. I had been looking at the picture of a young author in the book jacket of a first novel. "Damn it, born in 1933," I said. "Only four years older than me."

Neil gave me what you might call a grateful smile (except his smile was only a slight stretching of his lips). "Oh? It's comforting to know someone else notices those dates on the backs of book covers," he said.

Colonel and Mrs. West told me Neil sold office furniture.

It is a terrible thing to see a person who has not become what he wanted to be. Is that going to happen to me? Have I, by casting off one life already, freed myself or become more entangled in my own selfishness? Is it wrong to want everything? What am I doing in this South Kensington boardinghouse for young professionals? Are they, are we, the ones who could not bear to be shackled with ordinary responsibilities and thus wound up in a kind of prison of selfishness which gives us meals, linen & maid service for 7 guineas a week and demands nothing of us, no agonizing choices, not even the burden of selecting a head of lettuce at the greengrocer's.

The girl at the office, I *must* learn at least her first name tomorrow, is exactly my age. Twenty-four. She and her Mississippi husband have a flat in Hampstead. The bathroom is under an eave in the kitchen and her feet have not been warm once in the eight months they've been in London.

Yesterday her husband met her for lunch & then they went to buy a teapot. (Imagine, a real shopping jaunt for one teapot. I can hear them discussing it over breakfast: "Now we've returned these people's invitation for tea, so we have to buy a teapot. Do you think it will cost much?") She kept thanking me over & over for explaining why one should scald the pot. I think she regards me as terribly cosmopolitan. She is a comfort to talk to.

So here I am, getting back to me, and who kids himself into thinking he ever puts others first? Here I am in this "youth brothel," as Mr. West chucklingly labeled it in a burst of American humor. The room is never warm enough. I am in walking distance of Chelsea. I can hear background music of Haydn & Bach from Michel's attic concert hall, and I am truly alone. Very much alone. It follows, doesn't it, that I have all the prerequisites from time immemorial in order to scour my soul & allow my creative impulses to flourish. Oscar Wilde lived only down the street and I have an urgent rather desperate feeling that, for this chick, it is either now or never. I have borrowed too many laters. My account is overdue as it is.

APRIL 9

Eugenio & I are trading rooms—he's converting mine into two & I will feel much cozier in his. I shall allot a sum of, say, $50 to decorate it. I need curtains (velvet from Mrs. West) & a damn striking bedspread. The mantel is there for me & I shall need a bookshelf, which I'll paint dark on the inside & white around the edges. I want one *centerpiece* picture (a sketch or a print) to dominate the room & to inspire me. Then on that private wall by my bed I'm going to put a lot of small, framed pictures of the Canary Islands to weep over. After I get the room the way I want it, I should be able to concentrate more. Andrew will paint the room for a price ($5?).

APRIL 11

Doreen W., my supervisor.

About thirty years old—seven and a half years, airline stewardess; two years as information-on-U.S. director with TWA in Britain. Was skiing in Switzerland when she decided to stop. Virtuous, etc. "How can a girl live with herself if . . . ?" Calm, always the right answer—works late every night, a "girl's girl." Not impeccably dressed nor even fashionable. Striking, Indian-like face. Cheekbones, black hair.

If I could get three stories in clean, finished working condition—then take them to an agent—I might have a better chance.

APRIL 12

Today I assisted a gentleman by telephone.

"Much obliged," he snapped cheerily. "I hope you have a lovely lunch."

This is England.

opened a bank account

paid Wests

planned first revised page of "Roxanne" on the bus going home

I just have to get settled materially first and then set up a schedule.

I am going through an "action cycle."

APRIL 14

Every time a person really feels like Mr. Smug, something ridiculous happens. Like tonight. I was on my way to the toilet, smugly disgusted with my complete capture of poor C., when the door clicked shut behind me. A brisk run through the dark in pajama top & no bra to get a key from the Wests brought me firmly back to earth.

(The Wests hang their clothes over the couch & chairs when they go to bed at night.)

Block to my writing. I am too immersed in myself—am going to read all my journals over and make notes. Perhaps it would be a good enema.

Bought:

an Italian typewriter

an original drawing from Durrell's *Stiff Upper Lip.*[29]

a sweater

Feeling vaguely guilty. My impulses ran away with me, or did they?

APRIL 18
WEDNESDAY

Dinner in Soho with Doreen last night—she is very diplomatic, interesting but somehow has not pierced the barrier. Friday—Jas. Montgomerie is taking us all riding in his new convertible. Tomorrow night I'm going to the pub with Mike, the Yorkshire "turf accountant," and get good & drunk. Ahh, I have moved & instantly feel at home in this room—especially with Eugenio's wonderful electric blanket. I must get one next winter.

APRIL 19
THURSDAY

Last night went to the Prospect of Whitby[30] with Mike, Andrew, Judy, Simon, and McClosky. All of us are being evicted from 31 Tregunter in one month.[31] We got tipsy, sang songs, and told jokes.

29. In order to connect herself to an important inspiration, Gail splurges on a Ronald Searle drawing of a Durrell character.

30. The Prospect of Whitby pub is located on the Thames River in a building constructed in the 1520s. Nautical features and bric-a-brac overwhelm the décor, which also boasts references to famous patrons (such as Charles Dickens) and public hangings.

31. The Wests had just received word from their landlord, Michael Heseltine, that he wanted to remodel his houses, leaving the Wests and their family of tenants with one month to vacate. Thus began the Wests' search for another "youth brothel." Heseltine was just beginning to chart his career as a controversial Conservative politician and urban renewer. He eventually rose to the position of deputy prime minister, but his greatest success ended up being in publishing (with Haymarket Group), by which he became a multimillionaire.

APRIL 22

SUNDAY

Springtime in London is worth waiting for. This new feeling—of being in a place I've wanted to be a part of for longer than I can remember. The houses open up, gardens sprout everywhere, the jets whine out over my roof toward vacation lands. How long have I waited to sit in my own room on a bed in the window, my back to the sun, surrounded by type-writer and books, new ideals and a new love all in the present.[32]

APRIL 26

THURSDAY

Bad bout with a cold, but the U.S. Navy doctor with the crew cut diag-nosed "the London crud," and fortified me with "a bunch of stuff." The week has passed quickly. I can see the end of the letters,[33] although Doreen can't. Tomorrow night—James. I have a sneaking suspicion he is one of those hopeless cases—a WH, an AF[34]—I think he can jolly well live without me.[35] The Wests still haven't found a house. If they don't, I'll have to go to a horrible little hotel.

Judy stayed up all night typing Mr. West's Greek incident.[36]

APRIL 27

Like a damned ass I volunteered to work tomorrow. It's five till eight and dear James hasn't showed up. If he doesn't come tonight I shall (1) eat something—even at Wimpy's; (2) write Crowther[37]; (3) go to bed early.

32. Gail's bed ran parallel to a double window, which practically embraced the bed. When she sat on it at her worktable, her back was to the sun.

33. One of Gail's jobs was to answer letters from English people planning trips to the United States. At the beginning, there were a lot of ads for the U.S. Travel Service, and a huge volume of mail—maybe seventy queries a day.

34. WH and AF were two men whom Gail had known and whom she'd thought were inherently unavailable as partners.

35. James Montgomerie was a thirty-eight-year-old barrister with the Rank Organisation on his way to becoming a vice president. He had been very kind toward Gail and protective of her.

36. At Gail's encouragement, Colonel West had begun writing his memoirs. He had received a DSO in World War II for blowing up a Greek train.

37. Frank Crowther, a friend from Chapel Hill, had been at the U.S. Travel Service in Washington.

So it worked out. He thought I was late, etc. A slow uncoiling over Black & White. Learning new things about each other, dinner at Alexandre's, then we went to his place and he read me the first half of a short story and one act of a musical, "Why Buy When You Can Rent?"[38]

APRIL 29

SUNDAY

I find it necessary to become more involved with "living" (or should I say living it up) to get off by myself and remember what it is I'm planning to do. This weekend read like a storybook. Honestly, I'm so high-pitchedly happy I wait for disaster to strike any minute. Worked until thirteen o'clock at the office, didn't get as much done as I'd wanted because Bob Briggs, the assistant director, came in, several phone inquiries, the marine from Greensboro, etc. James came about two. He had brought me flowers & I gave him an octopus made of glass with blue eyes. We drove to the lake & ate a lunch of rabbit food, bread & cheese, Algerian wine & coffee & then drove the new motorboats around the lake for thirty minutes. After that we went to Bob Briggs's luxury flat (huge but rather empty) for the celebration of the new baby, Felicity. We appeared in our red sweaters & I could see the longing look in Doreen's eyes. ("A well-balanced girl, but not too exciting," James commented later.) Jas. made an excellent impression—the Oxford barrister, well-traveled, easy-spoken, always in command, never making a fool of himself. Briggs got pretty drunk. We went out to some Chelsea pubs & then back to James's apt. Doreen put on his white sweater & more drinks were served & I went to sleep. Spent the night with James (he didn't touch me) & I must say it was good being close to him. We have such a tremendous affinity. Real Geminis in every sense. He says the things I wish people would say oftener—quiet, unaffected statements filled with unself-conscious love. ("You're a nice person. I think you're unselfish in a lot of ways.")

This morning we lay in bed & talked from nine until twelve (he

---

38. James also was writing stories and plays, but had had no luck publishing.

asked me if I was a virgin and I firmly denied it but I think he suspects I am). How nice to have a little convertible waiting under the window again! Then he fixed breakfast & played *Pictures at an Exhibition*[39] and we read the papers. This sort of situation has always seemed one of the happiest to me.

39. *Pictures at an Exhibition* is Modest Mussorgsky's famous piano composition that connects musical interpretations of artworks by Victor A. Hartmann with a promenade theme.

MY VOCATION

Tregunter Road to Old Church Street,

London, with an Excursion to Amsterdam

MAY 8–SEPTEMBER 30, 1962

"*Tonight… listening to Van Cliburn & Mozart's* Requiem, *I regained my vocational spur," Gail writes on May 12 as Saturday night crosses into Sunday morning. Her fellow boarders had been playing music all day. Now she is alone in her wakefulness, conjuring up the right frame of mind to do nothing less than fulfill her destiny.*

Three and a half weeks had passed since Gail had traded her room for Eugenio's, bought a typewriter, and set herself up, expecting an inspirational flow. With music providing a background, she bears down, giving herself pep talks and pouring her energies into several works: three versions of her Florida-based novel ("Halcyone and the Lighthouse," "The Gall Crab," and "Gull Key"); the novels "Roxanne" and "Kim"; and two short stories. While these works will not find publication, they give us an opportunity to see the young Godwin at work, figuring out her craft.

Also gestating during this intense period was a work that would wait until 1983 to find expression and publication: the novella "Mr. Bedford." Gail was recording in her journals the observations and impressions that would be used to describe the essence of her sometimes hilarious, always vivid London boardinghouse experience.

MAY 8, 1962

Last night I went home with Doreen for dinner. I *try* and *try* and *try* to like her, but always there is that reservation. I'm sorry. I can't help it. I'm trying a work experiment which I shall record in this book. I don't actually give a damn about this job & therefore I can experiment with organization techniques. I've succeeded in getting into the inner room, where I have access to all reference material & get to listen to the management end of the business. Doreen has now asked me to open the mail & sort it. I have started trying to do little deeds to "take the weight off your shoulders." After all, I tell her, you're management. You shouldn't have to do these pedestrian things. *I'll do them.* The thing is to get people to depend on me to find things for them. That's the first step. We shall see. A Mrs. Gilbert came in today & I helped her & she ended up inviting me down to her seashore home. I may just go.

Jeremy is lying on my bed with his brown suede shoes on my sink; Andrew has fixed my typewriter & is applying for a job on it. Eugenio is coughing in the other room & we have been sending each other notes in Spanish.

MAY 12

James has gone to see his Scottish parents this weekend—William[1] said last night that he was completely fed up with the Rank Organisation[2] and had come back to the flat disillusioned & threatening to quit. We went out to a play Thursday night—it was one of those evenings that start off disastrously & end quietly & happily. We are both tense & the

1. William was James's roommate.

2. The Rank Organisation, founded in the 1930s, grew to monopolize the British film industry through its ownership of studios and movie theaters. In 1956, it branched out, through a venture with Xerox, into the manufacture of business machines, and then into the development of hotels and vacation centers.

play *Blitz*[3] wasn't really too light even though a comedy, because of its theme. Afterwards we stopped by the flat to have a drink & William had some character there that was the epitome of everything I hate about the English. Tight little mouth; snide remarks; a sort of constipation of the spirit. He proceeded to invite James on some cruise & then proceeded to decide out loud which girl would be best for James. I resented it & felt I *shouldn't* (now I know I am justified because he was just plain rude). So went to the Gigolo for a late dinner & I felt the need to retaliate & really let J. have it with both barrels. I made it very clear that I didn't like him at first, he was too old—and he looked suddenly very tired & old. Then I was attacked by a real tenderness & would have handed over my life to him in an instant. (I had even said, "I wish I could like somebody like you—you're what everyone says I need." What a bitch.) We went back to the flat again "for just one drink" and I lay on the bed feeling thoroughly sorry for myself & very dramatic & he fixed one Scotch & one coffee. Then he came & sat beside me & we talked seriously without any jabs. I ended up spending the night . . . it was one of those times when two humans need each other's warmth. He said finally, and sincerely, to my great surprise: "You're so sweet & very natural & I love you very much . . ." Also, "I want to take care of you & protect you," and with that I slipped away and we both fell asleep holding on to that warmth. He hasn't made love to me. And then we took the bus to work together & he left me in Hyde Park. That's when I realized what he was to me . . . walking away with that lumbering stomping walk, head bent slightly forward, carrying his umbrella. I watched him until I couldn't see him any longer & then turned & looked at the rows of tulips against the green of Hyde Park & the early morning riders on their dappled grays & roans & chestnuts—and there was the usual lemon & gray haze over my adopted city & I felt at once lonely and exhilarated; caught & free. I even stepped away from the queue to isolate myself for a little longer.

· · ·

3. *Blitz!* opened at the Adelphi Theatre on May 8, 1962. It was a musical about Jewish and Protestant stall owners at an East End market. Their children fall in love during World War II—as bombs are hitting London.

Tonight afterwards, listening to Van Cliburn & Mozart's *Requiem*, I regained my vocational spur. Thomas Wolfe still makes the others look sick. No little compositions of manners for him.

> *Each of us is all the sums he has not counted: subtract us into naked-*
> *ness and night again, and you shall see begin in Crete four thousand*
> *years ago the love that ended yesterday in Texas.*[4]

MAY 16

9:30 WEDNESDAY EVENING

It's still light outside & I have gone to bed. So much has happened. Where to begin?

James came Sunday evening and we went to 49 Mossup Place[5] & discussed his new decision to leave Rank. He said he was prepared to lower his standard of living, sell his car, etc. "I'm feeling particularly fond of you tonight." Was it that I had spent a self-sufficient weekend & looked radiant because of it? Was it because he read my clippings & decided I could write? Who knows? But anyway the wine flowed & the feelings got warmer. I'm not rationalizing when I say I'm not sorry. I know so much about him that he's never told me. First of all, he has not had a spectacular life. Father was civil service, Mother (I think) is a little over-loving. He was in the Navy—Australia, etc.—and then came back to study law at Oxford. From there it was a firm & then another (must ask about those in-between years). He's been to the continent but I really don't know how much he's traveled. I know he's *never* experienced the excitement I have in twenty-four years. I wouldn't trade my life with anybody's. Also, I wonder how he feels about my having been married. I don't think he minds, it makes me less of a desperate woman. "One of the things I find most attractive about you is that you're mentally honest." He knows how I feel about separateness. I have never had

---

4. This quote from the beginning of *Look Homeward, Angel* also includes the line "our lives are haunted by a Georgia slattern, because a London cutpurse went unhung." See Appendix 2, on literary influences.

5. Forty-nine Mossup Place was a chic new restaurant a half mile northeast of Tregunter Road, just outside Chelsea in Brompton, heading toward Buckingham Palace.

such a perfect relationship with anybody. It's a short time but it still sets a precedent. Monday night late, we fixed dinner (cold chicken, beans, peas & mint, cheese, bread & wine), had a good talk—mostly about the pressures of organization life & single people being pressured by their married friends.

MAY 17

This is one of those days when I cannot compromise to pacify the smiling mediocres with their stock of speech & thought patterns. I am finished with DW as a person. I was silly to think we could get along. She is not imaginative & not extremely brilliant. She is not appealing to men. She is not really a good manager. Today we clashed twice: once about a letter I had written and once about my paying American income tax. I rode home on the bus blue with hate. When I get extremely mad my face goes numb all over. I really wish I had the benefit of an older & cleverer person's advice but I don't. Not tonight anyway. Besides, there are only two people whose opinions I'd really value: B.'s & James's. Neither is available now. So: I know *not* to handle this situation as I did the Beverly Paulson case.[6] In other words, (1) *never let anyone suspect that I dislike her;* (2) *don't let her have anything to criticize;* (3) forget she exists as much as possible—if I come to work on time (*always nine!*) & start typing madly, reading every bit of material that comes in. Always have a stock of available literature in my desk if Miller[7] asks for it. FROM NOW ON BE QUIETER & don't talk to anyone in the office unless necessary— be utterly charming (never brief or surly) to the visitors and phoners.

MAY 18

The work problem somewhat alleviated. I kept it strictly business until the middle of the morning, when Doreen said: "Are you sick or something?" Then later she was forced to say: "Gee, Gail, you've really been

---

6. At the *Miami Herald,* assistant Lauderdale Bureau Chief Paulson had been Gail's nemesis. By this time, Gail had learned not to be ruled solely by her emotions, and thus be trapped in a predetermined fate.

7. Gail was responsible for having a large stock of travel-related materials to give out to potential tourists. Beverly Miller was Gail's boss at the U.S. Travel Service.

doing a lot lately . . . ," then she went to lunch & to the bank & to the hairdresser & was out all afternoon. Oh well, we shall see whether or not she is another BP.

Church bells are ringing somewhere, the air is cool, we have been cheated of spring. Is there anywhere like Chapel Hill in the early spring or Asheville in the late spring?

Now for a quiet rest . . . oblivion . . . and then the happy time . . . Shostakovich's Eleventh[8] is supplementing me. Thirty-one Tregunter closes down soon. The framework of the new venture will be myself, Eugenio, Jeremy, Colin & a few others. Rosemary left a thief; poor Alec must leave his piano. Fidgeting, his hands clasping and unclasping on an English novel, Neil, who isn't going, said: "You know, I'm glad it happened in a way. I was getting in sort of a rut." The lightheaded girls—Geraldine, etc.—rushed out to Flats (Raymond Kerry Share-a-Flat) & are now complaining miserably about basement dampness & old furniture. Michel is still in his room with the velvet curtains & double bed, counting his pennies like Midas, hoarding his unpaid tax money. Andrew will not find another passage, I don't think. He is at a party, owing me & everyone else money.

MAY 21

VAMOS A PARECER CACAHUETES EN CHAROLA EN LA CASA NUEVA[9]
"We are going to seem like peanuts on a tray in the new house."

MAY 23

It is 12:50 and I have completed the first six typewritten pages of "The Gall Crab." I am enthusiastic—it reads like pro stuff and I am having

8. Dmitri Shostakovich completed his Symphony no. 11 in G Minor in 1957. Taking Tsar Nicholas II's 1905 massacre of Russian protestors as his text, he incorporated many workers' songs, some of which Gail had been hearing on recordings by the Red Army Choir.

9. The "new house" Eugenio refers to in his note to Gail is 21 Old Church Street in Chelsea, which the Wests had just rented to resituate their displaced "youth brothel."

fun writing it. I know exactly where I am going and what I plan to do. I think this will be about fifty pages—that's four hundred words a page, twenty thousand words, which is a novelette. I haven't had this wonderful productive feeling since December in Copenhagen.

MAY 24

THURSDAY

If tomorrow weren't Friday I would be at the end of my rope. Complete exhaustion. My job is not the center of my life. Spent the evening with the Wests. We had a good conversation and I told them the Kennedy story.[10] Mr. West said I should relax more, said I was attractive and walked well. But they both think I should marry an American.

MAY 27

SUNDAY NIGHT

Another weekend gone. I have ten thousand words of "The Gall Crab" and have finished as far as the art class. Evan is emerging as a sympathetic character & I think everything will be all right. The next scene will be Wednesday at the library & largely a thought chapter. She will see Al at the library & they will go to Bayfront Park where he will tell her the story of the old man who fell in & then discovered he could swim. Al is emerging as a glamorous, intelligent character, but a little phony.

"Halcyone and the Lighthouse"; "The Gall Crab"; "Gull Key"—these three titles represent the evolution of Godwin's efforts to come to terms with her experiences in South Florida. In the end, "Gull Key" prevailed, but not without incorporating parts of the other drafts, and then falling short of publication, due, perhaps, to inconsistencies in the mixture.

"Gull Key" underwent tremendous transformations on its way to completion, eventually deriving its dramatic substance from a story not found in early versions: the dissolution of a marriage. Initially, the story,

10. This was the story of Gail's short marriage to Douglas Kennedy in Miami.

in its Halcyone mode, involved an ex-reporter who falls in love with a sea captain. Aside from the setting, the main element that "Halcyone and the Lighthouse" shares with "Gull Key" is the symbolism of the lighthouse.

Any one person has far more experience in his or her life than is required for any one book, yet few come away with classic tales. Any group of people will come away from a common experience with different reports, yielding unequal candidates for print. Godwin's process in writing "Gull Key" demonstrates that one of the most critical aspects of writing fiction is finding the essence of a story.

JUNE 1

Beautiful sunny June 1. I am in London. Reassured by outside noises of garbage cans clanging and the ragman calling down Cathcart Road. Inside, Eugenio is shaving. I am in bed with God-knows-what. I now have a natural necklace of graduated glands. Dr. Kennedy (a clean, white-haired English practitioner with just the astringency of an Irish brogue) says it's either poisoning from scratching my scalp or glandular fever.

> ANDREW: I get a kink in my throat whenever I see a beautiful girl driving an expensive car.
>
> EUGENIO: But *why?* That's so stupid.
>
> ANDREW: Simply because it's annoying. Too much.
>
> EUGENIO: But if you go around being so stupid you will make little squares of your life.
>
> MICHEL: But at seventy-two one does not need three or four silver teapots.[11]
>
> ANDREW (putting on Michel's soiled raincoat): You know, it's amazing how quickly one can make oneself look like nobody.

JUNE 4

I do not have time to write my book. James read it and liked it, falling asleep calling me his "little genius." It makes one wonder if one

---

11. Michel, like Andrew, was responding to instances of well-off people's excesses. He was adding another example, gifts given to people upon their retirement.

shouldn't get rid of one's own very polished, calculated style. Saw *All Fall Down*[12] tonight alone. Enjoyed being alone for a change. I like Gail. Must think about my book—haven't resolved it yet. Must be true to oneself. God, how I've improved since last year.

How to recapture . . .

JUNE 8

So many triumphs this week and I am too sick to care. I got to go to the *Daily Mirror* luncheon, not Doreen. My writing is better than ever. All that remains is to copy over part 1 and send it to the *Atlantic,* then proceed to finish the novel.

JUNE 12

Part 1 is all typed. I've prayed over it & tomorrow I write a very courteous letter to the editor, address it to the *Atlantic First* competition,[13] buy international postage coupons & mail without another thought. I must make clear that this is only a small segment of a novel.

At least I've got the entire book planned. I can submit an outline to anyone who wants it. Good grief. How can one *ever* know for sure?

JUNE 13

Wednesday—milestones: (1) I mailed my story and will either be rejoicing or be shattered a month from now; (2) I *detest* my job; (3) went to see *Jules & Jim*[14] with Andrew. The girl simply succeeded (for a time) at what I've been doing for years. Andrew's suggestion for skyrocketing the national economy: make fertilizer, marrow jelly & gloves out of corpses.

12. The movie, based on James Leo Herlihy's novel, which Gail had liked, was adapted by playwright William Inge. Warren Beatty starred as the incorrigible stud who betrays both his lover and his brother.

13. *Atlantic Monthly* published two very short stories by young writers in each issue, and awarded a monetary prize to the best one in each six-month period. *Atlantic Monthly* surpassed the *New Yorker* at the time for its representation of fiction.

14. François Truffaut's film *Jules and Jim* features a woman who maintains a relationship with two men, who are friends. She is both flirtatious and palsy, and seemingly mysterious, eventually leading her consorts to a mysterious tragic ending.

JUNE 14

Tonight it becomes necessary to set down (in order of importance) a few maxims in order to save my own life: (1) the story will probably come back. If it does, you must STILL finish the novel; (2) you must throw yourself into your job tomorrow and do all the letters and keep busy; (3) you must put James in his proper perspective. He is thirty-eight years old. Has never married, will probably never marry.

Seeing James tonight walking down King's Road, with that brown face, briefcase, that special walk, I thought: It isn't fair that someone like him should be running around loose.

Andrew: "Michel—your laugh just shattered three panes of glass in my window."

JUNE 17

Sunday—I am alone to assess myself & my progress (OR LACK OF IT). Today is the last day I can say I am twenty-four years old. Although the number 25 terrifies me, there's not very much I can do about it. Time certainly sneaks by. I have everything I want in life except the writing success and that will either come or won't. I have escaped Key Biscayne & the failure of a job & I have escaped Asheville & Frank. I have a man that I seldom tire of, a man that can get more tenderness from me than anyone else on earth; and this same man lies with his face buried in my neck and says, "I'd rather be with you than anyone else on earth." I am writing a novel, it is a good & honest novel, and the end is in sight. I was just thinking, sitting here by this window enjoying a pre-storm breeze: It is so very necessary to have privacy. I need meditation, I need to rearm myself for the never-ending battle of WE vs. THEY.

This weekend was a funny half-and-half one: James was standing on the steps waiting when George[15] brought me home from work. We went out to eat with Wm. & Anne-Marie and then came back, got sloshed, and James told me just how disillusioned he was. He apologized later but said, "I wanted you to know, anyway."

15. George was the U.S. Travel Service chauffeur.

I know that the answer is simple—for both of us. We must live the best truth we know.

JUNE 18

Twenty-fifth birthday. B., of course, forgot—but then that's B. Mother sent me a box with three little Mountain Craft animals and I am very fond of the bear. I am going to ask them to mail the mountaineer. Monie[16] sent me a card with a little girl on the front (the kind she's been sending for twenty-four years) and I felt curiously timeless—as if I never really grew up. James told me about himself when he was little. He had a face, he said, like a big balloon. God, I know how he suffered. A lady came to the door when he was three and said, "Hello, fatty, where's your mother?" And he looked at her and then quietly shut the door in her face.

And he used to climb to precarious heights to get some black-and-white-striped candy balls. "When everybody found out, they were so nice to me and let me have as many as I wanted." I told him about the goldfish. "Here he comes . . ."[17]

James is good in many ways—except that he's not sure of his future (who is?) and doesn't really know what he wants. I think I will know more about him when (if) he finally breaks away from his job & strikes out on his own. I wonder how our relationship will go. Is it now as strong as the one with B. & me? That's pretty damn strong. I think that tonight I will see how happy I can make James. He needs it ($38 - 25 = 13$, that's not too bad). Doug was fifteen years older.

16. Monie was Gail's maternal grandmother.

17. At the age of three in Weaverville, Gail swallowed a goldfish and was rushed to the hospital. "Here it comes," said the doctor. At age fourteen, she wrote a story about the incident, "Red Letter Day." The grandmother in the story, by forbidding her intellectually advanced three-year-old granddaughter to drink from the fishbowl, makes her feel that she is unfairly being treated like a child. Her hunger for experience becomes do-or-die. She drinks the entire contents of the bowl and then swallows sleeping pills. When the doctor pumps her stomach, a goldfish pops out, and he faints. Back home, the girl again puts the world of imagination above the real world by pretending to be an insurrectionist, crying, "Down with Prince Albert!" and igniting curtains with a flaming hearth broom. A few years later, Gail wrote the story "The Accomplice," in which a similar theme is developed. Innocently, a convent-school girl enacts a scene from *Arsenic and Old Lace*, yelling "Charge" as she runs upstairs, and is punished for her uncontrolled imagination.

JUNE 27

WEDNESDAY

Middle-of-the-week slump. I ride to work on the bus with nothing to look forward to. I ride home on the bus (feet aching) with nothing to look forward to. I have faith in my novel. It will be done well. It is honest. I am taking it slow and will prune the words carefully. I have to get her thoughts down as they are and yet not copy James Joyce or any of the others. I am getting more and more withdrawn about James.

JULY 2

Monday again. Riding home on the bus was particularly unpleasant— smells of body odor, Vicks VapoRub, the cheap print of the *Evening Standard.* A man got up for an old lady & then insisted that everybody else get up for old ladies. The old lady in question kept grumbling, "Is this Earl's Court? Is this Earl's Court? Will everybody please get off my clothes!"

Must make some resolutions about the office, in order to survive. I think the only way I can enjoy it is to be a martyr and work harder than everybody else. Doreen & I almost came to blows.

James took me out in the country for a picnic on Saturday and we slowly uncoiled. Came back & I took a hot bath & fell asleep at nine, no good for the rest of the evening. He slept, too, and then got up at midnight & fixed omelets & fried bananas & then we went back to bed. We also went to some small village to rent a punt (only there wasn't one) & sat in the pub and listened to the locals.

Sunday was better. We went waterskiing and I came home and worked on my book. Then he returned in the evening, bathed, exercised, and got three pages of "Lucan" done.[18] He's finished "George" and started a second story. They are both good and I am so proud of him.

Dinner in the new Italian restaurant, Trattoria Pigliatelli, or something like that. We talked about "Lucan" and my "Bentley," drank wine, and listened to the guitarist, whose voice was much older than he was.

---

18. Lucan was a rakish character in a new story that James had just begun.

Then we came home and listened to the Russians[19] and went through the *New Yorker*s.

Every energy I have is directed toward the successful completion of this novel. It is my passport out of these doldrums. Until then I must hold on.

JULY 4

Independence Day and for me, too—I have enjoyed this free day to the utmost. Up at 9:30, breakfast; wrote until 12:00; went for a walk to W. H. Smith's, where I bought this pen because it was old-fashioned and looked like one my grandmother used to have.[20] Then I walked back through Redcliffe Gardens[21]—dog turds; the slap, slap of wet feet on pavement; a child's voice saying, "Aeeoh! Wot a *nice* television." And a woman standing in a door saying, "I wonder if you could give me a rough idea how much it will be."

The sounds of my London on a day off. I drank wine & had Ry-Krisps + Camembert and thought about the triumph of going home & my novel is good. I know it.

Tomorrow is Thursday. Friday, Jas. & I escape. I need a skirt & blouse, raincoat & slacks & a sweater—& a writing pad. Tomorrow I must apply myself. Can't get fired, it wouldn't be good policy. Got one of B.'s cold love letters. He's the only person I know who can write an affectionate letter with ice dripping from every line.

19. They're listening to the Red Army Choir.

20. After using ballpoints for a long time, Gail experimented with a fountain pen that had beckoned to her at W. H. Smith. A large ink blot on the July 4 page signifies her struggle with the new medium. She avoided messes by writing in a back-slanting way until July 23, when she returned to ballpoints.

21. Tregunter Road, on which Gail's lodging was situated, led into Redcliffe Gardens, a larger thoroughfare in Chelsea and a neighborhood that had been built on the old Redcliffe Estate. The development of the estate had been engineered in the 1860s by architects George and Henry Godwin, namesakes whom Gail is happy to adopt, but with whom she has not made a documented connection. The status of the area, distinguished by Georgian brownstones, has fluctuated over the years, and it is now quite fashionable. In 1966, Tara Browne, heir to the Guinness fortune and pal to the Beatles, died in a car crash in Redcliffe Gardens, inspiring one of the lyrics in the song "A Day in the Life": "He blew his mind out in a car / He didn't notice that the lights had changed."

. . .

This pen does not work well. I shall take it back. The funny thing is that it works at certain angles—when I write counterclockwise. Stay with me.[22] It has taken me ten years to even begin saying things on paper.

Happy Fourth. The dinner was a success. Mrs. West took her shoes off and ran home barefooted. I feel truly free & somehow know that I am leading the kind of life I am meant to be leading.

JULY 9

It came back in the worst way possible—with a printed note signed "the editors."[23]

Somehow, I know I'll keep on trying and there won't be an end to it. The worst thing that can happen is that I will persist and lose. The chances are that I'll persist and win. James is coming by tonight to bring the accumulated clothes & souvenirs from the wonderful weekend. At least if everything else goes wrong, I will remember that there was somebody who enjoyed three days in Bath as much as I did. I think of us standing down in that pasture in our dinner clothes, waiting for our table to be ready. I have James as much as anybody has anybody. And he has me. Now is not the time for games. We are both standing on the border of uncertain, unpleasant times. I shall have to console him when *his* stories come back. Somehow I can't bear to think of how they'll hurt him, too.

I will not know just how short of the mark I came on this rejection. Was it too long? Too autobiographical? Was the subject matter not right? Was the writing faulty? All I know to do is to finish this novel and then find a patient agent who will at least tell me what I lack.

I do *not* feel like a failure. I will keep writing, harder than ever. I will stop hoping. I *have* stopped hoping, I think. One day, if I push on hard enough, I'll get there and it will be worth all the hell. Or will it? What a funny thing if it doesn't matter at all. Other people had to go through hell. Why should I be exempt?

---

22. Gail's journals are at times expressions of encouragement from her "cowriter," her other self. She uses the code phrase "PBWM," a prayer meaning "Please be with me," in her journals today.

23. Gail had submitted a part of "Gull Key" to *Atlantic Monthly* for Atlantic First.

JULY 11

I will spend fifty years, if I live that long, will prune, cut, rewrite & be my own worst critic. I am redoing "Roxanne" & cutting all the crap. I am (1) too wordy, (2) too obvious. When I finish rewriting this (over the weekend) I shall start mailing it again & while it is out I will have enough Dutch courage to finish the novel. Then that will be subjected to the same ruthless treatment. I am not afraid anymore, because I know what I can do. My trouble has been trying to do too much with words. For a while I shall simply set down what I see. Nothing more. I shall try to quit trying to trim off life's edges, like a piecrust. This is simply the story of Roxanne. A girl with a problem. Let the reader decide what that problem is.

JULY 17

At 6:15 p.m. tonight in the alley between South Hadley & Park Lane, I came within two yards of James. I was in a taxi & he didn't see me. He was wearing the suit with red in it, he was turning a corner and he was trying very hard to stifle a yawn. In that instant, I was stunned with my own feeling for him & rode the rest of the way home feeling keen pleasure. A rare moment. The kind we all wish to have. The pleasure of spying invisibly upon a loved one.

JULY 22

It is almost Monday again. The entire weekend spent skiing. The Princess & her husband were at the Lake.[24] James & I have reached the doldrums. If we can survive them we can survive anything. I have no illusions left about him but I love him. If all goes well our gang moves into Old Church Street next Tuesday—then there will be a double bed, food & I can *write*.

---

24. Princess Margaret and Lord Snowdon were in the waterskiing club. Gail based a funny scene in "Mr. Bedford" on the arrival of a similarly royal couple at the club's skiing pond, a water-filled quarry outside of London. As the couple drive up in their Bentley, the heroine, Carrie, overhears someone grumble about how the f-ing Joneses are going to monopolize the pool. Carrie assumes that the couple's name is Effing-Jones.

JULY 23

Wrote a poem entitled ODE TO SELFISHNESS.

> *Happy, Happy Ennui*
> > *Sailing down the River Me*
> > > *Please pour me a glass of wine*
> > > > *Please be clever and divine*
> > > > > *Tell me you are only mine.*
> > > > > > *Yes. Now Everything is fine.*
> *When we reach the other banks*
> > *You shall get your word of thanks.*
> > *Thanks.*
> > > *Splash.*

—Wentworth Talon[25]

JULY 26

Occasionally, I find out some distressing things about me. Running into Lydia Fish after three years, as soon as I had milked her of all Chapel Hill gossip I began wondering, "Now, how is she going to inconvenience me?" I don't seem to want to take responsibility for anyone.

JULY 27

Monie's birthday! I mustn't forget. I have finished my novel. Ended it with Bentley saying B.'s words "AND SO RISES THE INDESTRUC- TIBLE PYRAMID." Now comes the task. I think I will type three car- bons of the last chapter & of the psychiatrist chapter—send it to three agents. This one is good. I know it.

JULY 30

Eugenio is leaving as of this minute, trim and polite as ever. He was my favorite person in this house and I will miss him. While at Wests'

25. "Wentworth Talon" was an alias that Gail made up for herself on this occasion. "Wentworth" sounded aristocratic to her, and "Talon" represented the need to hold on. Gail's joy at writing verse is also evident in *A Southern Family,* in which Julia, history professor and best friend of the novelist Clare, composes playground rhymes on mordant subjects.

tonight I saw the date Jas. & I met—April 6. I have known him not quite four months. Wednesday I move to 21 Old Church Street.

AUGUST 1

Moving day—waiting for George to come & help me move. I have decided several things:

1. to rewrite my novel, not skimping anywhere and always keeping the ring of authenticity, always the right word. I'll have it done by September 1—in this new house.

2. to stay away from James for a while. We are both fed up with each other. There is no point in seeing him (or, for that matter, of him seeing me) if it is mutually unpleasant.

3. I will write him from Amsterdam and tell him simply that I will be away for a month. Or I will work out a similar compromise.

This novel is good, but it needs work.

—7:50 same day. When I look back on London, if I ever leave, I will remember this evening. I must get some books on English history and learn the area so I can write about it. It is the color of the sky and the people coming into and going out of pubs. Tonight, after dinner, I am going through all my old notebooks. Amsterdam Friday evening. Money tomorrow. Calculate budget. I am so comfortable in here I can't decide what to do first. I feel bad about the way things turned out for James & myself, but I'd rather be away from him & remember how nice he can be, than be with him and think how hateful he can be. August 1. August 1. Last year at this time I didn't ever imagine this.

I went for a walk. Down by the river. Into the Black Lion[26] with the Wests.

26. The Black Lion, one of several pubs near the Wests' place, was their favorite.

AUGUST 2

Amsterdam tomorrow. Bought a pair of comfortable walking shoes for £1.19 & an orange skirt for Holland, £2.19. Washed my hair after Mrs. West's delicious salmon trout dinner. Broke down & wrote James a note at his office because I'd left my bathing suit in the trunk of his car. Met him coming down King's Road & had a drink with him. Those blue eyes coming toward you in the white light of 6:30 p.m. on a summer night! He was going on to a party and was tired and didn't want to go. He'd bought me a gift, a book called *Style*, by F. L. Lucas,[27] which I will read later. He kissed me on the cheek outside by his car and said, "Have a nice holiday, sweetie, and if you get into any trouble, give me an SOS." I feel awful about my extremes of temper—if I can learn to live with any man, it's James, and who am I to expect perfection? He is perfection most of the time and that's why I get stunned when he so much as snaps at me. I'm taking my novel to work tomorrow. This ennui is terrible.

AUGUST 7

Amsterdam had no tulips but it had Van Goghs (173 of them) and a blond peach-cheeked canal-boat guide named Joost who said, "I'll make you an evening in Amsterdam that you'll never forget." I filled several pages with on-the-spot impressions in my travel notebook,[28] so no use to repeat myself.

It was a weekend in parentheses—complete in itself. Walking over the bridges in the rain, always the smooth green canals below. He is saying now: "To the right you see the Twin Sisters . . ."[29]

Staying out until dawn on a continual party—it just occurred to me that this is the first time I ever did this. We went first to the Farmyard and had two beers. It was in the second place, where the bartender told riddles and three men played instruments, that he first showed preference. Then we went to the Students' Beer Parlor & I played Ella Fitzger-

27. *Style*, published in 1955 and republished in 1962, is a writers' book, full of charming asides on various aspects of the narrator's voice. Lucas takes a long time moving from one point to another, enjoying, as he does, his own style in explicating good style.

28. The travel notebook was one that Gail was required to fill out for her job.

29. The Twin Sisters in Amsterdam was a nightclub.

ald's "You're Driving Me Crazy"—from there to a nicer bar, full of intellectuals, laughs, good jokes (sickness or disease), and a Dutchman with loads of teeth who kept saying, "American women smash their men . . ." Then to the Lucky Star, where we began dancing; then to a duller, mellower place for a rest; then to a very high-priced nightclub with an orchestra where we bought a bottle of wine & did the twist—then to the Café du Paris. When we came out, it was growing light.

AUGUST 8

Style by F. L. Lucas was another of the reasons I love James. One must first master all the rules in order to break them effectively.

AUGUST 13

Sometimes if I didn't have this notebook to resort to, I would go crazy. A dozen little hells since yesterday. When will I learn? On top of everything, I am tired. Where to begin? James did come by yesterday. Said he was "slightly alarmed" at my disappearance. We went to the lake & I skied twice. Everyone was in a fine mood. I was almost orientally relaxed. Driving back we heard Berlioz's *Fantastique*, which put a seal on the very pleasant outing. The evening. That's where it started. We ate at home (an omelet) and drank Macon (again). It all started when we began talking about his job. The more we talked, the more hopeless it seemed for him. If the television thing fails, what does he really have left? If the story from the *New Yorker* comes back (it's been gone five weeks), he will be very depressed. He mentioned several things he'd *thought about* doing (asking the man down at Pinewood Studios if there was anything in the production end; telling Davis the company simply was not using his talents). But then, in the course of the conversation, he ended up deciding *not* to do these things. I finally started crying and said far too much, including the fact that I loved him about fifty thousand times. I said I sometimes didn't think it would make much difference to him if I was simply erased tomorrow. He said it would make a big difference. I then got worse & worse and he said he felt inadequate and didn't take care of me and not to expect too much, and that I was harboring an image. He was so right but I didn't want to hear it. He brought me home at eleven and I had private hysterics in the bedroom. He will never know. He said, among other things, that he didn't have a great desire to *be loved* as Wm. did. I said, "Well, I love you, you'll have to accept that." I forget what he answered.

AUGUST 16

Planning the trip to Leeds, Bradford & Sheffield.[30] Doreen is no help. Disorganized & can't really get to the core of things. Heard Miller tell her that her report was "too general." I talk to him tomorrow morning. Mine is all planned. I am also learning how to stand up to her in her own language. "Haven't we?" "Don't we?" etc. He used a lot of my suggestions.

The Japanese film with James. I fell asleep twice. "Don't you pretend that you haven't been asleep," he said when I woke up and said, "Isn't that funny?" I was seeing two of everything. Afterwards we went to his apartment & talked & then I went to bed after a hot bath. He was very good to me in the way he sometimes is, being very protective. I could tell he was glad to have me around.

While we were standing in the kitchen next morning, his rejected story came through the slot.

What is to become of us both?

I wish we could get away together.

Andrew & I went to see *The Premise*.[31] I laughed so hard the man behind me told me to keep still. Pleasant bus ride home. London at night makes me happy. The lighted double-decker buses, the Times Square–like splash of lights & advertisements in Piccadilly. I want to know this town well. Today I stumbled into Shepherd Market by accident. Must get a good guidebook about London. Maybe I will set my next book there. Keep your eyes open. Put down what you see in the simplest way.

30. Gail's territory was the north of England. She traveled first-class by train, carrying Mr. Miller's briefcase, and visited travel agents, distributing information about trips to the United States.

31. *The Premise* was a show by an off-Broadway improvisational theater group of the same name that crossed the Atlantic and played for six months in London. Gene Hackman was part of the troupe at that time, and he credits it with teaching him how to make people laugh through the use of timing, delivery, and voice.

AUGUST 19

Sounds on Old Church Street on a Sunday afternoon: footsteps on the carpeted stairs; a bus rolling down King's Road; voices outside the Black Lion; someone singing; a bird chirping; a lorry bumping up this narrow street; Bob Hope in the living room below; a taxi—the unmistakable rattle of a London taxi.

AUGUST 24

The hunter is home from the hill.[32] Triumphant. If only I were in the mood to write my report for Mr. Miller. But I'm not. Before Monday, however, I must get the orders all ready to be sent out with library copy requests on a separate list for me to fill. Called James when I got into St. Pancras station. He was going to a party but sounded genuinely glad to see me. He had surprised me by telephoning to Bradford. I wrote him two letters, one from Leeds, one from Sheffield. Tomorrow we go to the lake.

It is time to start another story. Not a novel, I don't think. But then what? Maybe I need this "think" period.

This week has convinced me of one thing: I do things awfully fast.

AUGUST 27

One thing I know.

Exhaustion. Twenty visitors, tension with Doreen, Betty Hughes and Pat gone away. I have completed my report on the trip & on the Canberra interviews.[33] Tomorrow will be spent typing labels, filling orders, plus my regular job.

Miller was impressed. Heard him tell Bob Briggs, "Gail had a fabulous trip." Doreen came in almost two hours late. Re my U.S.A. trip: Miller reiterated, "Just be sure & come back."

---

32. Gail had returned from her trip to Yorkshire. She quotes the Robert Louis Stevenson poem "Requiem," which is engraved on his tombstone. The last two lines are "Home is the sailor, home from the sea, / And the hunter home from the hill."

33. The appearance of tourists with kangaroo pins on their lapels signaled a long and exhausting day to come. Australians wanting to travel to America generally required the retrieval and perusal of dozens of brochures and train schedules. After that, the Travel Service agents had to log the interactions in their reports.

SEPTEMBER 7

If I could capture the feeling I had when reading last year's entry for September 7, I would be another Wolfe, another Proust.[34] I can lie here in my bed in Chelsea and still be lying above the treetops in Blowing Rock—like last September 7. Just for the record, my novel is with Eric Glass.[35]

The reason I am not myself and very upset is because I am afraid if a mere agent rejects my book then what chance do I have? I know I will keep on trying but still it hurts. I haven't the slightest idea whether or not it is good.

SEPTEMBER 10

Mrs. West gave me Proust and I am embarking on a new world.

James

hairdresser tomorrow

Stella comes Wednesday[36]

Eric Glass

Proust

SEPTEMBER 11

Proust fascinates me. Of course, here is where my darling Durrell got his training. I have found rather he has expressed for me the thing I want to get across in "Kim."[37]

34. September 1961 had marked the end of Gail's time at Mayview Manor. At that point she had reflected, "And I must think of last September, about this time. How far I was from here! In spirit, in confidence, in every way, I came back from that navy reconnaissance flight into Donna."

35. Eric Glass was a London literary agent.

36. Stella Anderson, Gail's good friend from Chapel Hill, was arriving in London to stay at 21 Old Church Street for an indefinite period while she had surgery on her leg.

37. "Kim" was a story that Gail was beginning to write based on a formidable little girl in second grade at St. Genevieve's. This character later inspired the creation of Freddy Stratton in *A Southern Family* as well as Lisa Gudger in "Over the Mountain," a short story published only in the anthology *Evening Games: Chronicles of Parents and Children* (Penguin, 1986). In the latter tale, the young protagonist says of a problematic classmate,

None of us can be said to constitute a material whole, which is identical for everyone and need only be turned like a page in an account book or the record of a will; our social personality is created by the thoughts of other people . . .[38]

And:

So that even now I have the feeling of leaving someone I know for another quite different person when, going back in memory, I pass from the Swann whom I knew later . . . to this earlier Swann.

Saw Lillian Hellman's *The Children's Hour,*[39] only now called *The Loudest Whisper.* Excellent. Must get my ducks in a row to go home. All clothes ready. Buy a sweater for under the suit—Jaeger tomorrow.

I am thinking so much; but always too tired to write it down.

When I woke this morning the first thing I thought about was James and I walking down Old Church Street to the river; only now the skies were gray and the streets were clear in daylight. Yet which is realer? The actual minute-to-minute we stood there or the hundred times I turn it over in my mind, examining it for new meanings?

Don't let Proust run away with you.

His style is not your style.[40]

"We're friends, but I hate her. I hate her and she fascinates me at the same time. What has she got that makes everybody do what she wants?" The narrator's mother replies, "You are smarter than Lisa Gudger . . . But Lisa likes herself better than you like yourself." The daughter tries to believe her mother's counsel that once she figures the dominating girl out, she will lose her fascination.

38. This passage and the one following are from Marcel Proust's *Swann's Way,* chapter 13. Gail astutely zeroes in on Durrellian ideas, namely, that one's personality changes depending on who's doing the viewing and on when in their lives they're doing the viewing.

39. *The Children's Hour,* Lillian Hellman's 1934 play about two teachers rumored by a malicious child to be lesbians, encountered severe censorship and heavy editing when director William Wyler made it into the movie *These Three* in 1936. In 1961, Wyler chose to remake the movie, and it was released as *The Children's Hour* in the United States and *The Loudest Whisper* in Great Britain.

40. Gail, at this time, felt that Proust sacrificed plot too much in his efforts to represent characters' multilevel thoughts.

SEPTEMBER 13

Last night James and I met Stella at the airport. Funny crosscurrents—
Chapel Hill & London. All cementing my individuality—so much to
think about—must get something done.

Scene to be utilized at some time or another:

I am lying in bed in this room that I have always imagined in stories, only it is real now, my blue room.[41] Michel comes in and stands in
the doorway. He is wearing a white high-collared shirt and braces and
the pants to his gray suit. Eighteenth-century music is playing. He is
talking about his stocks. He props one knee on my bed. For a minute I
am the heroine of a romantic novel. He is my romantic husband. It is
after a party. But the fantasy cannot last because I know that behind
the wavy hair, the Byronic face, is a disorganized vagueness, Catholic
provincialism, no room for growth.

Viridiana[42] with Stella. Mr. West expounding afterwards.

SEPTEMBER 15

SATURDAY

How to begin? One has to start somewhere in summing up a philosophy
one has fashioned while walking along the Embankment acutely conscious of oneself, making literature out of every smell of river; the
Chelsea pensioner watching the rugby game; the leaves starting to fall,
which remind one of other leaves in other places. The thing is to be patient. Without patience I will go crazy. I want to write and I know
vaguely, in snatches, what I want to say. Saying it is something else. See.
In this page I have skimped through the afternoon. I didn't put the
meaning or even the feeling in the words. Meaning? Feeling? Hell.
James is suffering alone at some expensive hotel away from London. His
"George" was returned with a printed slip from the BBC. We can at
present be of no help to each other. When I think of how we would have
spent the day—the lake, too much wine, too much food, each brooding

---

41. The Wests had given Gail the master bedroom at 21 Old Church Street.

42. *Viridiana,* a 1961 film by cult celebrity Luis Buñuel, tells the story of a saintlike woman
who immerses herself in a society of beggars in order to help them.

over separate losses—I am fully aware that we had no business being together. But each time I think *James*, I am conscious of a vestigial sadness. Like waking and thinking for a minute the dream was real. We would have walked, talked, been bored and uninspired. And, I admit, it is healthy for me to be alone. I think I will soon consciously accept the maxim of complete self-sufficiency (as much as is possible in my kind of world), and when that acceptance comes, I will wake up and quit receding into the habits of the *other* maxim: the one of dependence. No one could understand that last sentence but me. The day when I *can* write sentences of this kind in a way that others can understand, I will be a writer.

Inertia impedes. The Kim novel. How long will it take? I feel pressed in. October 1, the Spanish girl comes.[43] What *guilt*, what perversity makes me offer to do the antithesis of what I want? I shall be miserable.

SEPTEMBER 17

There is no way out of it. She comes October 1. If I can't stand it, I will go to a hotel. James will lend me the money. Tonight we walked till I was ready to drop. He took a taxi back to the flat. He loves me. I must not be a bitch. He had a story rejected by *Cosmopolitan*.

SEPTEMBER 19

After dinner, Casa Neurotica householders played charades. I will not forget (a) Mrs. West with her paper wig doling out "Justice Walk";[44] (b) Michel laughing so hard about his successful rendition of Winston Churchill (after clanging tongs against the brass fire grate failed to elicit the proper response—"church"—he put his feet on the table, puffed out his cheeks, and made the V sign). It was interesting to see how praise affects him. He warmed to the game immediately, suggesting we introduce it to all forthcoming guests at 21, "now that we are experts."

43. In a weak moment, Gail had agreed to share her room with Isabel, whom Shell Oil was sending to the Wests from Madrid to improve her English.

44. Justice Walk is the walkway directly across the street from 21 Old Church Street.

Andrew is very artistically inclined. For someone who says "Of all the characters in literature, I would most like to be Swann," he does all right. Too bad I can't remember everything he says. Tonight, re Susan: "I am just discovering how miserable it feels when you know you have hurt someone." He and Michel are always at it. Yet I am sure when Michel goes back to France it will be Andrew more than any of us who will feel the loss.

Returns from the subconscious are beginning to come in the Kim project.

Always after, the whiff of a sweaty tennis shoe, a chlorinated pool, a tube of a certain brand of lipstick elicited in me a distinct feeling of uneasiness. I was again dressing for a gym period (Kim was much better at athletics than I and I always dreaded gym); back at the country club the horrible day of betrayal; standing at the bus stop watching Kim expertly outline her lips . . . The thing to do is to finish the first chapter with Mother Hardee,[45] then just write, start anywhere. Have a little summing-up first. Get the reader sufficiently interested so that he will want to know every detail about Kim.

Some people like Kim are so very definitely themselves; others, like me, write about them.

Framework: that year, eighth grade, interspersed with reassessments.

While it's true we gradually become disenchanted—the child's images linger on in the adult mind . . . certain images formed as a child linger on in our adult minds—we are all bound to our pasts.

SEPTEMBER 21

I am falling into a very bad habit of going to bed after dinner; but there is nowhere else to go. I just realized: when the Spanish girl comes I will have no place on earth I can go to be alone. I won't be able to write at all.

I am in the Wests' black book—

Everything I say is wrong—

45. Mother Hardee was an early fictional name for Mother Winters.

Michel laughs—

The weekend looms—

James is silent.

SEPTEMBER 23

Brisk wintery weekend. I went waterskiing for the last time this season. The water was icy. Saturday, Kokoschka at the Tate,[46] came back in the late afternoon and called James (he said he was going to call me later anyway) . . . We went out to eat (I had already eaten) and then did tape recordings in his flat. He told me a story about a little sea serpent. It was just the kind of story a child would love.

SEPTEMBER 24

Walked the streets for USTS today. Mr. Briggs may play the fool but his mind is in the right place. Had a long talk with Andrew. It is good sometimes to have other people's views.

SEPTEMBER 26

Wrote out in detail—the anatomy of a habit: James. Was finishing my cold process of mental dissection when he called the office and asked me did I want to go to Cornwall. Resolutions went out the window. I bumbled around and accepted. Stella is fabulous. She is a devil in her own way. It is good to have a girl to talk with about everything.

It will be fun riding down on the train to Cornwall Friday night. Tomorrow I must pack underclothes, slacks, heavy shoes, raincoat.

Things to remember: Bob Briggs cussing the cab driver. (During the last week we have worked together so well. Everyone says we are so alike, which isn't a compliment for either of us. But we can talk freely and be buffoons.)

Yesterday afternoon: the fall sunshine, Hill Street, and someone

46. Oskar Kokoschka, along with Gustav Klimt and Egon Schiele, formed an early twentieth-century triumvirate of avant-garde Viennese artists. Kokoschka's violent expressionism—in his paintings as well as his theater pieces—set him apart.

walking like James. I turned the corner sharply and headed on to Berkeley Square. I had decided to be strong and give him up. I went into a bookshop and concentrated on titles, hearing a street-accordion man play "Waltzing Matilda." I felt pangs of endings, loneliness, poignancy, separation, and was incredibly restless. It was as if I caught a glimpse of life passing me by.

Am continuing on "Kim." It is only that I hit a stale point earlier than in "Gull Key." It was discouraging but now I'm okay.

SEPTEMBER 27

The pub regulars teeter down Old Church Street at 12:30 a.m. This is the first time I have been sufficiently awake to hear what they say. Usually their voices have a hollow, dreamlike quality and no matter how I try, I cannot retain the message. James stopped by to pick up my bag. Eugenio is back and I am glad. He is thinner, has a French haircut, and is still the little gentleman. Stella, Eugenio, Andrew, Numela,[47] James, and I sitting in Nannie's kitchen.[48] James is smooth with them all, a slightly amused look on his face. He is always tender with me in public.

SEPTEMBER 30

The weekend in Cornwall was, from a purely personal and imaginative viewpoint, perfect. I will describe it more accurately tomorrow because much of it is good grist for the mill. I think I know two things now: (1) I am in love with J.; (2) it would never *possibly* work out.

So many nuances of feeling here; so many reinforced impressions.

God, these next two weeks. The Spanish girl coming to share my room.

---

47. Numela was an Indian girl whom Andrew was dating.

48. "Nannie's kitchen" was Mrs. West's term for the basement floor "kitchen," where the boarders made tea. It was outfitted with a hot plate and sink. Mrs. West's upstairs kitchen was off-limits, and the refrigerator was padlocked—wisely, Gail says.

Part seven

PERSONAL POLITICS

Old Church Street to Green Street, London,

with a Trip to Asheville, North Carolina

OCTOBER 1–DECEMBER 26, 1962

"Why do relationships fall short of the ideal?"

This riddle engaged Godwin as a writer in her mid-twenties. The answer, she discovered, has to do with the pervasive spirit of the times as much as with the complexities of the characters involved.

Enmeshed in her own place and time, Gail had personal riddles to solve as well as sociological ones. She had to figure out how the "Zeitgeist" had trapped and misguided her in her dealings with people. This journal part candidly chronicles Gail's struggles and ends with the calm assessment, "I see that I haven't progressed as far as I thought."

Featured are three romantic interests: B., the Asheville beau, who offered physical passion, material security, and separate existences; James, the British companion, who lacked passion; and Peter W., the intellectual poseur, who put Gail on the defensive with his D. H. Lawrence manifestoes. You could not have a better threesome to represent 1960s turmoil regarding male-female relations.

Nineteen sixty-two had been the year that Helen Gurley Brown hit the best-seller list with Sex and the Single Girl. Popular culture was catching up with intellectuals' breakdown of gender barriers. The time and place to which many were connected rested on shifting sands.

Gail Godwin was the product of three contending traditions: the modern intellectual tradition, in which she was thoroughly immersed; an upbringing in a three-woman household; and the 1950s South. When Gail wonders if B. will rescue her, when she yearns for a mysterious man who will worship her, and when she contemplates her thoughts about her friend Lorraine's coffee-colored skin, she is responding to aches conditioned by her foundation culture.

The problem is, the spirit of the times cannot easily be distinguished from intimate aspects of one's self.

OCTOBER 1, 1962

LONDON

Notebook number 7 in one year. Much must be sorted out. The only thing is to keep pressing on. Letter from B. today. He put a PS: "I say—a masterful letter." And was perfectly correct in this assumption. The letter began without a date or salutation, discussing the marriage difficulties of a couple at home.

About R. he says: "I like her. She's college grad, very attractive—rich—intelligent—even though addicted to tranquils—patent medicines—and 'high strung.'[1] I just can't understand where she got the vain notion that 'I do' meant I quit—you take over & entertain me for the next years. She's the proud cultivator of that women-invented VD emotionalism . . .

". . . most of all, give him the benefit of the doubt—have confidence—respect—knowing whatever he does or *writes in a letter* is not calculated to upset you emotionally and doesn't necessarily have overtones of lack of interest. In summary, stay off his arse emotionally though not physically . . .

". . . me, I prefer the un's—unhurried, unmarried, unengaged, un-acceptable, unproblemed . . . I only have to keep up with what I've got: new sofa payments, car pays, golf balls, physical stamina, and lawsuits. I prefer the simple unhurried life of a complete cynic—"

Masterful!

". . . Maugham's remark: Don't be shocked, reader—your overly dramatic & nauseating search for a meaning to life has been in vain. Life has no meaning."

·   ·   ·

1. The R. referred to here is a woman whose unbalanced marriage eventually ended in tragedy.

Then, one's moods are affected by one's position: *where* I have been the day before, what has been said or done to me. One ought to, I suppose, keep a daily chart over a period of years, recording thereon one's uppermost needs & desires each day. Thus, if I kept such a record for five years, I could go back and *count*. If there were more *I-am-happy-single*s than *I-wish-I-were-married*s, then I would know my best bargain for the greatest number of satisfactory days would be the unmarried state. It's a great subject.

OCTOBER 3

I have an idea, at last, about what I want to do. It is this: I want to say things on paper that will give expression to my own discoveries and at the same time make a reader richer in perception & enjoyment or awareness of his life. I want to experiment, I want to write the first things of their kind. I do not want the *almost*s. I do not want a good imitation that reads smoothly but does not bear up under scrutiny. I want to profit from the writing (not so much to "enjoy life," per se, but to put back into writing what I gain)—my own literary stock market, so to speak. It *would* help if I had a decent pen.

Eugenio's mother, Mrs. Martinez-Ostos, came for dinner. She's the kind of woman that can sit in the center of a room and have the men pressing their cigarette lighters like mad and the women, suddenly quite content with being women, wondering if they should go out and buy her brand of perfume the next day. After dinner I walked down to the Embankment and leaned over the wall and played optical games with the lights and the dark water. I created a few upside-down shimmering worlds aglow with electric-red splashes (from the Hovis clock); quivering white-hot spikes (street lamps reflected); and ghostly houses with two floors of lighted windows sailing over and against watery backgrounds (the buses).

OCTOBER 5

Weighed down with physical exhaustion. Worked on window displays all day. Mr. Miller asked me point-blank if I'd rather do what I've been doing these past two weeks. I said yes. He said he'd see if it could be done legally, but it would mean a *raise*. (!) Bought B. a golf sweater & me a black turtleneck. I sat in a hot tub and read all his old love letters. He *does*. When I was in the Canaries, he wrote: "I hope you get tired sometime . . ."

OCTOBER 8

Eric Glass sent MS back.

OCTOBER 12

NEWARK AIR TERMINAL, COLUMBUS DAY, 1962

First impression from the air was the incredible number of cars. Shiny blocks of color in mammoth parking lots, or spinning up and down wide-lane concrete highways. The customs official was a young Negro who asked my address, my proposed length of stay in the U.S.A. (the immigration official had said "Welcome home"), and what gifts I had brought. I said only toys & he asked if I would list the value, which I did at $5. He discreetly fingered through my stacks of clothes and then said, "Okay, go on through." The first thing I did was to buy a large Coke with ice in it (20¢); the second was to buy a *New York Herald Tribune* in which the major story was that President Kennedy had just approved a postal raise. Stamps will now be 5¢. And then to the bookstore, where I saw all the best sellers I was unable to buy in England. Philip Roth's *Letting Go*,[2] *The JFK Coloring Book*, and even one called *The John Birch Society Coloring Book*.

I noticed that I was reluctant to speak up in the midst of this cacophony of Americanese. But, then, wasn't that always the case? And a little apprehension about seeing people I haven't seen in a year. I have been moving in an outward course. They have been going on with the same lives. Or was that a fair statement?

My chief fear is that, upon arriving home and experiencing the nov-

---

2. *Letting Go,* Philip Roth's second published work and first novel, involves a narrator, Gabriel Wallach, whose empathetic nature and fear of emotional commitment leads him to meddle in others' lives. One of the main characters in whom he takes an interest is Libby Herz, an uneasily married woman. Gail saw in Libby a variation of the story of Bentley, a woman trapped in a marriage.

elty of bright faces, just because *I* have chosen to be among them, will I then become restless and nervous to be "moving on"? I have already decided after being in New York two hours that I must be submerged in competition—even though it is grueling.

In forty minutes they will call my flight. The last lap of the journey. A strange sense of mastering time. Arriving in New York, it seemed perfectly natural that it was just sunset when in England it would be 11:00 p.m. One *big impression* when helicoptering over Manhattan, from Idlewild to Newark: It is really a *very small island.* After the sprawling, endlessly joined cities within the city of London, this is a breeze.

I don't think people who see New York from an altitude for the first time will be half as frightened as those deposited at a dark wharf or in between hulking skyscrapers at midday. New York is a must: if only to prove that one isn't afraid. The heat is about 10 degrees more than expected. I am roasting in my dear old Jaeger tweed suit. There is an Ivy league–looking type stealing glances over my shoulder as I write. The Newark terminal is crowded. Didn't succumb to the fresh original Lady Manhattan blouses ($13) in a store. God, people are nosey. Water fountains! That's another asset. Will B. be the same? By that I mean, Will he have grown with me so that he seems the same? At any rate, it should be an interesting experience and certainly one badly needed. The thing is *not to let them know* if I find I can't go home again.

OCTOBER 17

Okay, get it all down while it's all fresh and hot. It will be a long wet London winter. There will be time to hash & rehash the meanings of words, nuances, little actions. I've done all the things I set out to do, nagged only by little prickly guilts that I ought to be in more places.

There were the tasteless lunches in GV & BP[3] with Kathleen (I look out at my requested view and instead see London); I bought shoes that fit at Edwin Burge, drip-dry blouses. Started on a campaign to rid myself of corns. Waited for—and hated—B. He came at 4:30 instead of

---

3. GV and BP were the George Vanderbilt and the Battery Park, tall brick hotels in downtown Asheville that served as the sites of conventions and club meetings as well as lodgings for medium-budget travelers.

12:00 (court case) and we went to Hendersonville, me shooting barbs all the way. But I finally looked out at the Indian colors, the haystacks, the mountains, and thought how silly and pulled out my knives. The dinner at the Little Chef was good. B. drinks Sanka with his meal instead of wine, but B. is a Southerner, U.S.A., not an Italian, Frenchman, or educated Englishman. Somehow he finally started talking. With B., I hang on hungrily, waiting for him to say something personal. It was the Navy first, but that's what shaped him. ("Before those eighteen months I had no identity.") It was things like "Goddammit, did you think you could get away without putting croutons in my soup?" and "Goddammit, you mean to say you let us leave the port of Norfolk without filling up the Kotex machine!"

That made B. the man he is today.[4] He cried, he clenched his fists, he got off the ship in Oran & bought a box of multicolored Kotex, but he survived and came back with the embryo of his philosophy. And, something I could not understand before, he is a good lawyer & happy in his work. His golf is his creative outlet. Christ, do I want everyone I know to yearn for publication?

But tonight we came as close as we ever will and I ought to busy myself on lonely Sundays during the next few years asking myself if that was close enough. He drove to all the high places, the places that construct my dream image of Asheville. Beaucatcher Mountain. Sunset Drive. Grove Park Inn. He talked of houses. We saw the lights & felt the same things about the lights. Later, waiting for a traffic light at the end of Charlotte Street, he said, "We'll have a den and a studio in the second house and you can come home and write." He put a firm hand on my knee and I was speechless. Then he quickly went on to another topic. All the other was expected.

The first day, a Saturday, he called (I was at Monie's) and just said, Mmm-mmm. He came later to Happy Valley[5] and when I walked into the room the sparks flew.

4. B. went into the military with the expectation that being an officer and a gentleman would not involve petty duties and attitudes. He had never experienced being treated as a servant and ultimately he learned to bide his time until he was the one giving the orders.

5. Happy Valley was, at the time, a new subdivision east of Asheville in which Gail's stepfather, Frank Cole, built houses. There, he provided his family—Gail's mother and

OCTOBER 21

Both weekends are gone & I have spent them with the wrong people. Called B. & had tearful hysterics over the phone; he said that nothing was that pressing. That was the best advice he could give me but I wouldn't listen.

1. Go back to London, live each day, work *quietly* & *intelligently*—MAKE A CHANGE.

2. Write at night; keep sending MSS out.

3. Remember that if I do my share, then it's still up to chance & can't be changed. I'm going to get older & will either win, lose, or get rained out.

OCTOBER 23

—Two more days. Lorraine called from Boston but I wasn't in. Last night I went to B.'s while he was at Reserve & cataloged all the contents of his apartment. He came in wearing that devastating navy uniform & we talked of Kennedy's tough move.[6] He said, "You never cease to amaze me."

Lunch with Mother at Grove Park Inn. Think the reason I love this town the way I do is because I learned to appreciate it from a purely objective viewpoint after I no longer lived here. Once that was done, then, appreciating it, I was eager to reinstate myself as a native-born soul.

It is hard to describe it because when I am looking at it I am seeing not only its physical beauty but also reexperiencing the hundreds of other thoughts & attitudes once entertained while looking at this same scene a hundred other times. I would like to live here someday and I would like to live here with *him,* but so many crosscurrents make things

---

Gail's two brothers and one sister by Frank—with their first ample accommodations. Gail's grandmother, Monie, with whom Gail and her mother had lived in Weaverville and then in a Charlotte Street apartment in Asheville, had moved to an apartment on Katherine Place.

6. The day before, on October 22, President Kennedy made an announcement that the Soviet Union was building missile bases in Cuba; on October 23, he ordered a naval blockade of Cuba.

either very simple or completely impossible. I would like to live with him on that mountain, but not now. It would be sudden death. I am not above-it-all enough to freely take action, write, live my own life as well as his. Not yet. From all outward signs, he is safe as can be from the snakelike clutches of local femme fatales. But accidents will happen. There might be a lonely night or a good meal or a careless tumble. He lives to eat. Well, I'll speak to him before I leave. Let him know my feelings & then smolder over them these next long winter nights. James & the wet, green summer, the trips to Somerset & Cornwall are more a part of another world than I ever realized. That, however, is a good world, and I will go back to it happily—at least for the present. There are good times with James & he & I have an affinity no other couple can match. I know James & James knows me. A pity about all those cold baths at Haileybury.[7] There will be more trips this winter & maybe James & I will go away for Christmas.

B. pays $8,000 a year income tax! Great God, he must be loaded. I never knew. Ah, well, no use to chafe. Either he'll wait or he won't. After all, who's to guarantee *I'll* wait?

OCTOBER 26

MORNING—

I think B. was extremely right in parting with "See you next week." He came around and we went out to Black Mountain to the Coach House for our Summit Meeting. He said it was ridiculous to regard my trip as a negative and that our relationship was anything but negative. He said he didn't have one person in his world who had faith in his good judgment to be where he wanted to be (that was aimed at me). He said he thought it was fine we had completely separate interests, that he could think of nothing better than a woman writer & a man lawyer living together, each with their own interests & with one common bond: bed. I used all kinds of bait but he didn't fall. He said, "If you ever fashioned

7. Haileybury is a boys' boarding school. When James was a student there, boys were required to take cold baths.

that clay man you couldn't get rid of him fast enough. You don't want a carbon copy of yourself?"

OCTOBER 27
BACK IN LONDON

Back from the New World with my New Philosophy. There has been plenty to test its strength.

1. James got fouled up on the time, the plane was early & we missed each other.

2. Came home and opened a letter from the bank telling me I was £3 overdrawn.

3. Called Peter W.[8] & received the classic rebuff of the self-assured Englishman. He soared in my estimation. I had played dirty & he wasn't having any. I wrote him a letter tonight. I will probably never see him again & it will be my loss.

4. Had it out with the Wests. The sad thing is, Mrs. West & I could make it okay again but Mr. West did not play square & I can't say this to her. We have gotten into a real tight spot, like Kennedy & Khrushchev, and somebody's going to lose face & that's why it won't work because they'll always resent it / or I'll always resent it. Now that I'm tired, I wish I could forget about the whole thing.

The thing about this new philosophy is that it saves unnecessary wear and tear on the human machine. If I do not have to think through other people's lives, how simple it will be. This way, I will have a definite framework. It is basically this: Regarding other people in category 1, demand absolutely nothing—ever. When it seems they have done something unfair to the relationship, decide whether or not I have the faith

---

8. Peter W. was a reporter on a London newspaper and a former student of F. R. Leauis's at Cambridge.

in their judgment to accept the act *unflinchingly.* If so: The relationship goes on. If not: Stop. Don't second-guess if I can help it. Weigh a situation as honestly as possible in view of all the factors available, then decide & act. Don't second-guess.

Do during each day an honest amount of work. At USTS, this means enough to earn my salary, and enough to satisfy Miller's faith in me. About the writing, know what has to be said. Then attempt to say it. Don't think in terms of finished products but simply of a few good sentences that say exactly what was meant.

Regarding people in category 2: This includes people like Peter W. in relation to category 1 person James. This includes people like Uncle William, etc.—people that I like, that have more than a temporary meaning to my life, but people that I can live without. Fair play is the recipe here, but no concessions *ever* at the expense of a category 1 person. (I am in category 1; that must not be overlooked.) Duties & obligations to category 2s must be defined & adhered to.

Category 3 people do not include neutrals, shadows passing through, or semi-people. Category 3 is an important one. It consists of those persons who, for some reason, either by proximity or relation to 1s & 2s, are an undeniable part of my day-to-day life. To these people I owe nothing of myself. Courtesy is the byword here. Respect their territory but don't let them invade mine.

Lorraine's forty pages were good. She thought it out. I enjoyed reading them. They were not slop.

OCTOBER 30

They were two very separate beings, vitally connected, knowing nothing of each other, yet living in their separate ways from one root.
—D. H. LAWRENCE

I can think of no better relationship than one where the wife is a writer or whatever she wants to be & the husband is a doctor or lawyer or

whatever he wants to be & they live in the same house, make love in the
same bed, but go their separate ways.

B.

Emotionalism & inward gazing. That is what's wrong with my life
& my writing. Did I think I could separate the two, keep one clear of the
other?

Walking to the bus stop on Haymarket at 5:30 is, I think, my most
unpleasant experience to undergo daily. I have given up taxis for the
present (no money). There is something so desolate about darkness at
5:00. I join the fast-walking crowds hunched down into their coats,
necks receding, like turtles, and we all hike for the bus stops. Then there
is the queue and finally I am aboard a 19 or 22, breathe a moment of relief upon entering the lighted interior, upon finding a seat, crossing my
legs, scrunching down into my warm clothes & looking first at everybody else on the bus and then out the window. Sometimes I can look
from my top-deck seat into the top deck of another bus drawn up along
beside us. This is almost like spying and I turn away if anyone in the
other bus returns the look. Often I forget all about paying until the clip-
pie is standing over me saying, "Any more fares, please."

Walking down Old Church Street from King's Road, I thought of
Peter W. Through what may have been a sincere indifference to me and
my kind, he has made himself an image to be attained at all costs. His
simple act of rejection has turned him into a new person and I now
want to go back and reassess all the things he said and did in the light of
my new opinion of him. Whereas before he seemed an overintense,
little-bit-strange D. H. Lawrence fan with too-curly reddish hair (I
would have said carrotty before!), he is now a thwarted request for an
unsolitary winter, good talk and romance. I have a feeling he is one of
those inscrutable men. And so for the thousandth time, one second-
guesses. At least that first night he made it quite clear what he wanted.

One of the reasons I called him when I returned was that I was
ready for a new section of experience. No nostalgia is felt for Asheville.

I was there and now I'm here. That's all. B. will always be my hero. James will always be a friend. Now I simply want a good winter friend to keep me warm and talk with me about the poets and various assorted ethereal subjects.

The West situation has eased. I wonder what will happen next. I shall pay the rent and wait for the Spanish girl. She will not receive a hearty reception from me. I have gotten on the Black List by (1) this incident, (2) my indiscretion, (3) with James, of all people. I think courtesy is the byword for November. And no confidences.

So much now seems superfluous. I can't even write B. because I feel everything has been said.

I am reading DHL's *The Rainbow*.⁹ Where will I find this secret of writing?

James said the other night, the night I had just returned from New York, "Darling, don't ever cry again like you did that night." I said, "It would be sad if I did, even sadder if I didn't."

OCTOBER 31

MIDNIGHT

Peter W. called. I answered the phone (7:45) and knew it was him because he said, "Just a minute," and I heard newspaper sounds. Dinner with Charles and Jill¹⁰ and Michel. Fun. Light. This winter I am going to have a romance with Peter W. I am in London. He said, "Don't think too much." I said, "I've quit thinking. Nothing's urgent." He laughed. Tomorrow!

---

9. D. H. Lawrence published *The Rainbow*, his fourth novel, in 1915, when he was thirty. Stepping away from his autobiographical third novel, *Sons and Lovers*, to portray a family straddling the years of the Industrial Revolution, he felt he had achieved a literary landmark. Embracing three generations, Lawrence placed Ursula Brangwen, granddaughter of stolid, earthy Tom Brangwen, in a key position, for it is she who provides the link to *Women in Love* and who represents women's struggle for equality in society and within marriage.

10. Charles and Jill were a mismatched couple that Gail knew. Jill had once been considered a child prodigy ballerina, but she lost that promise, gaining weight, and no longer danced. She had been unhappy, Gail knew, and now Jill was facing the rejection of Charles's French family, who opposed Charles's marriage to her despite Jill's efforts to prove her merit. She had moved to Paris to learn French, but to no avail. When Gail went shopping in Paris, already feeling like a "lout-ess," Gail says, in comparison to the couture-sophisticated French women, Jill went with her, making the experience a depressing one, for Jill had no money. Gail took advantage of the revolution in femininity and perfume that had developed in France at this time. Her appreciation of this is revealed in this journal part.

NOVEMBER 1

Damn time anyway. I arrived here about three minutes too late and Peter W. had called and left the message that he couldn't come and would call Monday. Monday is eons away, but he's such a busy man and I have no right to anybody on this earth. I took a giant step for me today.[11] Now apply B.'s maxim: Don't ever second-guess yourself. So I've done it and there must be no what-ifs. I won't be a six minutes' walk from James, but then neither will Mr. West ever get the chance to feel my bottom or Mrs. West say "I think it's just AWFUL, your staying out all night." I will have to cook, but then I've done it before and I can do it again. The indestructible pyramid! I will have to watch my finances but I've already added it up.

£24 weekly salary

£4 for tax

£10 for apartment rent

£3 for food

= £17 for expenses

I will have £7 a week to live it up on. That's $20. I should certainly manage and manage well. What is more, I could get someone else in and charge them £6 and then I will be saving £6 a week myself. I walk to work, so some savings there. I shall sell my foolish gold and diamond watch. It will be nice to be completely independent for a year. And I should get some writing done. It will be lonely as hell at times but I will manage. Who knows after that?

James. My test of maturity soon arrives. The weekend looms. Stella may or may not want to move. That makes no difference either way. I told the landlady November 13. As soon as she confirms it, I shall tell the Wests. I hope there are no cold words. I like them, but I can't tolerate

---

11. Gail is referring to making a down payment on her own apartment, away from the Wests.

this infernal, everlasting gossip. Ah, and Peter W. can come and see me in my new apartment.

It would have been good to see him tonight. It is cold, wet, rainy. It would have been good to talk to him in a calm voice, feel the affection, think of the enjoyments of exploring the mystery.

Another step I thought I might take: inquiring about journalism careers. I would have to pay English taxes. Horrible. But at least to get away from this stultifying job.

He came after all and it's all on a new level. A challenge again. When he talks, I have sometimes to admit I don't understand his words or his word combinations. He hates clever women who edit magazines and teach in universities.

When he comes toward me, I feel repulsed, frightened, and passionate, all at the same time.

He is ridiculous, virile, honest, self-possessed. He was pleased when he saw *The Rainbow*. "You'll learn more about England from that book than from any of these silly persons you meet in London."

Thirty-one, not twenty-seven. Cambridge, lit.; Manchester, logic and degree in philosophy.

One does love the flaws, too. Can it possibly be that one loves MINE?

- "Marshmallow you called it?"

- "I don't want to talk about it." I had been describing what I hated about my writing.

- "I shouldn't stop writing. Writing is a way of existence."

He suggested I try some short stories first.

This is a man to be careful with.

"I might call you next week if you promise not to put perfume on my clothes." (My Givenchy Le De had left its aroma on his tweed jacket.)

I said, "You don't have to come if you don't like. I can live without you."

"How wonderful this is," he said.

"For me or for you?"

"For us both."

NOVEMBER 2

It's all done. Now, as B. says, there must be *no* second-guessing myself. I know I did the right thing and it is amazing what this knowledge does. I went into the kitchen after dinner. Mr. West was doing the dishes. I put my hand on his shoulder (did I have to do that?) and said, "Look. I'm giving two weeks' notice. Is that okay?" He said, almost without batting an eye, "*Uh-huh.* Fine." He was then very anxious to know just when I was leaving. I told him November 13. After that it was only a matter of minutes until I had reached the top of the stairs, Mrs. W. had returned to the kitchen, he mumbled & she said (a bit too loud): "Oh, I'm so glad." How one misjudges one's own popularity at times! I had actually thought they would be a little distressed! Then very shortly afterward they headed out of the house (with Andrew, I think), probably for a pub. I can picture the very zest with which they walked up Old Church Street. They are going to have a pint of bitters. And there is something new to talk about. Something even more exciting than the Cuban situation, because I was a part of their lives and now will no longer be. There will be speculations, the opinions will range. There will be a crescendo of faultfinding until one of them, feeling subhuman, will say: "Oh, wait a minute. That's not really fair." "No, you are right," the others will chime. There will then be qualifications. Soon they'll be digging in again. The funny thing is, I feel nothing at all. Rather I have to fight against the old urge: to please people I don't really like.

NOVEMBER 3

SATURDAY

Guy Fawkes Day. The English Halloween. Worked until 12:30 at the Fishbowl, then came home, ate lunch, & went to the shoe repair shop. When I returned around 3:00, the "European haze" had started to fall. It really *is* smoke-lemon. The weak sun straining through actual chimney smoke, I suppose. Anyway, it gives me a sense of unreality. Not at all unpleasant. The cold is worse, but I really do not mind that either. In fact, I haven't been desperate about anything since I returned.

Re the Wests: This was a good lesson, the complete value of which will be recognized later on. Until one becomes adroit, the best rule is to go entirely by past evidence. I have seen them switch loyalties on and off like light bulbs; I have caught him in fibs; I have felt the insincerity of some of their remarks. They are desperate people living on a now basis. Therefore it is both logical and necessary to them that their friends also be on a now basis. When the friend (?) ceases to fit in with the demands of the NOW, they MUST TURN AWAY IN ORDER TO SURVIVE.

I believe more and more that people do change . . . and on a day-to-day, place-to-place basis. As Proust says, our social images are created entirely by other people's thoughts. I think that our images of ourselves are influenced tremendously by our surroundings at each given time. We are all perfecting our act. We are living in a social world where an act is a survival.[12]

Sunday means sleep late, write Greenwich Village section of "Roxanne," drink effervescent vitamin C. I no longer wish to be where I'm not. I can get my stuff over next Saturday, Sunday. By taxi, return by bus. Two trips will do it.

GREENWICH VILLAGE[13]

On my way back to London, exactly a year later, I stopped overnight in New York. Roxanne & I had been corresponding on the average of once a month &, after several months of tentative meeting plans, we had agreed in our last letters to meet at the information booth in Penn Station at 9:00 p.m. that Friday.

I had not planned on being physically exhausted. After a

12. Five days later, Gail would write her grandmother, Monie, "I am sorry to say that I am not leaving the Wests on friendly terms."

13. Godwin's story "Roxanne" was never published, and no copy of the manuscript survives.

five-hour plane trip on a rough windy day from my mountains
to Newark Airport (it takes only five and three-quarters hours
to get from or to London!), fifteen miles and $9 worth of taxi
into the city (the driver never stopped talking once), and two
aspirins and one Scotch on the rocks at J.'s, I was fit for no
human company. I lay on J.'s sofa in a stupor, talking to my
host in monosyllables, listening to the Brothers Four singing
mountain ballads,[14] and leisurely examining J.'s living
quarters. He had reinforced my belief that New York, unlike
any other capital of the world, while boasting ceaselessly of its
melting-pot status is nothing more than an island of well-
defined groups. Even in Greenwich Village, reputed to be the
home of the different, the unusual, the artist and the outsider,
the inhabitants were living in uniform apartness. J.'s
apartment, for instance: the travel posters on the wall, the
bookshelves filled with paperbacks and Henry Miller ("I had
to go all the way to Mexico to buy those"), the daybed with
multicolored cushions, the old portable typewriter on the desk,
the Paul Klee reproduction, all this I expected before I ever
stepped inside. But that deadly tiring Friday evening, its
familiarity was comforting to me & I lay there against the
colored cushions, sipping my whiskey, thinking of the hundred
other apartments like this one where I had paused for an
afternoon or night. It was raining outside and it was 8:30 & I
wished I hadn't promised to meet Roxanne. I thought of the
many times during the past year when I had genuinely longed
for her company and wondered why so many of life's events
are ill-timed.

She was sitting on a vast marble pillar which marked the
foot of the stairs under the clock at Penn Station. I heard the
bored-assured "Hi-i-i-i" before I saw her. She was prettier

14. The Brothers Four were one of the most popular groups propelling the "folk revival"
movement from 1959 to 1964. The movement involved the "discovery" of traditional
Southern mountain music as well as the development of the college-campus circuit for
musicians.

than I remembered and also, I noted, not as dark as I had *expected.* I was a little disappointed to note that this was the girl I'd been telling people was black. Her skin was far from coffee-colored. It was the same color as light light butterscotch. She was wearing a knitted suit which I remembered from Copenhagen. I went up to her and awkwardly offered my cheek and then stood back and looked busily at everyone milling through the vast hollow terminal and said: "God, I'm exhausted. It's been too much in one day." She seemed a complete stranger, someone utterly different from the girl with whom I'd exchanged long personal letters for almost a year, and I was embarrassed by her actual presence. She wasn't a bit embarrassed.

Looking me over, she said: "You look great. So . . . I don't know . . . European. Did you have that coat made for you in London?"

I said, "No, I bought it."

"Well, it's still nice. Let's go and sit down somewhere."

We walked a complete circle around the station. Nothing was open except a gigantic chilly waiting room with rows of long brown counters. Three or four people sat at stools in front of the first counter. The rest were closed. The waitress, a hag who looked as if her life had been one disappointment after another, handed us two menus.

"I'm starved," Roxanne said. "I think I'll have a sandwich."

"No sandwiches at this hour," the woman snapped.

Roxanne looked displeased. "Oh hell, then coffee. Bring us two coffees."

The woman nodded & went away. Roxanne & I waited. Once or twice we began, "So, here we are . . . after a year" or "Well, what's new," but each time we stopped & looked after the waitress, as if the arrival of our cups of coffee were the only proper beginning of this conversation for which we had both waited so long. I was in a daze. My heart throbbed and although I knew I was not drunk, I felt drunk. I thought of sleep. I wondered how soon I could politely tell Roxanne that I had to go back to the Village and get some sleep. At the same time I was afraid to tell her I had a place to sleep, afraid that she might say "Well, I don't. Look, can I come with you?" She didn't however. She said she was spending the night with an old classmate who worked at the UN. I was vastly relieved.

She had not changed at all. She spoke in the peculiar way she had, always showing her teeth, which were large, square & slightly crooked, but very white. She jangled her bracelets as she talked, occasionally spreading her fingers wide and staring at her slender flexed hands. She varied her conversation between recounting her experiences in Spain & Copenhagen & finally Boston and extracting from me any little secrets which she thought she might find interesting.

"So, how's, uh, B.?" she would say through her white teeth. "Did you ever sleep with him?"

She tucked away my answers and continued her own chronicle. She had sickened, she said, of the Latin men "with their hot gnashing pearly little teeth, their Sacred Heart medals banging against you in bed." There had been one in Sevilla—she had gone there for Holy Week—who had asked her to marry him.

"He took me to church & to meet his mother. D'you know what? She thought I was Mexican! I almost *did* marry him, you know, then he started talking about how he wanted to make children with me. I saw myself shut up all day, every day, in some little hacienda, walking around & around with a big belly. He was terribly possessive. It would never have worked. But, then, sometimes I wish I had. I had a birthday. I'm twenty-nine, y'know." She paused, letting these words sink in (as if she had said, "I have leprosy, you know").

We left each other at exactly ten o'clock because the big counter had a "Closed" sign on it and the waitress glared at us,

the lone survivors. Roxanne fumbled in her pockets. "Gosh, I
don't have any change. Could you?" I paid the check, tipped
the woman 15¢, and went out of the big hall. Penn Station
bustled with late-night travelers & commuters. There was the
color of Broadway playbills & windows full of pipes, perfumes,
magazines & transistor radios. Roxanne left me at my subway
entrance. I gave her the number of J.'s telephone & she
promised to call at ten o'clock the next morning. She wanted
me to read the parts of the novel she had finished &
reworked.

J. was waiting for me at his apartment. He gave me another
Scotch & had one himself. He had been reading & drinking
while I was gone, he said. He was pleasantly alcoholic & we
exchanged whimsical talk, tinged with the late-night flavor of
the unreal. "Seeing you in such a rapid fashion, 'between
continents,' has the necessary otherworldly quality for my
makeup," he said. "I wish we could slice time into something
besides days. But wait. Perhaps we have."

NOVEMBER 4
SUNDAY

The new philosophy, the non-urgency, has helped my writing. I have no
need to say anything now, other than what I have to say. The Wests are
entertaining Lord & Lady Somebody, complete with Nanny and their
children. The Wests are in their act, they are in the image they have of
themselves. The gracious, well-informed American wife in tweeds, the
rather eccentric husband—oh, but he was a colonel and has a DSO. Eugenio was sitting erect in a chair in his cold room, reading history with
earplugs. Stella composes letters in her room or dozes under the eider-
down. Andrew & Michel have gone to the Budapest String Quartet.
Peter,[15] nineteen, has good study habits. He sits at his desk and reads to

---

15. This Peter is not Gail's journalist acquaintance, Peter W., but a young boarder at 21 Old
Church Street. He fell in love with Stella, which caused Peter's parents to make a fuss and
the Wests to turn against Stella.

Beethoven. It has been nice, the Chelsea experience, but I have been far too comfortable here and it is time to go.

Mr. West exaggerating to Stella: "Gail's been with us for TWO YEARS and then bang! Seven days notice. Snap! Just like that."

Tomorrow the Spanish girl encroaches and I will have no place to call my own until next weekend.

This place reeks with intrigue of the most amateurish category. A continual buzzing. Stella has been chosen as go-between. She will probably come with me. Now the Wests are worried. They wish I would leave immediately. It is uncomfortable for them, they say. WHEN, exactly, did I say I was leaving? It can't be quick enough. But I have worked at "the friendship" too long. This time it will not be easy. They read this journal. I think it is comical. I do not put anything past them. Their loyalties have the endurance of an eighteen-year-old boy's orgasm. What a damn pity. Still, I am not going to inconvenience myself. I have absolute assurance in this situation that they have been underhanded about the whole thing. Let them writhe in their uncertain hearts.

Sleep all day, one won't sleep all night. What if Peter W. is married? I certainly shouldn't want him. The group chortles downstairs. There is something subhuman about people grouped before a shadow box capable of eliciting their deepest responses. No use to worry about anything. What good will it do? It's bad for my machine. If James calls this week, I can give him some of my luggage. Will it be cold in the new apartment? Will it be badly furnished? Will it be lonely? Chortle, fools, chortle.

NOVEMBER 5

This is Guy Fawkes Day. The firecrackers have begun. Peter hasn't called. Two clocks are ticking away—8:15 p.m. Work tomorrow and the cold goes on. I am utterly exhausted. Mrs. West asked if I would mind sleeping in Michel's room—he is away—so the French girl could start off in my room. I said yes, I would mind. They know, I think, to leave well enough alone. Where, by the way, is James?

NOVEMBER 6

What a test for the New Attitude. No word from B. No word from James. No word from Peter W. Half-dead with a cold. Have to pick up stakes on Saturday and move. Hate my job.

BUT:

I can still see that I have myself—every bone, brain tissue, and blood cell dedicated to one cause: my preservation.

I have enough faith in B. and James to refrain from misinterpreting their silence.

I do not even KNOW Peter W. All I know is the image I created out of my own fancy.

The cold will go away.

The job, even though frustrating, pays well.

So shut up, shut out the world, and live till 7:00 a.m., November 7, when you have your day mapped out for you.

NOVEMBER 7

It is one of those times when things are happening to everybody. On November 20, Sir Reginald Watson-Jones operates on Stella's leg. She has gone about it quietly, patiently, & efficiently. We talked about the accident, the great unmentioned subject. When Stella said "Did we ever talk about the accident?" it was her way of admitting me past the last barrier. So I have another friend in the world.

And Miss Patricia Jane Farmer is quitting. Ostensibly to marry Pepe. The Faithful One back home. But did I detect resignation rather than the above-it-all rapture expected from a future bride? And if she desperately loved him, would she go skiing in Austria for a month before jetting back to him? It does sound as if her "I do" will be, in effect, "I quit."

Late last night, the shock of transatlantic travel wore off and I knew that Asheville was all over and the fall of '62 is a reality only in a part of my brain cells. It hurt like hell. There is something diabolical about jet travel. Monie sent a note (a flowered card with "I miss you"). How could she know what that pastel sentimentality did to my calm cool sublimity?

"Haven't anything to say that's different or new; just thought I'd like to let you know how much I'm missing you" was the verse. And the whole fabric of that life was there in her note.

I suppose you are back in London though we have not heard. K. mailed your package last week. The pipe is in a little box with your things. It's very nice. I finally nagged (her words) K. into shopping for a real little overcoat for Rebel. She said he looked lovely in Sunday School today. Hope you are feeling fine—we all are—your mother said tell you she would write as soon as the election was over.[16] They are all still running wild. Still some very beautiful trees; across the street from me are two very large ones. One a lovely rose and the other gold. We saw B. a few days ago. K. talked to him. I was coming from the library with books so only said good morning—he gave me a big smile—said he had not heard from you. Though I suppose it was too soon as it was about Tuesday. Please let us hear.

On the back of the card, just to get it all squeezed out, it says "American Greetings."

How can they be there and I be here? And then one of them writes a few words & sticks a 15¢ stamp with the Statue of Liberty on the front and ploomp! I am all choked up.

But this is the right way for me. I'm certain of it. It's better to hurt & appreciate than to stultify and not feel.

But not to feel so much. I haven't written B. and I won't until I get control.

Next week I will be tucked away on Green Street. It will be warm,

---

16. The Republican Party began making steady gains in the South in 1962, turning away from race and developing such key issues as budgetary conservatism and decentralized government. Lawrence Brown, Buncombe County sheriff and, to some, a feared political boss, was defeated in that year, and Kathleen started the Republican Women of Asheville. She became enamored of Senator Barry Goldwater of Arizona, the Republican candidate for president in 1964.

at least, and I will then write, since there will be no other choice, no people at all.

James leaves for Spain Friday unless his plans have changed. I probably won't see him until he gets back. Wonder if he'll come around to 21 Old Church Street and Mr. West will meet him stony-faced at the door with the little bit of news? But no, James will write from his little jaunt down the Costa del Sol. He has to share his discoveries, if nothing else.

Brahms's Violin Sonata no. 3[17]—

If Peter W. has slipped out of my orbit, well, he never was really IN, was he?

NOVEMBER 8

James took me to dinner tonight. He leaves for Spain tomorrow. The thing that disturbs me is that there is absolutely no passion between us.

I must admit my calm is shattered.

The fact is, I feel real affection for him, and there are the shared experiences of the wet gray unreal summer. It won't be like that again. I needed him this summer and he was there. I don't need him now. Oh, but he is nice. There is only one Gemini.[18]

What the hell am I going to do? I think it may be a mistake to let men know I can take care of myself.

NOVEMBER 9

On the credit side of the ledger, tomorrow is Saturday and no problems. I have only to pack and wash out some underclothes, wash my hair. On the debit side: B. hasn't written and I don't think Peter W. ever planned to make another entrance. Thus I have the few hours of gray daylight, the frightening prospect of survival and all alone.

·   ·   ·

17. Brahms's Sonata no. 3 in D minor for Violin and Piano is a masterpiece of sustained passion within the normally conservative chamber music form.

18. James was the only man with a Gemini astrological sign with whom she had formed a close relationship.

The woman who came into the office today made a deep impression on me. If *Dr. No*[19] hadn't purged me of all energy, I would write it out. However, there is the long, long weekend. Damn Peter W.

This retreat for the winter is just about the best thing that could happen. I actually want to write stories and to live in them. How nice to know! I'll be supporting myself & writing & living. That is a lot to ask. That is better than being married.

NOVEMBER 10

SATURDAY

Rain of the kind that doesn't drip. It scrapes against your face. Outside is pneumonia weather. Each day I like other people less and less, God forgive me, but I sat downstairs in the living room making every effort to be sociable & the sound of Stella's lilting voice going on and on about popcorn, punctuated by Mrs. West's "Oh, we *will*, we *will*," sent me rushing back to my retreat.

Tomorrow morning, I get up, dress, collect my little odds & ends, & take off in a taxi. It is stifling in here. Absolutely. The new flat is big, spacious, clean, warm & convenient. I do not like the chintz curtains or bedspread, but that can certainly be changed. I shall ask for Tuesday afternoon off & go to get some material at Pontings & have them put hanging tapes on them; then paint the desk, get a mirror from my antique-dealer friend, & I'll be comfortable for the winter. There is no time here for self-pity. I am a big girl now and have learned that (1) one can't have everything perfect in one day, (2) nobody can be relied on 100 percent to do anything right. This afternoon I took a walk up one side of King's Road & down the other, looking in antique shops, watching a small "area parade" (it's Memorial Day): Englishmen in overcoats with their war ribbons pinned on the lapels marching briskly, terribly soberly down the King's Road. Winter is really here. Stella & I are at lance points. I came in from lunch saying that such-and-such was not in

19. *Dr. No*, the first James Bond movie, was a huge hit in England.

good taste and then Peter chimes in with his nineteen-year-old know-it-all "Good taste is relative." And then Stella sings, "I'm inclined to agree with Peter." She's always inclined to agree with anyone, except me. So, I must now concentrate on doing things as well as possible, as cheaply as possible, making a completely independent life for myself. I cannot count on anyone: not B. to rescue me, nor James to come regularly to the flat, nor any novel I write to sell. Not yet. I somehow think this winter would be made increasingly brighter with the return of Peter W. However, I can't guarantee that. And when he calls here again I will be gone. Oh, well. I'm alive & don't owe any money—except to the government.

How does living reality become journal reality, and then, years later, story reality? Nowhere in her 1962 journals does Gail Godwin indicate that she will be writing a story that will have as its core the Wests' behavior and place in history, yet years later they will form the basis of the title novella in her collection Mr. Bedford and the Muses.

Carrie Ames, the narrator of the novella "Mr. Bedford," reflects, "I am still far from 'figuring out' the Eastons [the Wests' counterparts], which is why, I suppose, they have remained so tantalizing to my imagination." For Gail, the figuring out took shape through the medium of her journals.

About ten years after her U.S. Travel Service years, a dream caused Gail to consult her youthful record and transform it. "I wanted to live in that English time again—but with the perspective that time and distance and imagination can bestow," she reflected in the "Author's Note" at the end of Mr. Bedford and the Muses. *"There were memory gaps, but I would fill them in with fiction, which, as every writer knows, is often the best way to get at the important truths that lie beneath 'what really happened.'"*

A comparison of Gail's journals and her story shows how particularly she selected details to maintain the right tone in "Mr. Bedford." She doesn't mirror journal entries until page 25, when Carrie starts her job at the Travel Service, and page 28, when Carrie gets a glimpse of the Eastons' ready-to-travel bedroom setup, a sight "both touching and sinister."

Preceding these references, Godwin places two curious stories: a look into the distant future, when Carrie sees Nigel, a hapless fellow boarder, acting in a soap opera; and the retelling of Mr. Easton's story about a woman whose dress lifted while she was playing the piano to reveal a tail whipping around. The first story is so incidental, its inclusion can only be for effect, to blur reality and fantasy. The second story plays a different role. The Wests were living in a delusion outside of their present time.

NOVEMBER 14

London is the best purgatory I know of. My first morning on Green Street, I emerged to find the blue sky back again & all Grosvenor Square shimmered with golden smoke & morning promise. It was invigorating.

The Wests almost pulled me under. I felt for a while there that I was a completely undesirable person.

Peter W. is silence itself. I wonder if I shall ever see him again. Well, at least he got me into DHL and that is a real find. Of course, there could be all sorts of excuses: (1) parents in town, (2) hard work, (3) giving me a hard time, (4) disinterest. However, there is absolutely nothing I can do to make him do anything he doesn't want to. Therefore there is really no point in thinking further about it. Either he has reasons and will call when he is free, or he does not wish to see me again. What "either/or" could be simpler?

NOVEMBER 15

It is such an ordeal just taking care of what are commonly called "incidentals." One has to learn that a can of soup is too much for one person. And Jaffa-sweetened orange juice is *foul.* And there must be a lamp. I saw a very nice floor lamp for 67s. 9d. and a shade for 35s. Then to buy bulbs (150-watt small for overhead); then Indian madras and white rickrack and I shall make something interesting—6s. a yard, four yards, and voila! Also the paint. Then everything will be fine. One has to make things habitable. Tomorrow: paint, £1; madras, £1; rickrack, 10s.

I've lost all drive to write. Just round and round, dear diary, like a stargazing teenager with tunnel vision. I can't remember when I have wanted to have my own man so much. B. asks Mother if she's heard from me. She says he's puzzled because he hasn't heard. But she may be exaggerating. I can't believe Peter W. didn't accept the challenge. This is just a time of waiting. God, November is a bitter month.

NOVEMBER 17

Bought a lamp and am not sorry, walked across Grosvenor Square and had tea in the Italian restaurant where I cussed the girl out once last summer. Back across the square. Nobody but the lone bobbies patrolling the Embassy.

Edwards[20] is sanding the floors. I keep making conversation because it is the easiest way out. He tells a good story. Sarah Churchill never paid him £40 for redecorating her flat; a rich antique-collector, horse-breeder homosexual lies on my left, a Chihuahua-owning one on my right. Landlords rent flats in London with the provisions (1) you completely redecorate them (2) you agree to leave on a week's notice. They get the suckers to decorate the flats & then give them notice. It seems smart not to pay bills here & to get away with cheating the other guy. I'm not having any. Thank God the Southrons[21] are human beings as well as landlords.

NOVEMBER 18

Sunday—it gets easier and pleasanter to be alone. Edwards did the floors. The place looks decent, but I mustn't go overboard. If I got it finished perfectly, then it would trap me. If B. has meant it all this time, then I won't be in England after April or May. I was sitting at my desk this afternoon and it came in a flash of intuition that he has known all this time.[22] Little snatches of memory fell into place (or did I FORCE them into an ill-fitting symmetry?). The phone call that morning when I was working in Blowing Rock: "I looked in the Sunday paper and saw a picture that looked like you and thought you were getting married again. You're not

20. Edwards was the handyman for 5 Green Street, Mayfair.
21. The Southrons were Gail's landlords at 5 Green Street.
22. Gail believes that B. has known for a long while that he's wanted Gail for a permanent relationship.

getting married again, are you?" And: "There's nothing negative about this relationship." Only I know I made a huge mistake spending my one free weekend in Asheville with L. That is the last time I will ever allow pity to overrule good judgment. B: "Don't ever think *I* don't have feelings. Just because they don't show doesn't mean they're not there." And: "We'll have a den and a study and you can come home and write."

But: can B. make my life in Asheville? For I would NOT be a Junior Leaguer, country clubber, etc. I would have only the relationship with B. and my own amusements.

He once said, "I'd give up my freedom if I were in danger of losing you."

Soon it will be time to write. There is absolutely no excuse not to now. I love the subways underneath my floor. It's the Oxford Circus, Bond Street, Marble Arch run—the Central Line. Thursday, Thanksgiving. I shall (1) paint this desk, do other things to be done, (2) buy scatter cushions, (3) get gold, purple madras & white braid for sofa cover, (4) buy an adapter, (5) buy a low table for other room—very cheap—get a BASKET.

I am going to stop worrying about money. The only thing I owe to anyone is $200 to the U.S. government.

NOVEMBER 20

TUESDAY

Each morning I start off so full of zest and beginnings. Walked through Rupert Street at noon, wide-eyed at the vendors' stalls, thinking, What marvelous eating if one had the desire. I hope I can cook for James this winter. He will be a good weekend companion if nothing else. As of tonight, Peter W. goes off the list. It was a bad gamble, there is nothing I can do about it—and keep my dignity—so better forget. Came dangerously near exploding in Doreen's presence over a silly remark I was supposed to have said to a customer. For survival in that job, I must put down these remembrance points: (1) it's a cushy job, (2) without which I would not have a penny in the world, (3) I must do my best at it—at least appear to, (4) I must be pleasant, but quit talking to everybody. Too much boredom leads to exchanging confidences. Better not to. This I must do, or all else fails.

Finished *Women in Love*. If nothing else, PW gave me that. It was my need to read something he had read, to connect myself with him through a common object. Big Ben is chiming over my transistor,[23] the train is running underneath. China is pushing into India.[24] I feel smothered by space in this flat. I think now I shall shut off the other room. I am in a state of dangerous calm about B.'s reaction to my letter, which he should receive tomorrow or Friday, since Thanksgiving is a holiday. Will he save me? If he doesn't, there must be a *complete* break—I hate to think of the life without him always there in writing distance. But if I feel this way & he has any real relation to me, he will want to do it too. AM I RUNNING AWAY AGAIN? Was the English winter a factor? Peter W.'s flagrant evil rejection after his commitment? Pat Farmer's influence?[25] The desire to "nest" whetted by the furnishing of this flat? Now is the time to be brutally honest. And what of the writing? That gnaws. What is the answer? I think, first, to get past caring about people's reaction to my writing, but to satisfy myself . . .

NOVEMBER 21

WEDNESDAY

Tomorrow is a holiday. Painted a desk (so-so). When will I learn? You can't break the rules until you're a pro.[26] Mr. Smith, the servants' chef at Buckingham Palace, re the efficiency survey: Some bloke was taking Queen Victoria her bottle of Scotch until twenty-five years after she was dead.

23. Gail is referring to her transistor radio.

24. On October 20, 1962, China attacked India along the Himalayan border following the failure of efforts to negotiate disputed territory.

25. Pat Farmer was one of the three original guides at the U.S. Travel Service office along with Gail and Betty Hughes. Pat left to marry her Mexican boyfriend, Betty married Howard Melton, and Gail stayed the longest.

26. Gail skipped the primer coat.

Reading Lawrence's biography by Harry Moore.[27] That remark PW made on the last night. "Do you think it helps to live in one place all your life and write about that place?" I think, instead of being a detriment, it is very definitely an asset. Your vision becomes sharper because the distractions are fewer—or is that true?

I sat in that office again, it began to grow dark, the ceiling lights got redder and redder in the bank across the street. I wondered what in hell Peter W. was up to, until I finally decided that any rebuff, any ridicule, any loss of dignity would be better than this maddening ignorance. So I wrote him a note, typewritten, unsigned, which said: "Not that I don't mind the other implications, but to start someone on DHL and then disappear at question time is inexcusable. Or was the Givenchy too rich for your blood?" That last to injure his male pride. Mysteries madden me. He is probably a sickening little overeducated boy. I didn't like his narrow ankles or the green socks or the same suit every time I saw him. I thought he was much too serious about everything. I didn't really like his looks. What I do like is the fact that I can't look him in the eye for very long without gravitating toward him *in spite of a definite revulsion*. At least, action, for me, is better than suspense. If I don't hear from him NOW, I'll know he found me loathsome or "clever" ("I hate clever women"). But I've got to get him down to human proportions.

After my "renovations" tomorrow, I am doing nothing but (1) writing, (2) eating, (3) sleeping, (4) saving money.

This is a dark period. If I can't concentrate on any one thing, I will have to write snatches—to practice. I must learn to get *real* people (who are always unbelievable) down on paper.

NOVEMBER 23

FRIDAY

Thanksgiving was pleasant—pale sun and not too cold. Spent money, made curtains, & saw Samuel Beckett's *Happy Days*,[28] which I didn't

27. Harry T. Moore's biography, *The Intelligent Heart: The Story of D. H. Lawrence*, originally published in 1954. Moore was also a scholar of Lawrence Durrell and Henry James.

28. *Happy Days*, Samuel Beckett's 1961 play, presents a woman, Winnie, buried in sand amid a scorched, postnuclear environment. The play's circular dramatic monologue, creating suspense without a plotline, corresponds to musical form.

understand completely. But he stripped a subject down to its rare nakedness. Sometimes I think ambiguity is a virtue. People insist upon reading their own meaning into things anyway.

This journal has no earthly use or interest to anyone but Number One. I remember looking through James's night book, where he had recorded ideas and epigrams at random. Most of them just missed the boat. I could understand how he'd felt so clever at the time of coining them.

Walking home tonight I asked myself, Could it possibly get any worse? I think one must find out his capacity for solitude. I am always adamant about being alone when I know I am in a house with other people. And it's another thing to be alone in a town where you have friends, commitments, where you only have to pick up a telephone. But I'd like to see old recluse B. living alone in London with no Asheville Country Club set, no small coterie of social elite to tide him over. Music, he says, and golf, and good hard work are the panaceas. One or all of them is/are effective. What are some more? Good creative activity. Try to forge something shapely and valuable from this experience. Wondering (on this same walk home, instead of shrinking from the rain, I finally stuck my face into it and let it come at me) what attitude one could take regarding these purgatory periods. I decided that this, more than anything, shows one's progress along the road. One must first stop dividing time into units, whether one is having a "good period" or a "bad period." It does not help to say "This has gone on for three weeks, will it last another?" or "In two weeks, I'll be doing such & such" or "This time two weeks ago, I was doing such & such . . ."

Then one must gather around oneself all available resources: namely whatever work is at hand, however menial, whatever experiences are open to one, however limited. Then one must function & partake, function & partake, without hoping for more, without regretting the times there had been more, simply keeping the machine in running condition, leaving oneself spread out not expectantly but availably for any unforeseen "extra" which might come along, thus breaking the chain of bad luck—for the time being.

I know how I must write now—it only remains to start somewhere and keep at it until I regain the lost confidence.

Peter W. was a good lesson. Something to remember: When you detect the spark, don't treat it carelessly. If I had been more human at that time (October 10–11), I might have kept a valuable friend and who knows what else? But the habit of James was too strong. And yet I can't think PW will never make a reappearance—could I be that boring?

NOVEMBER 25
SUNDAY

Do I have the courage to write? I do everything to put it off. I am afraid to get close to it—afraid of what I might say. This weekend: Preparing for a two-day abyss of loneliness, I stocked up on wine, groceries, made lists of chores to be done. I walked miles, went to the Tate, roamed through the huddles of lost causes in Hyde Park.[29] But I never got free; I was always thinking: I am doing something; look, I am spending my day; I am gathering impressions; I am not wasting my time.

At the Tate, he had something but I was not sure what.[30] A kind of elemental form, color stacked against color. But how sick I am of these thin-lipped esthetes with their ragged hair who glibly shoot out statements like "Those colors, rather Braque-ish, don't you think." These people used to frighten me in America. Now that I see them pouring out from the source, I would not bother to answer them—unless, perhaps, just to say cooly, abstractedly: "I don't like to talk about art." In Hyde Park there were various outcasts on platforms & stepladders; as soon as one mounted, a curious crowd gathered. Refreshments were being sold, & I think most people simply come to snicker.

This week will be rugged, wet & physically demoralizing—calling on agents.[31] I saw D.'s little list for Monday's meeting—she is going to give each of us a little project. The humiliation of having someone I consider an inferior in every way bossing me. Last night I dreamed consecutive

29. Gail is referring to people preaching from soapboxes, and their listeners.

30. The artist in question was Jean Arp (1887–1966), of whose works there had been a special exhibit. He was cofounder of Dada and later a Surrealist.

31. Gail had to pack a suitcase with brochures and go door to door like a salesman. Women generally didn't go door to door except to sell cosmetics. Gail presented herself at travel agencies wearing a tweed suit, scarf, high heels, stockings, and black kid gloves.

terrors—Beverly Paulson reappeared (she is like D.) to tell me not to use the good pillowcases. I said, "Oh, I won't," knowing I had one on the bed at that moment. "But you have one on the bed now," she said chidingly, triumphantly. Then I dreamed I had TB and had to be sent away for a year—then Franchelle lied & said we had a school holiday & I got terribly behind in my work.

Oh, I crave the plan for a book in which I can exorcise all these people. The trouble with anything faintly autobiographical is that it is so unreal. I have moved in so many groups of people, gone to so many places, that it is impossible to regionalize. Even in the relationship (basic) between boy & girl, I find I start leaving things out because they are preposterous & do not pertain to my story and then the whole story ravels away to nothing.

Even during my "active" weekend, I searched for my mad rusty-haired little journalist. I have spent so much time building my image of him, he could not possibly live up to it. He is another Rupert Birkin (who was Lawrence's idealized version of himself!). He is the strange, silent boy in the raincoat walking down Fleet Street with some highly unreadable paperback under his arm; he has a sullen, bright Swedish mistress waiting for him in his flat, where she whiles away his absences by making copper enamel ashtrays. He never utters a foolish statement. He has a partly finished manuscript on his desk and at this he works lovingly, sparingly, in the nighttime to a background of Mahler, Berlioz, Stravinsky, Bartók, and perhaps Beethoven when he needs soothing. I have thought of every reason why nothing came after that night. I suppose the most logical but hardest to face is that he saw nothing else he wanted. "You're uncertain of yourself, aren't you?" he forced me to admit.

"And you?" I asked.

"No," he said.

"Are you saying that because you mean it or because you know I would hate you if you said anything else?"

He thought a minute and said: "Because I mean it."

A woman sat down at my table in the Tate restaurant and smiled at me, helping herself to a sugar cube. I got up and left. It is not the companionship of a woman, nor of smart, attractive people. I want one man who is a mystery to me, who will worship me and give some direction to my life. But, what is there to worship? I suppose James is back now. He may call this week and we will have dinner and talk the old merry-go-round things into the ground. Then I won't see him for two more weeks. B.'s positiveness cancels James out. What did I love about him? Or was it just the shock of my first educated Englishman with his feminine-tinged thought processes? I think we loved each other because it vaunted our own egos—yet it was never as good even toward the end of the summer. I don't want to talk about his things anymore. I want something bigger. Something that will trail off in wonder and detour to sex.

What really fabulous men have I known in the last five years? How many times have I been submerged?

S. Burman and Bill Hamilton—Chapel Hill

Paul Trinchieri—Miami

AF—Pompano

B.—Asheville

Niels—Copenhagen

Antonio—Las Palmas

James—London

Will there be a next, or will it stop with B.? Are there to be no affairs?

When there is no one to talk to and nothing to expect, one must either bury oneself in a creative fury, have a good book, do something.

A passage from *Aïda*—B. sitting through the performance in the Blowing Rock Theater—those long dusky summer evenings, B. putt-putting around the curve in the old Ford convertible, slouching over the banister, unseen by me in my waitress uniform, talking tripe with the other girls. Blowing Rock was a specially good segment. The air was so fresh, it took your breath away, the work was purely physical & exhausting. The nights driving by myself in the Falcon, listening that time to Rachmaninoff's Third, knowing that the power was turned on, that I was about to have great adventures. And they have been good, at that. The freighter to Oslo & Copenhagen. The motor trip to Berlin. The bus trip from Copenhagen down through Germany, Colmar, Nîmes ("God, you go to the most unheard-of places") & on over the Pyrenees to Barcelona—Berlioz's *Fantastique*, second movement. The brief hell in Málaga. The cold interiors of churches—then on to Las Palmas—the balmy night air as the taxi rattled around the curves, the taste of almond & apricot pastries, the appalling white of my legs as I took off my stockings that first night. Antonio & I made the bed together because it was late. "I can only let you have this room until tomorrow," he said. His teeth were broken & uneven. But his eyes had that hot brown fire of a real tropical giant. "Don't worry, I won't put you out on the street," he added. It was healing, unlike any other place I had been & he took good care of me. Bananas, sandy beaches; the other language; & then on to London, which I cursed and anticipated. And B., sitting across from me in the Dogwood Room at Grove Park Inn. Jotted down the entire year on a napkin. At first I saw a little story in everything. It was all new & fascinating because I could still view it from the other side, my former longing-for-adventure side. Then, one day, my way of living became the most natural thing. The boy in J.'s Greenwich Village apartment who said "God, aren't you excited? You're leaving for *London* in forty-five *minutes*!" seemed so overdramatic. But, fortunately or unfortunately, I had to come back to London in order to realize I was finished with it. I had to taste the sleepless fatigue after jetting into the sunrise and waiting for James at the airport for an hour. I had to return & distribute all my presents and be welcomed back to the expatriate fold. I had to see the English winter for myself. I had to have this experience of living in a foreign country by myself with no human companionship to lean on; and be forced by the sheer absence of anything else to face my own predicament. I honestly saw, sitting in the kitchen in Happy Valley, savoring every minute of that too-short vacation, that I must come back to England & finish here, finish what—I don't know.

At times I seem to myself so incredibly narrow, so immature, so full of childish visions had at one time or another by every gray-faced intellectual under forty. I wonder, to what extent do I really care about pleasing other people? The writing, for instance. Do I want to write & try to publish "almosts" or to keep hitting for that real transfusion from life to paper? . . . Yet something still hankers to be said. I don't know the answers to anything—& I don't know where emotion stops being emotion & becomes emotionalism. I do know certain things have the power to elicit passion in me over & over again. There was something in that Copenhagen winter that I want to go back to. And there was something sinister & horrible, a reckoning, in that Málaga hotel room, and again there is the haunting balmy sensuality of Las Palmas, except at the end when I reduced it to a waiting period—the awful fight in the hotel room in Tenerife, the closed in feeling, then waking up the next morning and seeing the great white Teide[32] outside the window & realizing it was there the night before & *knowing* that it would have made a difference had I known. And then the smoky Sundays, listening to the BBC, reading novels by the fire, being puzzled by England & the Englishman. James made a period all by himself—the strange half-relationship matched the strange half-summer—wet, green, dreamy—never really warm, never really bright. The half-people at the lake. Old Church Street, the Thames. The many times I told James "I adore you" because I thought he needed to be adored. But it was good to dream together, to write in comfort, to rebel in safety.

NOVEMBER 26

As long as there is this outlet, I can survive. There are worse things than being in a room by oneself. These journals, while seemingly overpersonal & dead-end, are a panacea—and may, someday, serve as references when I find a route.

---

32. Seeing "the great white Teide," the Canary Islands' snow-topped volcanic mountain, Pico de Teide, made the fight Gail had with Antonio seem trivial in comparison.

Today, there occurred a situation so typically feminine that I must record it in its entirety. It involves the four of us at work.

Doreen came down at 9:30 carrying her usual scatter-mass of notes, spiral tablet, brochures & timetables & called her meeting to order. The meeting consisted of herself, Pat & me, since BH was late. She came straight to the point. She said, "G. & I had a little talk Friday & I've been thinking about it ever since. I know no one likes little 'Joe' jobs but, quite honestly, that's all there's been to give anybody." She then gave me charge of the files, adding sweetly, "It's a big job & you'll get credit for it." Then she said we weren't going to replace Pat when she left. "Also, Gail said you'd all discussed it among yourselves how irresponsible I am, and I'd like for you to tell me how I am irresponsible." This was really a nasty jolt for so early in the morning. As Pat said later, "Here I was, on a Monday morning, feeling wonderfully businesslike, untouched & impersonal, and crash! Down comes this large dose of female pettiness. I thought for a minute I was back at the sorority house. Only there, I could refuse to attend meetings." But we bore up pretty well & didn't retreat very much, but told her in hot ill-devised little stammers what she'd asked for: why we thought she was irresponsible. Then Betty Hughes came in, looking pink, flustered & not too very sorry about being late. She had obviously had a very satisfying tumble in the sack with her strong-chinned Mississippi husband. It took her, under these circumstances, several minutes to recover from Doreen's very personal inquest. She stood her ground better than any of us, having spent the entire weekend (except for *those* moments) discussing it with Howard. She listed, one, two, three—it was quite refreshing. P. & I have a tendency to stammer. Fortunately, this uncomfortable little discussion was interrupted by a summons from Miller for Doreen to attend a meeting upstairs.

The three of us were left to rip her to shreds & to think of things we should have said. I had a cold, dangerous feeling of enjoying it tremendously. We would go the limit, then one of us, feeling we'd reached the absolute bounds of good taste, would veer the subject off office politics. After coating ourselves afresh with respectability, someone would launch a fresh attack: "And another thing about Doreen."

I was very shaken because of dear old security (again!). P. is leaving

December 29; BH, the last of January—one month from now & two months from now. "You must get out, too" they urged. "It's the only thing."

"That's easy for you to say, but I haven't got things so well worked out."

"Oh, but you can get another job! Go to Fleet Street, Paris, Geneva."

"Sure, sure."

Then in a rash of second-guessing, I thought: Perhaps I should go upstairs & settle this with her, smooth things over. Make the path easier for myself. But luckily I didn't. "You're like me," P. said as we sat camaraderie-style on our coffee-bar stools. "You blow up at her and make all these vows to be absolutely businesslike, cold & unresponsive. Then she comes back to you, placid & sunny, almost humble, for God's sake, asking you the name of your dressmaker or did you have fun with your boyfriend last night. You are flattered and almost sorry for her. After all, she is doing the coming back. But you see she wins hands down this way. It's just her method of keeping the boiling point down for awhile. *She* is the one who is regulating the steam then, don't you see? Also, she picks questions that vaunt your own idealized image of yourself. You find yourself warming as you advise her on seamstresses and dentists, or telling about that nice little supper club you discovered over the weekend. So, careful! I would say, if you're going to stay on here for any length of time, to decide on one relationship or another. Either have it all business, cut her short on the personal drivel, or be her friend and temper your job with good-natured give & take. Frankly, I can't see you doing the latter."

As soon as I got out on the job, down in the city of London, with real businessmen to see, a heavy case to carry, a map to follow, my head cleared sufficiently for me to see how absolutely "poor show" this had been, how degrading for the four of us. Here I was walking down streets hundreds of years old, visiting houses of business older than my own country. I thought back over four girls, three younger, bitchy-brilliant ones & a more settled safe thirty-fiver . . . I thought of the "she saids" and it all sounded pretty ladies' washroom–ish.

I can already recognize those farther along the way. For instance, the director at Holder Bros.—a Mr. Peter Warner. Of course, to start with, he was a good-looking, well-built Nordic type. But almost immediately our talk was on a larger scale. We eventually discussed what can USTS do for Holder Bros., and vice versa, but first was the effects of living in a land that is not your home. The intangibles missed, etc. I know I would like to talk to that man again. I would like to be the kind of woman *he* would like to talk to again.

What can be done now—

The facts: I am in London for at least six months more. I need the job. I have no outside resources in the world—financial or emotional. There are no more insurance policies, money from cars, care packages from rich relatives. James does not fit the big picture any longer.

What can be done: Keep the ship trim. Devote more time to your physical appearance. You have gotten sloppy! Buy some darker hose. Keep your hair in shape. Polish your shoes. Do a complete job with the agents. Try to get BH to let you do her agent visits, too.

Practice your act on every travel agent just to polish it.

Keep occupied upstairs: concerts, plays, keep active—try to begin writing something substantial, even if it is a small sketch, a perfect tile in a large mosaic.

Practice seeming self-contained: soon the *VIDERE* will become the *ESSE*, which is the N.C. motto, so that's all right, too.[33]

Rest of the week:

Get up at 7:30—eat breakfast at Embassy—buy *Guardian*—be at work at 9:00, in W.C.[34] by 10:00. See as many people as possible—keep your eyes open. Come back—write report & go home as if you're getting ready to go to a fancy dress ball with . . . No, I don't like fancy dress balls.

---

33. *Esse quam videre,* "to be rather than to seem," is the state motto of North Carolina.

34. W.C., or Westminster City, where Gail was distributing travel information, is the borough in London that contains Great Britain's government offices, its major shopping district, the clothing industry, Westminster Abbey, the major art galleries, and Paddington Station.

NOVEMBER 28

Finished the city (except for one on Milk Street), had lunch on Fleet Street. Dinner in a dark, friendly little place in Soho called Act One, Scene One, & then—expecting nothing—to see *How the West Was Won*,[35] which was really spectacular & filled me with pride (having come from such a place—or can I take credit, coming from the East Coast?— yes, because some ancestor went west even if it was from Switzerland or Denmark or England). I walked home bursting at the seams.

Coming across Mayfair, I felt London. Cities are so beautiful when the people have gone. Only the lights, the magnificent silks, wines, galleries, furs to tease the eye, hints of rain in a subtle, almost balmy air, the taxis, all lit up with "For Hire"—those pompous black sentinels cruising reassuringly through the night. A look through a thin curtain into a ground floor on Berkeley Square revealed a sumptuous bar with red carpets & waiter complete with tails.

Thinking back to Miami nightclubs & bars with Marty—padding across thick carpets to twining mahogany bars, sipping our Kiss of Deaths,[36] talking big talk in whispers.

Before one can rest, one *must have both.*[37] At least I have kept moving.

NOVEMBER 29

The Great Enlightenment looms no nearer. All I can do is keep my eyes open, never miss an opportunity to see anything offered—no matter how small, irrelevant, uncomfortable. Eugenio dined me at the Shepherd in Shepherd Market (now shadowed by the London Hilton). There was a King Charles spaniel in the pub, in spite of the "No Dogs Allowed" sign. [Eugenio] explained about the special rule made in 1640

35. *How the West Was Won* represented the apotheosis of certain cultural trends in America. It was filmed in Cinerama format, in which three projectors were used to show what had been recorded on three cameras at once. Based on a seven-article series published in *Life* magazine, the movie attempted to tell the American story through the story of the West, and it did so with a confidence in Manifest Destiny that would not survive the American public's disillusionment with the Vietnam War.

36. A Kiss of Death is a drink that mixes Scotch with tequila and dark rum.

37. Having both is enjoying the experience of being outside looking in and being inside having the direct experiences.

exempting the King's dogs from normal laws—nobody has bothered to repeal it. That was worth the whole lunch—not that it wasn't superb. At nineteen, this boy knows how to stage an occasion from start to finish.

The mornings are so alike. A small hope comes alive through the early hours, diminishes toward late afternoon. Each day is very much like the one before. What right have I, has anybody, to demand this be different? I get all tensed by my work, a dismal challenge, riding along in the taxi, to my first call of the morning. I daydream when I am walking. Rebuffs no longer touch me. I know that every odd one will be curt, maybe one a day will pierce the barrier and make up for all the rest.

NOVEMBER 30

Tomorrow will be 1 December—so let's hope only November was the jinxed month. I have started a new story. At least there is a framework. Las Palmas. Antonio. I am having to start from scratch, building my case. Once it is down, it will be easy to rewrite. I decided how I did not want to write after finishing K. A. Porter's *Ship of Fools*.[38] You can't write like that anymore. I want to break through. If I can't, then nothing is worth it. The headaches will probably be gone tomorrow & then I can proceed.

Antonio—he offered a solution—this is the whole point. He offered a solution, but it would have had to be followed 100 percent. I want to describe the earthy, sexy, basic feeling of those days. The new husband & wife (she already pregnant) standing outside on the mall (Paseo de Canteras) in the late afternoon.[39] Damn it, I am lazy.

DECEMBER 5

It took three quarters of an hour to scrub away the vast deposits the city of London left upon my person. And Americans wear *white* raincoats called London Fogs. Thirty-two people have died since it [the fog] fell upon the city yesterday. Probably they died from some other cause alto-

---

38. Gail's objection to Katherine Anne Porter's *Ship of Fools* was its subjugation of characterization to ideas.

39. On the main drag in Las Palmas in the Canary Islands, married couples would promenade, and Gail had noticed that the women were often pregnant.

gether or were going to die anyway. But they were just what the head-line writer at the *Daily Express* needed. People hulk about, scrunched deep into their coats, swathed in protective scarves & clutching their chests like advanced tuberculars. Bob Briggs took me to lunch at The Thistle & Pat & I went idol smashing after the office closed down at four. Funny how our ideas of people swing pendulum-like from one extreme to the other. We saw *The Manchurian Candidate*[40] & then dined in a Chinese restaurant, where we were positive the waiters were leering at us. Of course, the topics of discussion were the favorite ones. We turn the same people over & over in our minds, examining. Now BB is no longer the pleasant fool with good Washington connections. BB is a man who laughs at it all because he is untouched by it. BB is "the only genuine man in the organization—and his wife's nice, too." Then the big idol fell SMASH! Tonight. Pat said, "I think Mr. Miller is nervous sometimes," and crash, my own subterranean hunches blossomed. And poor Doreen. We have reduced her to a pulp because now, in our conversations, it is always "poor Doreen." Pat told of her half-tipsy attempt to hold on to the youngest member of the chamber of commerce at the cocktail party. "She tried one of your favorite tricks, being kittenish, only with her, it didn't work." So on it went. Turning them upside down, right side up, examining them as dispassionately as naked dolls. What a pity things always come into the open too late. Pat would have been a compatible roommate, namely because she would have kept to herself. Or would I have liked her then? I remember how, at first, we made a big thing about hating each other. "I'll certainly always tell you what I think of you," each was fond of saying to the other.

The only hope for sanity with Miss Shining Light[41] is to keep my distance. No use to confide in this meat-and-potatoes homebody. Rebels know their own kind. They can play dangerously, say insulting things,

---

40. *The Manchurian Candidate*, John Frankenheimer's film based on the 1959 Richard Condon novel, uses flashbacks to portray the discovery by a soldier (played by Frank Sinatra) that his fellow POW (Laurence Harvey) has been brainwashed to kill. The revelation about how governments work was deemed controversial enough to have the American government stop its production. President Kennedy gave the go-ahead to the film. Then, after Kennedy's assassination a year later, the film was taken out of distribution.

41. "Miss Shining Light" is Doreen.

go the limit. Not with Miss Shining Light. We are still in the dormitory stage with whispers after lights-out and stuffed animals on the bed.

Pat at Zermatt and St. Moritz: "I felt repulsed everywhere I turned. The Germans didn't like me, the English wouldn't even look at me; the more I drew inward in my shame and self-consciousness, the more repellent I grew to them."

This is one of those times when I cannot possibly imagine a future of any kind for myself. I don't see a continuation of the here and now and I don't see any great miracles occurring. For some reason I feel confident of myself, possibly because day by day it all matters less and less. What if a man, seeing me across a room, doesn't go for my type? Why should I force anything at all?

James came and took me to 19 Mossup Place. After a drunken walk through the fog all the way to Cadogan Square. It was so depressing. I still haven't recovered. His indecisiveness fills me with shame.

Damn it all, I am going to be very hard about it all. I shall do the repulsive little dailies, buy myself a red dress, and write away—even if the result is only a little piece of a big part. I am coming to terms with oneself—myself.

DECEMBER 7

A surfeit of cocktail parties, desperate people stalling for time. Never again. I refuse. I am tired of second-rate conversations, false hopes. Tomorrow I am going to the office at 12:30 and place a call to B. I shall tell him the truth and if he doesn't understand I shall break it off then and there and spend the rest of the winter keeping to myself as much as possible.

I am sick in my soul, or what is left of it. I see the stupidity of wanting to compete. There are too many others—others who appear outwardly to be the same skimmed-off neuroses as me.

DECEMBER 9

All done. I feel whitewashed. Either way, I feel qualified to continue the game—remember, it is *all* a game—he will say yes or no now & there will be no more delusions. Then I will go from there. Jill (the cocktail party hostess, the party at which I met Gordon) came by in controlled hysterics, looking utterly ravishing in that way only redheads can, as if they are about to burst into flame, smelling of Ma Griffe[42] & in a real panic about her Frenchman. I must admit that I was flattered she chose me instead of her flighty little cronies ("I just couldn't *bear* to face Sue at a time like this"). I enjoyed talking to her. I enjoy utterly selfish people who don't *need* me. There is no constraint. We simply ran everyone into the ground & she left feeling much better. But her foundations are shaky.

And we see another facet of the whole picture. She: "Giles & Davis were utterly furious when James found you this summer. He had teamed up with you instead of them—especially Giles—and they hated you."

And now it has run full circle. Said Giles Friday night, maliciously: "Are you still writing furiously?"

"Yes," I said.

"Are you still writing furiously with James?" he asked.

"No," I said. "James is not writing now."

"He's been ringing me furiously this past week," said Giles. "We're going tomorrow to look at boats for the lake next summer."

"You have a new pet word," I said.

I think Giles was justified in hating me.

McK.'s apartment.[43] Why was it so unsettling? Because it had not one shred of taste; and yet wasn't austere (*that* would have been bearable for a bachelor—ah, but he is dying to fall off his tree into the lap of some ready woman). I think it was the complete absence of any pictures, prints, etc. And those terrible heads of pretty girls for lamp bases & even one sticking out of the wall. And men's bathrooms are always such a mess. No huge cakes of colored soap, never a roll of soft toilet paper, and never a dry towel.

·   ·   ·

42. Ma Griffe, a woody, mossy fragrance, was developed by Carven in 1946.

43. McK. was a travel agent.

The enigma of Mr. Peter W. may be partially cleared up at six this evening. Or he may torment me by not showing. Oh, for some new insights. I want so much for him to be a master at the game. Will he provide me with enough material for another five pages? Oh, just to possess the ability to make other people *want* is an art. Will he come shambling in wearing his rumpled raincoat and the green and white polka-dotted scarf that I "ruined" with Givenchy? (Ah, and I have a brand-new 1 oz. bottle as a weapon this time—not too much. There is nothing so disgusting as too much scent, even if it's $21 an ounce.) Will he cast his aesthetic eye around my rooms and sneer inwardly at my abundance? Will he drop by at six and leave at seven?—this is the most likely guess. From what he says, he is *always* working. Or he will disappear as soon as he has sufficiently frustrated and intrigued me. I can't really prepare myself for the actuality. This phantom man, created mostly from my supercharged imagination, will appear out of seven weeks' silence and either smash or build higher my lovely image. Let us see.

Later:

First of all, when I say to him, "Help me to grow up," he says, "What a funny thing for you to say."

"I mean help me to realize and accept."

"It won't be easy. It won't be according to everybody else's solution."

We fought like tigers and it was exhilarating. He bruised my wrists and said, "Thanks for the exercise."

The note I sent him: He thought it had been sent by somebody else.

"Your face has two planes. The top part falls in a shadow. It is subtle and desirable."

Percy Wyndham Lewis, *Time and Western Man.*[44]

---

44. In *Time and Western Man*, published in 1927, Wyndham Lewis viciously attacked such writers as James Joyce and Ezra Pound, who had helped him in his career, and set himself apart from what he considered a deadening modern tradition.

DECEMBER 18

The Christmas frenzy beats faster and faster. Peter W. sent a one-page typewritten letter, full of Hamlet and DHL and a host of university quotes, all to say he didn't want to see me again. He ended it by saying, "I do this so that you can *live*." I was numb and crushed, empty and frightened. Walked all the way to Chelsea to see James, who was leaving for a date. His roommate William was there, smirking over a glass of wine, his gray hair sizzling silver under the lamplight. In exchange for my listening to several stories of his business ventures and ex-wives in Alexandria, he took Peter's letter and read it and with a mixture of calculated snobbery and existentialist humor he had me laughing at it ("Your main concern," wrote Peter, "should be how you're going to fill in the time between now and your funeral") and at PW. I was able to see that this boy had sat down on Sunday afternoon and written out an intellectual exercise to himself. This morning I thermofaxed it at the office and sent him the copy with a short letter telling him to read his own letter again in ten years. But the point is, I couldn't have written that letter last night.

DECEMBER 19

Another cocktail party—Albany Travel Agency—walking home tonight I knew that nothing *outside of me* could ever hurt again. B. will stay in Asheville.[45] The dentist's dogs can whine next door. Peter W. will write his book and masturbate. And I will go on here. There are worse places than London. I am beginning to like it. It stays still long enough for me to move.

I was thinking about PW tonight and decided that the man I was mad about never really existed. No man I could love could write a letter like that, and the letter came and his name was signed on the bottom.

DECEMBER 26

Boxing Day, they call it. I borrowed five days, paying for it only with the flu. Here I am, inside me, as usual, surrounded by little pink Kleenex

---

45. B. had told Gail by phone that he was not ready to commit and didn't think she was ready, either.

balls, a transistor playing half-baked music, "On the Sunny Side of the Street," sniffing and breathing hard, reviewing and distilling. Again. As usual. My party was a success. At least I say it was because they, my friends and enemies of the past nine months, surrounded me and gave me a pleasant image of what they saw: me, mature, complex, surrounded by the good things. But regarding them with whimsical indifference. Not striving for effect (when I have strived for the greatest effect of all—that of appearing not to have strived for any effect).

The two-bit radio is playing:

When people ask of me
what would you like to be
now that you're not a kid anymore
. . . I know just what to say . . .
I want to be Bobby's girl.

And that's about it.

James came by bringing a Christmas gift, a Scots beret. We spent Xmas Eve Day together, inflicting our silences on each other.

The upshot of all this is that I see that I haven't progressed as far as I thought.

Part eight

MY FATHER'S SOUL

Green Street, London

JANUARY 2–FEBRUARY 16, 1963

As this chapter in her journal opens, Gail finds herself alone in her "hermitage" on Green Street after having cleared away the traces of holiday parties. Her situation demands creative output, yet the project on which she has labored, "Gull Key," seems wrong. She needs to decide whether to continue working on "Gull Key" or to seek a new project.

Gail Godwin has said in interviews that she lives constantly in the shadow of failure, and it seems that her interviewers have misunderstood her attitude. It is not modesty. It is combativeness. Trap Godwin in an emotional, circumstantial, or writer's block and watch the reaction. She redoubles her ingenuity to find a way out, making sacrifices.

Gail's most remarkable embarkation happens on February 9, after she tells herself, "I must not take second-best plots, almost-stories. All my heroes & heroines must be looking for the main root. Not, not an offshoot, a facet, but the mainspring." The injunction comes on an auspicious day, which she marks in her journal as being the fifth anniversary of her father's death by suicide.

She then produces a story about a college girl's trip to a priest to reveal her anguish over the suicide of her father and the fate of his soul. Looking back on the swirl of Gail's concerns, experiences, and efforts in early 1963, it is easier now than it had been within the moment to see that the father-story was the one that was ready for expression.

Gail's postholiday solitude in her Green Street lodgings re-creates the circumstances of her aloneness at the University of North Carolina during midterm break, when she had had to digest the news of her father's death. The vacuum, by itself, invites spirits.

JANUARY 2, 1963

No. 5 Green Street is once again a hermitage. The party glasses are washed, all my possessions are in place, & there is only the ticking of the clock, the rumble of the underground to keep me company.

I had a New Year's Eve party & it was a fabulous success. No one went home senseless. James, drunk in a cool invisible way, sang "Beale Street Blues,"[1] many verses, with a voice fashioned from the incredible will that comes with alcohol. He just got promoted to secretary of the Rank Organisation. He was complaining bitterly, but was secretly flattered. Whenever I hear the bagpipes, I'll think of that night—for we had a real piper & the men in skirts almost outnumbered the pants.

Now I am here again, working toward that unconquerable soul B. preaches.

Ah, I have borrowed too long.[2] I must get my thoughts in order.

I am rewriting "Gull Key," salvaging a small bit of it, keeping the framework, illuminating characters & adding others.

Is Gull Key a place or a state of mind?

Reading over the other,[3] it seems so simple and shallow.

I want to hold the real flavor of Miami—a city of no return where you lose sight of values & mount the whirling dervish, the dangerous half-truth infallibility that comes over one in dark cocktail bars after too

---

1. Memphis blues music became very popular in the 1960s, thanks in part to B. B. King, whose initials stand for "Beale (Street) Boy." "Beale Street Blues," written by J. C. Handy in 1919, celebrates unrepressed life in the district and includes the lines:

If Beale Street could talk, if Beale Street could talk,
Married men would have to take their beds and walk,
Except one or two who never drink booze,
And the blind man on the corner singing "Beale Street Blues!"

2. Gail is being conscious of her use of time.

3. Gail started writing "Gull Key" fresh.

many gin & tonics. What was it that made the old ways so alluring? I can only find out as I write it.

My visual images are so strong.

JANUARY 5

A day of staying in. I began the study of logic.[4] Used my good old college study habits, underlining sentences, but I couldn't do the riddles at the end of the chapter. I mean, the reasoning problems. Reread *Franny & Zooey*. I found myself laughing out loud, or discovering a new meaning in some simple phrase like "wringing wet." The man has that genius.

JANUARY 14

Last night I was lying here in the dark wondering if there was a man in my life that I truly couldn't live without. There wasn't. What I then felt was no sense of deprivation.

I went to a palmist yesterday. She told me exactly what had happened, but we shall see.

The electricity was off when I came home, so I turned around & went to the Baker Classic to see *Jane Eyre*. It had Liz Taylor as a child & Margaret O'Brien as a baby and Orson Welles as a very Edward Rochester–desirable cynic.[5] I tried to analyze what it was about the character he portrayed, or, more than that, his facial expressions, that made me long for that perfect love and at the same time thank heaven

---

4. Gail was searching for a book on logic that improved upon the lessons she had received in a class at Chapel Hill. She may have been inspired, in part, by her confrontation with Peter W., who had a degree in philosophy and logic.

5. Edward Rochester, in the film version of *Jane Eyre*, conforms to one idea that Gail has of the ideal man. His cultured cynicism is so alluring that neither his disloyalty to his lunatic wife nor his disability (blindness caused by a climactic house fire) makes him unappealing as a marriage candidate. In this journal part, Gail views her relationships with men in many lights. In the next entry (January 20), she analyzes the character of and her attraction to H., whom she'd recently met, noting her concern about "when the music stops." His morality is his strongest point, though there are traces of his former physical beauty as a red-haired sprinter. Eight days later, James visits her—while she's in the midst of reading *Wuthering Heights*, Emily Brontë's melodrama about a passionate and vengeful lover—and presents himself as a male ideal free of sexual expectations. A week passes; Gail begins to write a story that balances her experiences with Neils and Antonio, with whom the physical component was key.

that I was still free to search. What is it that I so definitely want in a man & see only at times—even if it is a character in a hackneyed, romanticized film?

Was it the peculiar glint in his eyes?

His sharp jaded wit?

What, what, what?

No, it's not B., either. The nearest person I can think of is BH. What is it? Is it only possible in a film, in a book written by a lonely old maid? Do men like this exist only in the tortured minds of lonely women?

I am feeling so otherworldly, so afloat in possibilities. There's something about cities at night. I think now I shall turn off the light and think . . .

JANUARY 20

. . . This weekend I spent with H., whom I met last Tuesday. Actually, I met him (he says) at the Canadian Government Tourist Office party, but I chose not to acknowledge him until last Tuesday. I have paid closer attention to this relationship, and—more important—its beginning stages, than ever before. I am trying to find out when the music stops. Yet, it may be too late for such clinical procedures, for this is the first relationship I have had with anybody who I considered had just as much right to live as I did.

In the past, there has been a time when the person's resources were exhausted and anything further I gave was given out of pity, habit, or just plain old loneliness.

Ever since that first evening at Royal Festival Hall, I have been looking for a flaw that will allow me to discount him. I do not have far to look if it is a simple flaw I seek. He has several of the type I have never allowed before. He has a nervous tic, which is apparent to everyone. (But I have found, by a hidden watchfulness, that when he is in his own element, explaining something to me, listening to the second movement of Mahler's *Resurrection* Symphony, eating a steak, showing physical affection, this nervous flaw subsides.) He is going bald. He is losing his beautiful reddish curly hair, it will be gone within five years.

I think how he must have looked as his school's number-one sprinter, red hair streaming in the wind like Mercury. Speaking of Mercury, he is early Gemini.

I have tried and tried to categorize. When he took me to his room and showed me a collection of theater & concert programs covering a space of ten years & a span of miles from San Francisco to London, I felt a little sickening twinge (after all, he was *proud* of this collection). I thought I had found an irreconcilable flaw at last. So that was why he went to all of those concerts, to collect the programs. But, even while feeling this, I knew it wasn't so. That might have been my motive once upon a time, but not his.

Here is a man to whom money is not important, grand achievements are not important; just so he earns enough to enjoy the use of his five senses & to appreciate the genius of others. I think he is one of the few people who may have guessed right about himself. There are no self-delusions, H. is H., and I must take care not to try to inflict my goals upon him. He would be impervious and un-inflicted—if there is such a word. If I want to be a great writer and believe in myself, then it is my business and only I can achieve my self-set goal—if I achieve it. And if he enjoys his present work, his present life, his present location, that is his business. It isn't as if he never showed initiative or curiosity. His thirty-three years of history read proudly for any twentieth-century man:

a Jew who remembers it but does not dwell upon it;

an educated man who does not forget those who made it possible;

an army man who went after a commission and got it;

a traveler who made up his mind to try other cities, live there, work there, and did; who decided after two years that London was his city and returned to live & work there & has never second-guessed himself.

So, according to my standards, H. is a good man, a moral man, a man who carries his security inside himself.

His French windows had red velvet, floor-length curtains which, when opened, revealed a garden covered with snow. I sank into the velvet armchair & read & stopped & looked out at the snow drifting by, the occasional bird scavenging for food in the thick snow, listening to Brahms's Second, Fourth, Mahler's *Resurrection;* and he was always in touching distance, yet he does not give himself away. He does not demand too much, admit too much. I miss him already & won't see him until *Benvenuto Cellini* on Wednesday. He may not be the love of my life, but he is not a fool, does not fake his life, & we will be close, quiet friends.

("I hesitated to ask you to see *King Lear,* or to go out with me, because I thought you were much younger than you were.")

H. has already booked seats for Paris—April 13, 14, 15, 16. If I can only keep this on a calm basis & not try to devour him. God, we'll have a time in Paris . . . (*ha, ha*).[6]

JANUARY 21

Veeraswamys[7] for lunch. My tongue is still sweating. Mr. Miller got more money & more people, whatever that is supposed to mean. Peter W. called again, I wonder what his game is. I talked with Hilda, my palmist, on the telephone. She, too, is a human being. "Ah, Gail, it's so good to hear your voice!" Clairvoyant or not, she is lonely and needs the conversation & communication of kindred spirits.

JANUARY 23

Continued cold. The fog (smog) returns on little cat feet. Today I met a publisher[8] & he placed his electric heater at my feet & told me I could

---

6. The "ha, ha" was written in later as a postscript to the trip. "We didn't get along in Paris," Gail notes. "His twitch was worse than ever and he accused me of picking at my face and scalp. I was envious of all the perfectly groomed Frenchwomen, and disenchanted with H., as he with me."

7. Veeraswamys was considered the best Indian restaurant in England, and was the oldest, having been established in 1926.

8. Gordon Landsborough, publisher of action novels and military histories, had an office around the corner from the U.S. Travel Service agency. He became interested in Gail's work and recommended her to his friend Ursula Winant, a literary agent. He also took

write. Peter W., called away on busy-business, will return tomorrow at teatime. I am beginning to suspect he is ridiculous. Wonder why the change of heart after the passionate farewell? I refuse to worry about money before I am actually hungry. Letter from Kathleen. "A good, full life."[9] What a family of individuals they are. I can now say "they," looking on them from here, enjoying them.

What to write next, now that I have the man who will always read it.[10] ("One woman whose manuscript I'd rejected came in one day & asked me if I knew of a man about fifty years old who needed a wife.") I must go through my journals. Why is every subject I think of so womanish? ("A good writer never 'settles for' anything.")

I was impatient with H. tonight. Did he sense it? And yet he's 100 percent person. Lately, I have decided there are several other nice people in the world besides myself.

JANUARY 26

No. I have not been faithful to the record lately. Partially recovered after a second bout with flu. I have had several male nurses to assist. Peter W. dropped by yesterday about 5:30 but I was already occupied. It did him a world of good. The best line to take with someone like him is that of humor. It's the only way. He is forever on the brink of losing touch and I told him so.

Re the Writing:

1. Don't be false with yourself now. Don't wax all Jamesian but remember your heritage. Keep moving. Keep alive. Don't be poisoned by the English reserve.

2. Don't write with an eye cocked for the reader.

Gail beagling. Gail ran, walked, and ran, following the beagles in search of a prey she never identified. "We went the day after Kennedy's assassination," Gail recalls, "and I cried a lot, running through the fields."

9. "A good, full life" is the fairy-tale wish passed on to the prodigal daughter by her mother, who did not necessarily experience such a blessing herself.

10. Gail is referring to Gordon Landsborough.

I am bulging with the life force. I don't think I'll ever make any one person a matter of life & death again.

Release your fanatic grip on it, & it, so recently struggling in the opposite direction, boomerangs—practically breaking its neck to get back to you.

JANUARY 27

Dragged myself out of bed & to work. Everybody said, "Oh, but you shouldn't have . . ." So I came back home. Mr. Miller came around at 1:30 & said he was sending his own doctor by later. It is times like this when you see the real value of someone. He exacts a good bit from his staff, but he's there when they need him. I am enjoying the unreality of being sick. My ears are stopped up & I can't hear too much noise. The good things of life crowd round, pressing for admittance. Not yet, I say. Play it cool. A publisher thinks I can write, Peter W. has come back, I work for a man like Beverly Miller, & this is my life. So much is possible on this day of all days.

There are plenty of half-people, looters, qualifiers. Why not smoke out the rarities and set them to words?

JANUARY 28

Read . . . inhale . . . swallow . . . sniff . . . John Updike . . . lunch . . . nose drops . . . *Wuthering Heights*. Could I have enjoyed this complete aloneness five years ago? One year ago? Tick, tick . . . hammer, hammer . . . another building rises out of London's crowded ugly architecture. What are they all doing at the office? I'm glad I'm not there. James came by last night. At first, I was almost impatient for him to go. But we faithfully dredged up memories and built a temporary platform on which we sat, ate, and drank. One beautiful moment: when he lay stretched on the rug, leafing through a book, unconsciously graceful and young—for thirty-eight.

Miller's doctor is making a new girl out of me. There is a concert Thursday & a new "smart" play Friday. I think James has terrible taste in plays. He always chooses something very clever-clever. This one is about a man who turns into a bed-sitting room & about "fallout hampers" from Fortnum & Mason.[11]

JANUARY 29—OR IS IT 30?

The Dear Doctor informed me that he & Miller conspired to have me spend *the week* in bed. I am ashamed because I have not been writing. Nothing seems worth the effort of putting down. I have no strange romantic tales like the Brontë sisters because I have satisfied my tastes for the strange & romantic in the world of the real. I cannot write like Steinbeck because I'm not close enough to the earth. I don't know one town intimately like Carson McCullers or D. H. Lawrence. Surely there is a place in the searchings of literature for The Great Sampler. I have hungered all day for the simplest conversation with another human being. Even Stuart the Scotsman was welcome last night. Peter W. hasn't shown, & oh God! It's only ten till eight. Where are all my dear, kind friends? If I think any more thoughts, I will go insane. I even resorted to cleaning out drawers.

I know what is wrong. I cannot stand to write about anything that is not myself—how much have I lost by failing to look around me instead of *inward*, always *inward?*

SHIT.

AN EXERCISE IN PORNOGRAPHY

I am getting tired of reading, hearing, practicing, and talking
sex. Although I have not reached the Platonic state of one of
my closest friends, a cynical Englishman of forty who
proclaims sex is a function, no more or less noble than
defecating, I am ready to cry "False!" to almost any statement
anybody may choose to utter about this wearisome subject.
Politics, religion, segregation, nuclear disarmament—what

11. The play is *The Bed Sitting Room* by John Antrobus and Spike Milligan of *Goon Show* fame. It features characters who experience disconnected absurdities amid postnuclear British ruins, including one character's transformation into a bed-sitting room.

chance have they after the first gregarious hours of a cocktail party? In the end, the clusters break up into smaller molecular units. Number One takes over and it is like watching the reorganization of germs under a microscope.

I have been able to read for twenty years. At the age of eleven, I was informed of the reproductive process by a thirteen-year-old friend named Eugene who lived in the same apartment house. After that time, everything I read took on a new aspect. In books, the characters were no longer divided into good & bad; strong & weak; rich & poor—but they were either men or women. The men, whether they be called Hamlet, Heathcliff, Captain Marvel, or Heidi's grandfather, were the ones who "put it into" the women. The women, Scarlett O'Hara, Jane Eyre, Emma Bovary, existed for the inevitable occasion when it would be put into them. This sounds crude. I don't have the guts to read it over because I would be shocked & put down the pen, rip out the page, and rip out the unsavory thoughts. But no! Dear Reader, you clamor for just this sort of thing. You read out of the corner of your eye, the same way that you look at the victims of traffic accidents. You determine by your impeccable taste just what books will top the best-seller list. And to you, gentle reader, this book, a truthful, unbiased, unabridged account of my sexual research for the last five years, is affectionately dedicated. No fear of peeking ahead into future chapters with your nibbling eyes, hoping to spot the morsels without putting in honest reading time. I promise you satisfaction in every page. God, how you all worship a good lay.

THE GREAT SAMPLER

(To save you further speculation, I am one of the second category—the ones that have it put into them.)

JANUARY 31

After almost a solid week spent in the sometimes confused but never boring *GGK,*[12] I am beginning to get my bearings. I have tomorrow, Saturday & Sunday to think. Then the floating has to stop. I must begin somewhere.

Retrace all these notebooks & find what is significant in them.

What is sad is to read what I wrote about James one year ago. And he is taking me out tomorrow night. It isn't sad that we are unexciting to each other now, but it is sad that I could have written that last year to be read this year. Always telescoping, telescoping into past & future.

FEBRUARY 9—FIVE YEARS SINCE MG'S[13] SUICIDE

Another work point:

Father's car	Seeing the priest in Durham after the event—the evasions, the not-quite meshings.
Jack M.[14] in the intimate	The constant search for a premise that runs like a thread through our lives—I must find out the truth, we say—but how much can you hope to find? Everyone is looking madly.
The beach	The essence.

I must not take second-best plots, almost-stories. All my heroes & heroines must be looking for the main root. *Not, not* an offshoot, a facet, but the mainspring.

·   ·   ·

12. Gail Godwin Kennedy.

13. Mose Godwin.

14. Jack M. was a law student at Chapel Hill, an ex-Marine, and an older man. He was the inspiration for Jack Krazowski, the experienced outsider in "The Angry Year" who offers the heroine, Janie Lewis, an alternative to her appealing yet dishonest relationship with Graham, president of his fraternity. Janie, sensing the challenges of the 1960s, becomes angry with herself for caring about what others think and for tending toward conformity.

This whole day has been a failure because I've let myself be a football field for a lot of people's games. If I don't watch it, the spongers are going to get my smell & I'll find myself keeping them in whiskey, steaks, and sympathy. My most valuable commodity is time and I have spent it carelessly. The whole miserable day is my doing. To make it up to Henry for being curt to him after *King Lear*, I wrote him a note & invited him to lunch Saturday (today). He called yesterday (interrupting an intense conversation with Mr. Landsborough) to say he wasn't sure he could come because he'd had a headache for two days. So I said, "Well, see how you feel tomorrow," thus giving him leeway and trapping myself. Then Stella called & asked if she could "invite herself over," and of course I said yes. Then Henry calls at 12:30 & hedges, saying he still has his headache and he has to be home early if his sister has this friend to dinner, but he's not sure—so what shall we do? Meanwhile, a customer comes into the office & I'm talking more for his ears than Henry's & I'm tired of the whole bloody thing, so I say, "You decide. I can't make up your mind for you," and he says, "I wish I could put my head in the river," and I say, "I have to hang up," and do so. (I heard him say something else, but I hung up on it.) When I left the office, I felt distinctly annoyed & was perfectly aware I'd managed to do it again—please everybody but myself. So, Stella came & Stuart, the Scotsman, cooked & I was in the middle. Stella always makes me feel I have to "perform," what with her avid interest in my doings. I have a funny intuitive suspicion that Stuart wears thin with her & so I react to him the way she is politely not reacting to him. (Same situation as with Lorraine in Denmark when I thought they were snubbing her in the restaurant because she was colored & ended up crying & she was comforting me.) I hate being in the middle. Then Jim Jensen[15] came in & I was surprised at how glad I was to see him. He was the one sober positive element in the late afternoon. He went all too soon. So Stella has gone home, having had her afternoon; Stuart went out & got ornery-drunk & came back & made a farewell speech, during which he contra-

---

15. James Jensen, whose given name was Dmitri, was the son of an English engineer who had emigrated to Communist Russia. See the fuller entry on him on February 16 in this journal part.

dicted himself fifty times. I am in everyone's mind as an ill-tempered, fluffy bitch—if I am in their minds at all. Candidly speculating, I doubt if anyone is giving me a thought. Thus I lost this round, but gained an insight. The result of trying to please people out of a sense of guilt only leads to laying yourself on an altar, cutting a gash, & letting the suckers suck.

FEBRUARY 10

I am okay again. Leaning on people was bad for me. Got up at one—I can lie in on Sundays indulging viciously in dreams, half dreams, and finally daydreams. Then I had breakfast at Lyons Corner House,[16] came home & read the papers, cleaned up & washed my hair, and wrote from four until nine. It must have needed to come out. I did 14 3 280 = 3,920 words today, and I think it is the first un-bitter thing I have ever written. If only I'm not too tired tomorrow. I've gotten through the preliminaries and now need the priest scene & the beach scene. (End: "Listen, we'll try again in the morning. Okay?" "Okay," I said.) I brought these people to life today, now I've got to finish them.

> He [Jack] had a good face, the kind I would learn to appreciate later. There was nothing slick or collegiate cute about it. It was many-planed, complicated, and, when he took off his glasses, rather beautiful in its own way.

> Tomorrow—go to bank & get £5. Mail letters.

FATHER FLYNN: A SHORT STORY

> That weekend began desolately. After midterms, everyone went home. I could have gone to see my mother if I'd felt like

---

16. Lyons Corner House had emerged in 1909 as the only place in England to which people could go to nurse a cup of coffee in the morning. In 1954, with the end of food rationing, the chain began serving quick meals, such as "grill and cheese," prior to the entry of McDonald's and Burger King into the country.

spending most of the weekend on the bus. By Friday
afternoon, the campus was as silent as a ghost town.

I was miserable. It was not that I had many friends,
because I didn't. I tried to merge with the groups I thought I
ought to like while I secretly longed for the company of the
unacceptable and nonbelongers. Thus I hit somewhere in the
middle and touched neither side.

But I didn't mind my aloneness as long as there was a
background filled with people. Now that background was
removed for the weekend and I had nowhere to run. I had the
keys to my father's beach cottage, but 150 miles was too far
to drive alone, and what would I do when I got there? It was
cold & there were no heating facilities and nobody had been
down to inspect the damages since the hurricane.

I drove around the deserted university town in my father's
car (by this time the novelty of having a car had worn off),
wracking my mind for someplace to go. I passed the Gothic-
spired Episcopal church and it was thinking of churches that
led me to think of my father & the ominous religious
significance of taking one's own life (if he who loves life loves
God, then he who . . .), and then I remembered that a nun at
the convent school I'd attended for ten years had told me when
I visited there last summer about a priest in Durham. She said
when I went to the university, if I ever got a chance to go over
to Durham, some nine miles away, to be sure and look up
Father Flynn, who was a wonderful man of God and who had
helped her many times when he'd been in the local diocese.

"He has an insight into things," she had said, and this was
enough for me. I suddenly felt very lighthearted and
purposeful, and started for Durham at once. I drove fast,
enjoying the smooth-moving landscape ribboning away on
either side of me. I stopped at a Shell station outside of
Durham and looked up the rectory in the phone book and
called him.

I began by mentioning Mother Winters's name, and he

said, "Oh, yes." He said he would be glad to have me drop in
that afternoon, and gave me directions how to get to the
rectory, which was two traffic lights past a bakery, turn right.

Three standard black Cadillacs in the rectory parking lot
were aligned with pontifical exactness. My green-and-cream
Buick hadn't been washed since I'd inherited it, and looked
shabby beside God's gleaming automobiles.

Although it was located in an area of town that was going
downhill in real estate value, everything about the rectory was
new—its yellow brick, its large picture windows, even the
grass. A few trees in the yard would have certainly given it a
mellower, traditional look.

A priest answered my knock. He was dressed impeccably
in a black suit with the clerical collar and his face had that
unfocused puffy look of someone who has just awakened.

"I have an appointment with Father Flynn," I said.

"Oh, yes," he said, blinking. "You called from the filling
station, didn't you? I'm Father Flynn. Look, come in and have
a seat in there." He motioned to a sunlit room on the left, just
inside. "I'm on the telephone. I must apologize, but everybody
here is either away or down with that awful Asian flu. Have
you had it yet? No? Oh, good. Well, just wait in there, I'll try
not to be long." He flailed his arms in a gesture of despair and
almost ran from the room. His ankles looked fragile in their
black silk stockings and he wore a new pair of black Italian
loafers. I heard him continuing the telephone conversation,
which I had obviously interrupted, in a breezy, rather nervous
flow of words that sounded like a PR man talking to a client.

I had lost the initial fervor with which I had begun this
trip and thus began rehearsing my approach to nervous Father
Flynn. I felt that I should keep from boring him at all costs
and was relieved when I remembered that I did have a serious
problem and one which would surely not be taken lightly by
any Catholic clergyman. I sat in a soft beige armchair beside a
table with magazines, mostly *Catholic Digest*, and tried to

recapture the somber convent mood of incense and martyred saints, but it was a bit difficult when everything smelled of fresh paint.

"Well, I'm back," said Father Flynn, wheeling into the room. "I'm sorry, it's a madhouse today. Now, I'll just shut this door so we won't be interrupted. But I must warn you, if the phone rings again, I'll have to answer it. I'm expecting a call from one of our parishioners whose husband's in Duke Hospital with leukemia and we'll have to go over any time now to give the last sacraments. What a day." He passed his hand over his forehead and sat down in a chair facing me.

"That's terrible," I said.

"What is, my dear?"

"That . . . the woman's husband, I mean."

"Oh! Oh, yes it is. It certainly is. So much tragedy. But always for a purpose, for a purpose, you know."

"I'm glad you said that, because one of the reasons I came here . . ."

"How did you know Mother Winters?" he said.

"Oh, she was my favorite teacher at St. Genevieve's. I still go and see her whenever I'm up that way."

"Are you Catholic?"

"No, but I might be. I mean, I might become one."

"Mmm. Mother Winters is a fine woman. She has a real vocation."

"Yes, she said you helped her quite a lot in getting over some spiritual obstacles."

"I helped her? Oh, yes. I remember some of the sisters did come to me at times for recommended reading. Yes, maybe I did. Nice of her to mention it. Well"—he paused and fingered the ring on the third finger of his right hand—"so you were a pupil of Mother Winters. Where are you, at Duke now, or up at the Hill?"

"Yes, the university. I mean, not Duke, but Carolina."

"I see. How nice." He looked as if he were casting about for some more suitable questions so I decided to get to the point and not waste his time.

"I hope I haven't added to your hectic day, Father, but the truth is, I've been kind of mixed up about some things and I remembered Mother Winters saying that if ever I was over this way, you had a real insight (he was looking attentive now) into these things. So. Here I am."

"Well, I'll certainly try to help in any way I can. Do you, uh, know exactly what's bothering you? Can you put your finger on it? Little matter of faith, is it?"

"Well, no. I mean, it is in a way, but what started it all is my father committed suicide last month."

The telephone rang outside the door and Father let three rings go by while he gave me a look of deep sympathy. "Dear child, I'm so sorry for you. Do you know whatever drove your poor father to do this? He was ill, was he?"

"No, he . . ."

Father Flynn looked agonized. "There. I can't ignore it, can I? Do forgive me. I'll be right back. I'm so sorry about this." He bolted from the room and I soon heard the businesslike drone again. I picked up a *Catholic Digest* and leafed quickly through its pages, not really seeing anything.

"Now. Let's hope it was for the last time. You were telling me about your father's illness. Did it go on for very long?"

"No, he wasn't ill. I mean, he wasn't very stable in his work and he drank a lot, but nobody expected him to—well, you know."

"How did it happen? Sleeping pills?"

"No, he shot himself in the head. The first shot misfired, so he really killed himself twice. I keep thinking how much nerve it must have taken when he realized he wasn't dead and had to do it all over again."

"Brrr," said Father Flynn. "Well, my dear, you must

remember that when a man does something like this, he might not *seem* ill, but he could be very very sick and not really comprehend the seriousness of his action."

"But that's what I really wanted to ask you about. You see, I loved my father very much . . ."

"I'm sure you did."

". . . and, well, I had Catechism at St. Genevieve's and according to you, he's roasting in Hell right now . . ."

Father Flynn looked slightly annoyed. "Now, let's not be extreme about this thing, my dear, there are mitigating circumstances for everything. You must understand that if your father was . . . uh, mentally disturbed at the time of his action, and sometimes a person can be *temporarily* disturbed, then he was not entirely responsible, you know."

"Then, if he's not in Hell, where is he?"

"You must understand that he is not in a state of grace, but neither would we like to say he's, uh, roasting, as you put it. There are always circumstances. I can tell you for fairly certain that there are prayers for this sort of thing. There are prayers."

"Then I should pray?"

"Why, yes, pray. Certainly pray. That's the idea. I know it seems bigger than life to you now, you're probably still in a state of shock, but gradually things will fall into place for you."

"But where is my father's soul? I mean, you couldn't tell me definitely, could you?"

"Nobody could tell you one hundred percent definitely but God," said Father Flynn. "You must have enough faith in him to rely on his judgment. He's a pretty fair guy, you know."

"Oh." I had been waiting for the telephone in the hall to ring again, but it stayed silent. I heard a bus rumble by on the street outside and suddenly felt completely relaxed, almost stupefied, and unable to move or think further. Father Flynn had crossed his legs and seemed to be contemplating one of his thin silk-stockinged ankles.

"Well, you've been a big help," I said, not wanting to hurt his feelings. "You've said so much. It hasn't had time to sink in, but I'm very grateful."

Father Flynn straightened up like a released man and smiled warmly for the first time. "I don't know about that," he said, "but I'm only too glad if I have, and you're free to come back anytime. There is a very good man over in your neck of the woods, though, in case you're interested. Father Gregory. He's at the University Parish and terrific with young people. I can strongly recommend him. He seems to be closer to their problems, you know."

"Father Gregory," I repeated.

"That's right. I think you'll like him. Very understanding. Tell him about your father. He'll give you some prayers to say, maybe explain it better than I have."

"Oh, no, but you've . . ."

Now he was standing. "Tell you what. I'm going to give you a book that may help you. It's sort of a compact little rule book to let you know where we stand on a lot of matters. There's a very good section on marriage and the family in there and you look like a girl who may be needing that chapter before long." He attempted a robust wink and handed me a little paperback volume he'd taken from the book stand: *My Way of Life*, it was called.[17]

"Oh, but you must let me pay you for it," I said, also standing now.

"Why, I wouldn't think of it."

"Well, gosh, I mean, thanks."

He held my coat for me. "Did you drive? Yes, I guess you did. Could you follow my directions all right?"

17. *My Way of Life* is a pocketbook compendium of the wisdom of St. Thomas Aquinas's *Summa Theologica*, "simplified for everyone," the subtitle indicates.

"Oh, they were fine. No trouble at all."

"Good."

He shook hands with me at the door. "So nice to meet you," he said. "And next time you see Mother Winters give her my regards. Brrr." He looked up at the dull sky. "You'd better get back to the Hill before it pours."

"Oh, I love the rain."

"Do you? Well, that's a good way to be, I guess. So long, then."

"So long," I said.

Just before he closed the door, I heard the telephone ringing again. Poor thin, slangy Father Flynn. I hoped he wouldn't come down with the Asian flu.

Halfway back to campus, the sky opened and the rain came down in sheets. I slowed down to 30 mph and turned on the wipers and the radio. By some lucky coincidence, they were playing the *Pastoral* Symphony.

I ate supper at Harry's. There were plenty of others. There were only three girls sleeping in McIver that night. None were on my floor. It was enjoyable, in a way, the absence of shrill conversations in the showers, no telephone ringing every third minute, the after-rain smell of water dripping into leaves, etc. I cleaned out my desk drawer and got my laundry ready ahead of time. Then I read through the entire fifty pages of Mott's *History of Journalism* listening to the rain leftovers plip-plop onto the leaves outside, carefully underlining with a pen and ruler. By the time I had finished, it was late enough to go to bed.

After my supper at Harry's I had walked. The wet streets were clean and empty. I stopped in front of Kemp's to look at the new record albums displayed on a turning rack and then next door at the Intimate to look at the new book titles, the colorful dust jackets.

Walking past the post office, I had a brief realization that I loved my life that I was now living. But this flashed past so quickly that I was left with only the words: I will always remember this evening. And couldn't even decide why.

Saturday morning, I awoke to such quiet and beauty going on outside my window that I wondered what all the fuss had been about. I decided that, damn it, I was going to have fun this weekend all by myself. I would drive out to the country in this pre-spring air, and park by the side of the road, and walk, and maybe pray for my father. Then I would come back to town and go to a movie. I enjoyed going to the movies alone, anyway.

FEBRUARY 12

Ursula Winant, the agent, has invited me to her office on Monday to discuss my writing. Oh God.

FEBRUARY 16

Lorraine has said that my letters were beginning to sound like catalogues of lovers.

Jim Jensen. If anybody does not remind me of a Jim, it's Jim. I wish he could go by the name he was born with: Dmitri. He has, if not completely stolen my heart, at least set certain things clear for me. B. said, "I can see no better relationship possible than that of a man and woman who have no common interest." I accepted this because I (thought I) loved him. But I can see the possibilities of loving a man who has the *same* interests. My problems are, in a certain respect, J.'s. I can appreciate him because I have a better understanding than most of what efforts he has made to achieve what he has done. I also see why he is seriously concerned with a future in which lecturing & serious writing must be combined.

Jim: "It's not consciously 'writing,' and that's good. Remind me to discuss with you later ways you can *bring up* Father Flynn—even through the use of colors."

I can't sleep and I only want to think further of him. I may not run through him quite so quickly for the simple reason that he's progressing at an equal rate with me.

What almost put me off was, I think, his flip way of speaking. He seemed to me to be a "smarty." Some of the flip in his voice, I finally discovered, is simply a remnant of a Russian accent.

And funny how I am affected by little things like the fact that his jackets have two slits in the back. The fact that he is short. When I think that I actually deliberately stood him up one evening to have a drink with Bob Briggs. If he hadn't come around of his own curiosity the next day, I wouldn't have bothered again. The turning point came when I saw that he was human behind this flip exterior. He actually cooked for me one night. There was something in that offering of that very well cooked steak, something in the way he kissed the back of my hand (he has very warm lips) that made him at least welcome the next time he came by. Then when he came last Saturday, he seemed the only really *valid* person in the room. Stella & Stuart at cross-purposes, I in the role of nervous hostess.

By Wednesday, I wished he would telephone, and when he did on Thursday, I broke a dinner date to meet him. That was February 14 and the first time I was intensely aware of him. We went to the Embassy cocktail lounge & I began drinking Scotches to his lagers, even though the barman set the lager in front of me. J. doesn't miss much either with his eyes or his ears. And I love his fine appreciation of subtlety. I asked him about himself because I was now interested. His grandfather was an English engineer who became enamored with Communism and actually *immigrated* to Leningrad. J. was born Dmitri and was there until he was five. Then a German "work camp"—Canada—California. He is still stateless and has no passport. He's been through some damned inconveniences, but manages to see the humor in it all. (The four lawyers, British Passport Office & Embassy: nobody knew what to do when he'd run out of space on his travel document; finally, the fourth lawyer Scotch-taped a piece of ordinary paper to it.)

It was at the Barley Mow that I really began to see him. This is a very attractive pub. Something about the orange lights, the polished brass rail, the wood, the burnished copper pots & the carpet. There is music—a really tinny barroom kind—and a little stairway, which leads somewhere that looks interesting. There were several characters in there, including a sad-type peroxided female who kept nudging her man's gonads with the toe of her shoe. Three Scotches. And we're talking about masks.

"What makes me mad is when people take my mask at face value."

"But you must expect it. The most you should look for usually is for someone to see just far enough to perceive you *are* wearing a mask."

And he said Yeats had seen this & he should know since he did his thesis on Yeats.

He's got a consciousness that seems to match mine and therefore he's worth more. I can enjoy putting my face against his, touching him, because of an awareness that there's so much going on in that body. So much more than in most. I must offer something of the same to him because he said at the Barley Mow: "You seem to be able to enjoy things fully. That's why I wanted to see you tonight."

Today I went to Selfridges and bought things I wouldn't ordinarily have bought just so I could have packages to carry when I went to the lamp department to look for him. We went to the coffee bar (at his insistence), and then he came by later—about two. Not much "personal" talk, mostly about his doctorate and plans to teach. And Henry James. I think James has more to offer me than any other writer at this stage. He's so civilized, it's sheer joy to read him after so many lazy technicians.

I read *Portrait*[18] until 6:00 a.m. because it was entrancing & because I was afraid again. Went through some of my old writing & found it pretty sad. So conscious of itself. So clever. I think I am on the verge of some new philosophy. For the first time in about ten years, I don't *want* to be immoral or even amoral anymore. I want a set of guiding premises chosen by me & followed by me. The writing will come now, I think, because I'm not so obsessed with "catchy subjects." As soon as I finish "Mourning,"[19] I may try one on B. just to see if I can write from a man's point of view.

18. Gail's reading of *The Portrait of a Lady*, by Henry James, consciously addressed her feelings of aloneness, awakened in her by the anniversary of her father's death, as well as by her precarious status as an independent woman abroad.

19. The full manuscript of "Mourning" has not survived.

NIGHTWALK

London

FEBRUARY 27–MARCH 24, 1963

Each part of Gail's journals has offered us not only an example of her literary efforts and an account of her personal adventures but also something else: the kind of underlying, vital dynamic that serves an author in finding inspiration years later. Gail's trusting relationship with her journal enables her to bequeath herself material not fully recognized at the time of writing.

In this journal part, Gail continues to develop her story "Mourning," an important and valuable exploration, which, fourteen years later, will feed Violet Clay. *Meanwhile, unscripted, she lives out a story that is related to her imaginative output.*

Empathizing with her late father in order to describe the kind of man whose idealism leads to suicide, she falls prey to a succession of symptoms: writer's block, spiritual visitation, and motivational paralysis. As with Gail's experience of loneliness in the previous journal part, the reader must tell himself or herself, "This is Godwin's real life, not her invention!"

[NO DATE]

When Beth Learner's father committed suicide during the second semester of her junior year in college, she was shocked more from her own lack of grief than from the event which should have summoned it.[1]

The story of a man's suicide seen through his daughter's eyes—mind—point of view. Every fact remembered about it—their times together, father's past (insert this in the notebook). Cut out the slang; see if you can be original without it.

I

Ambrose Bradshaw has killed himself & he is the main person.[2] This is his story. In the first scene, we have the reactions of his immediate family to his death and, through their eyes, get a taste of his character . . . hopefully enough to make one love him, or at least take his side. We are also introduced to Lee, his twenty-year-old daughter by a long-since-dissolved first marriage. It is through her eyes we will know Ambrose.

II

Lee is at a party given by her glittering surgeon-lover. It is the eve of her father's death but she doesn't know it. We get a brief

1. Shortly, Gail will change the name of her heroine from Beth Learner to Lee Bradshaw.

2. Gail has begun to expand her short story "Mourning" to novel length. Readers will recognize the name Ambrose. It is the name of the heroine's uncle in *Violet Clay*. He, like the father in "Mourning," commits suicide. Here, Gail considers beginning "Mourning" with Ambrose's family's reaction to the news of Lee's father's death. In *Violet Clay*, the mention of Uncle Ambrose's death is delayed. Preceding it are Violet's memory of working in his studio as a budding artist, and her recollection, while drunk after a career setback, of his welcome when she'd arrived in New York City. The news of his death eventually comes to Violet via a telephone call that awakens her from an alcoholic blackout.

insight into her structure—nervous, unsure of her place intellectually and, most acutely, socially. She's intelligent, emotional—and between introductions to the other characters at this party, which includes the setups stamped with the approval of the Schultzes (explain their criteria & try not to be . . .)[3]

FEBRUARY 27, 1963

Went to see *This Sporting Life*[4]—very brutal, full of "truths," etc.—and I came home in a taxi feeling thoroughly depressed, trying to place myself, thinking all cities were the same at night after a depressing movie— Miami—Asheville—Blowing Rock—Copenhagen—London—

I want to cry or express some definite emotion & then seek further release in *The Golden Bowl*.[5] Dear civilized Henry James! I have never had any desire to rough it.

FEBRUARY 28

Sometimes I get a little bit hungry for "coziness." Farewell dinner with the Southrons who are emigrating to France & BH & Howard who leave London tomorrow.[6] She snuggles up to him so. Will I ever find a man who's inexhaustible? *"After a time, you get to recognize certain qualities repeating themselves in the men you like,"* said Dorothea, the new girl, who has run away from her English psychiatrist husband once already.

The National Anthem from Radio Frankfurt . . . *Am I staying away too long?* But where, then, is my place at home? I have no desire to go back

3. The entry breaks off at this point.

4. *This Sporting Life* was a 1963 film featuring Richard Harris in his first starring role. He played a coal miner's son who rises above his circumstances to become a celebrated rugby player. The game brutalizes him, and his resentful anger both inflames and saps.

5. Henry James's massive, late-career novel *The Golden Bowl* portrays four individuals who negotiate what easily could have become nasty conflicts within their close unit. The relief that this book offered Gail, after seeing a brutal movie and while feeling assaulted by aloneness, is equivocal. It violated both romantic love and father-daughter closeness, and it represented the kind of security found in safe marriages.

6. Betty Hughes Melton was one of Gail's coworkers at the U.S. Travel Service. Her husband, Howard, was employed at the London School of Economics for a year. They were returning home to the States to begin their home life; the coziness of their relationship had tempted Gail at times.

to newspapering. I don't want to go garretting in New York like Lorraine. What I must do, then, is stick here with the writing for a little longer (after tax & rent I still have about £10 a week & let's not kid ourselves, I can live higher off the hog here than in the U.S.A.) I think— no, I *know*—that B. is wrong for me. He's underdeveloped in many aspects. He, for one, would *never* understand the writing. And he dreams big but lives small. So that knocks him out. I must be brutal about this so as not to waste any more time.

The new book is on a scale bigger than anything I've attempted.

I am tired of people who overwrite. I was among the most guilty in this department.

I keep thinking—there's something just around the corner I should remember.

Hot summer sun. June 18, 1955 . . . her eighteenth birthday. And it *was* being born again. All traces of the old life had been swept away. The view, the people, the sounds, the smells, even the air was different. She had petitioned in her dreams to be rescued by a stranger, to be given a new life, and her request had been granted. For now, it was enough to *be*. For once, instead of dredging up past experiences or dreaming up new ones, she was content with What Is. She studied his face, line by line, knowing he was aware of her doing it, expecting her to do so. She was extra-conscious of her aliveness, felt the blood flowing through her limbs, felt the sun drawing it up out of its dark winter layers, tingling up to the surface of her skin. She was getting a tan. She compared her own arm with his. It was already darker, with fine golden hairs to his dark ones. But the blood, flowing beneath the skin of both arms, was the same blood. Upon this revelation, she could draw imaginative sustenance for literally hours.

Ambrose—[7]

7. Some of the material about the daughter's rediscovery of her biological father made it into Godwin's short story "Old Lovegood Girls," included in the Ballantine Reader's Circle

Part II must be oh so carefully tailored. Lee is comparing the pictures of Ambrose and Ben. Ambrose suggests (this must be *conveyed, not stated*) a love of life, a sense of humor, devil-may-care generosity—then she recalls the last time she saw him before Christmas. This must be superbly done with all of Ambrose's goodness showing but at the same time a hint of what was to come.

Ambrose retained the place of honor on her tidy desk in full
view of her bed. His crooked smile was the last thing she saw
before she closed her eyes.[8]

Then we go to the next day. She is in class. A messenger comes. Somehow (and this must be brought across by a hint, something during their last meeting), she knows he did not die of natural causes.

"How did he die?" she asked, not because she herself didn't know,
she had already guessed the minute the teacher had called her
name, but because she wanted to make sure this girl *did not know.*

Then to her room, collapses. Mrs. Stikeleather comforts her in a rather macabre but satisfying way by dredging up memories of her late

edition, *Evenings at Five: A Novel and Five Stories* (2004). Regarding her rescue by a stranger, Godwin's eighteen-year-old narrator, Christina, says, "I was still panting hard from my close brush with downward mobility." She notes her stepfather's unsure job status, her mother's pregnancy with her second child by her new husband, and her own failure to enroll in a college. Christina's invitation to her graduation reaches her father at a fatefully receptive moment. "It struck him suddenly," she muses, "that I might be a credit to him." Later he says, "I'm glad I found you while you were still fresh and unspoiled by life." Their time spent on a beach, which occupies a substantial part of "Mourning," contributes only to an aside in "Old Lovegood Girls." In the aside, Christina tells how she had invented short stories for her English teacher, Fiona Petrie, in order to attract Miss Petrie to her father. In reaction to one story—about "a girl and her father lying on the beach, discussing how thankful they were to have been reunited"—Miss Petrie comments, "This moved me very much." The story concluded with the father murmuring, against the sound of the waves, "Now I feel I have something to be good for again."

8. Gail is composing her story by assembling vivid segments, capturing what she can on the fly. Of note is the way that Lee Bradshaw reveres her father before going to sleep. In *Violet Clay*, Godwin worked a major change in approach. Idolatry became the province of Ambrose's girlfriends, for whom he was the Byronic hero. The daughter figure, now the niece, strives to empathize with him—to live through him—rather than admire him at a distance. This powerful tendency is developed to the utmost extent in *Violet Clay* and comes to a head when Violet visits and then takes possession of her dead uncle's bungalow.

husband, almost forgetting herself at times. She returns beaming, gives her (from her own hidden resources in some well-hidden corner of the white bedroom) what is known in Southern drinking circles as a "double jigger" of Kentucky Gentleman. Some real good homegrown philosophy should come across here. Then Mrs. S. takes the liberty of calling Ben.

MARCH 6

The dentist is over with and my well-cared-for healthy American teeth have been given a clean bill of health.

Dinner with Doreen. (How she hammers the head off a subject. "But, back to Kipling, don't you think he was a superb representative of his time?" She is so careful, she is almost not real.) And Dorothea & her psychiatrist husband. In the first place, I don't see why she married him; but once she did, she had to be able to find some redeeming qualities. I was able to draw him out a little bit. He is shy, wants to be thought clever (oh, desperately), and is a real gentleman. Also has a gentle sense of irony. At least Dorothea & I agreed upon one thing: It's nice to have a man to go home with.

The book is getting difficult, but now I love doing it.

This weekend, finish chapter 1—

I wrote a synopsis of "Ambrose." What the story is about & what I propose to do. I have always hated these (I used to labor over my proposals on college term papers) but it does force you to look where you are going.

I have still not worked out all the "relevant elements" in Ambrose's background. And I think just a few touches on the mother will be sufficient. Also, Ben must be "done."

MARCH 10

SHIT—SHIT—SHIT . . . It is Sunday and I haven't scratched the surface. I am beginning to think that I am a trite person with trite ideas. My damnation is to consider myself & my ideas unique. There are about seventy million as "unique" as Gail Godwin Cole Kennedy. There is *so much*—always increasing itself. I cannot catch greased lightning. In front of me are Webster's *New Collegiate Dictionary* and *Roget's*. I haven't even glimpsed *their* possibilities.

Everything is sad & unreasonable & I can't talk to anyone. Everything I have even glimpsed has already been thought of a million times by everybody else.

Went to *La Dolce Vita*[9] by myself. I have found that when I can't write, it is more profitable to go out, raise hell, sink myself into humanity (like Alden[10] & the jazz club last night) or go to see a good film. This was, perhaps, the best I've ever seen. It wasn't so neatly packaged. There were lots of people. It successfully reproduced life in the living of it. It was highly individual, no type-casting, etc.

Again tonight, the helplessness of communication struck me. There was a very pensive, high-cheek-boned boy in a white raincoat who walked down the aisle & sat two rows in front of me. If I had been brave, I would have gone and changed my seat & sat beside him. But while I was deciding, someone else took the empty seat. And besides, do many people even notice who sits next to them in movies? I feel the quiet, mysterious tension that settles over me before I meet someone new. That's the best time of all: when I've just discovered someone & have his whole depth to explore. Not all promise a challenge at first. These did. Most of them wore off, but it was great while it lasted.

Is it lack of imagination? Do I, did I, after all, have a bloated dream of triumph? I want to let myself go, to let it all come pouring out, but it won't come.

· · ·

9. *La Dolce Vita*, Federico Fellini's landmark film, follows a journalist on a surreal journey through a depersonalized modern city—a kind of nightwalk or dreamwalk.

10. Alden James, a Canadian, was a medical student who had come to London for both studies and play. Gail, Robin Challis (a man whom Gail met at her office), and he sought each other out for solace and went on camping trips together.

After you have given up all hope, go on trying *without* hope. Sometimes it turns out you were taking yourself so seriously that it clogged your work up.

MARCH 15

It passes. I am written out with Ambrose. Stood with Henry for a full five minutes *perceiving* Piccadilly Circus. Saw (heard) & clapped *Black Nativity*.[11]

Prokofiev's piano concerto.

The nature of the malaise.

Edifying—is this all we can do? If so, my book cannot be squashed into any preconceived pattern. People must seek their own destinies, never consciously intruding upon the other's orbit.

Here is a man who has lived in a corner of a little farm community. His orbit has been N.C.—Fla.—N.C. Seasonally. He had a dream, even though he could not name it; was vaguely dissatisfied; wandered to the end of his life not knowing, or perhaps he did know, with awful certainty, & this was the reason he chose the quiet, dark ultimate No-Life rather than any form of life open to him.

1963 Royal Film Performance with James. Princess Margaret was there.
Tiberio's, a Romanesque supper club with catacomb ceiling, strumming, breathing jazz band & the kitchen in view behind a sheet of red glass.

James & the ghost of last summer. Steadfast James. At least he knows how to arrange a proper evening.

11. *Black Nativity* is a gospel play that was written by famed African-American poet Langston Hughes in 1961. It inspires hand-clapping to such songs as "This Little Light of Mine."

MARCH 21

And the first day of spring and nothing is good enough for "Ambrose."
I see now what a joy, hazard & continued labor good multilayered writing is. I finished the first part—fifteen thousand words—& when it is
retyped I will send it to Ursula Winant with a short note.[12] She can give
me criticism & that's what I need at this point.

Lately I have been visited routinely by the unnameable. The best I can
do is describe it as an almost-touching, a lack, an intimation, a pale, *pale*
illumination. I see that, in my pursuit, although I'll never completely
understand All of It, I am due to discover so much more.

The dreaded time when the Home Service goes off the air—my eyes
itch & it is time to go to bed & face the dark.

Ambrose, after a trip to Pine Bluff Alcoholic Sanitorium, fishing out his
pack of Luckies: "They said I was . . . wait a minute, I wrote it on this
pack of cigarettes. Here: psycho-neurotic with compulsion to drink."

MARCH 24

SUNDAY

The paralysis came back. The same nullifying one that laid me out at
twenty-two in the Robert Clay Hotel in Miami in 1959 so that I could
not even read a book, write a letter, or go down & swim in the pool with
Tennessee Williams in his bathing cap.[13] I do not know what one does to
set this right. I am a displaced person in a world full of displaced persons, some of whom recognize the fact. I've got to get straightened out.
New York newspaper strike is over. Gale warnings from Shannon. It got
so bad at about 1:00 today that I saw no alternative but to go for a "purposeful walk." Up Baker Street with good intentions & then I came un-

12. Winant is the literary agent who had taken an interest in Gail's work a month before,
when Gail had presented "Gull Key" to her. Preparing to send her "Mourning," Gail had
not been aware that Winant's father had, like Gail's own and like the character in the
story, committed suicide.

13. Tennessee Williams was staying at the hotel while *The Night of the Iguana* was playing
at the Coconut Grove Playhouse in 1959.

expectedly upon Mme. Tussaud's. Paid my 4s. & went the rounds, following the program. One guard scared the daylights out of me; stood very still until I went up and inspected him. Then he moved. I said Jesus Christ. He had a good chortle, evil man, & followed me out into the hall, where we talked as I came out of the Royalty room heading for the horror chamber. He was a foreigner with flashy teeth. "You must have a lot of fun with these people," I said. "Yes, I do," he agreed. Then I went over to the Kenco Coffee House on Marylebone High Street and had a ham & mushroom sandwich (I ordered ham & cheese but did not feel like making a fuss with the waitress) and a glass of Russian tea. The place was full of Sunday malaise. Scattered DPs[14] in ones and twos. There was a rather dissipated man in a drab green sweater that I would have liked to discuss dyspepsia with, the Sunday kind. We sat, facing our separate views, stealing discreet glances at each other. He got up first and paid his bill, looked back toward my corner as if weighing something, then went out the door where a girl in orange slacks washed her TR-3. Cutting back, I noticed a church & went inside. It was cavernous, with tiers of candles & a man's face staring at me from behind some candles.[15] It was more terrifying than Mme. Tussaud's. I came out into the sunlight quickly ("Masses Said in Spanish") and a plane droned overhead, jet engines cutting through a nice cumulus cloud. I thought of the afternoon worshipers coming outside, feeling suddenly uplifted in the fresh air, attributing it to their visit with God, the touching of match to candle. I came home & finished James Baldwin's novel,[16] eat-

14. Displaced persons.

15. In *The Perfectionists*, Dane Empson encounters a similar specter in a dark church in a very different context. On a resort island, Dane walks out on her husband, John, following a disturbing experience with his monstrous little son, and recalls the time she had walked out on him after having met his estranged mother. After a lonesome lunch, she takes refuge in a church, which reminds her of her non-churchgoing father and her mother's abandonment of him. She sits down in a pew, contemplating how her marriage has fallen short of the "Big Event" for which she'd longed. "Frowning hard into the incense-laden murk, she met a pair of wise black eyes staring back at her. She practically leaped out of her skin. It was an old priest, spying on her from behind a statue of the Virgin Mary. Momentarily, she expected him to whisk down the aisle and accuse her of something. But when he saw he'd been seen, he hurried away, a quick black wraith, into the restricted sanctity of the chancel."

16. James Baldwin's *Another Country* was a controversial book when it was published in 1962, drawing both extreme praise and condemnation, whereby Gail was alerted to its value. The title suggests another point of interest to her—the novel's concern with displaced people, including those wandering in a large city and those going overseas.

ing cookies, peanut butter sandwiches, dreading the time when the book would be finished. It was. Then I crawled into bed with the Sunday papers & three magazines & two books. Finally, I dozed into a swollen, terrifying sleep. All my thoughts & problems & visions appeared in the forms of neat rows of paperback books orderly arranged on the shelves—like the Bumpus bookstore on Baker Street. Woke in a state of near-faint, remembering Tussaud's eerie profession,[17] decrying my unfinished book.

Said Bruce Hogg,[18] taking my hand, "Look, may I take you out sometime?"

"Why?"

"What do you mean, why? Wouldn't you like to go to the theater with me?"

"What's the use to start all over again? Oh, yes. I'd like to go to the theater with you."

And tomorrow I'll wake, full of Monday-morning bravado because I have five days of forced labor. Then "Ambrose" will become incredibly dear.

On Saturday, there is much to
be done.
Supplies must be gotten in:
the milk, bread, and eggs
for the weekend;
and the sheets must be
changed.
There is probably even somewhere
to go.
Spinning along in a convertible;

17. Madame Tussaud's first wax figures—of Jean Jacques Rousseau, Voltaire, and Benjamin Franklin—were eerie enough with their arrested liveliness. In 1844, Tussaud added her museum's Chamber of Horrors, featuring French Revolution victims and serial-murder characters, achieving a level of unequalled ghoulishness.

18. Bruce Hogg, a British official, visited the travel office on business occasionally. Gail remembers him particularly for the phrase "I blotted my copybook."

drinks in someone's flat, listening
to Beethoven or some jazz.
The beat moves toward Saturday
night and is limned with
Possibility, the chance encounter—
quick, to the wine merchant.
He closes at six
even on Saturday.[19]

Sunday is a different story.
Sunday is a day of falling back on oneself.
Whoever made the day of worship a non-
Working day was no fool. We have no choice.
We will arise early, put on clean underwear
& sit in hot churches to be cleared of
part of the burden.
Then there are the walks,
the parks, for some.
There are afternoon concerts
& window shopping—only look, you can't
buy anything.
And there is the zoo.
And there are one hundred & forty-nine
cinemas in London.
There is something good at the Kilburn
Classic.
But where is Kilburn
& how does one get there?

If I had an underground map . . .
but it is too risky to walk to the
nearest underground.

---

19. The format of the lines replicates the handwritten entries in the journal.

It is too far & what if I change
my mind on the way, decide I do
not want to see the film in Kilburn?
Look once more through the newspapers.
Sunday victims, combing the
Newsprint for salvation?
I have a pound in my pocket. The door
key. Take my glasses, just in case
I should come across a film on my way
to somewhere.

There are many like me. Note the
long queues outside the cinemas
—even in the rain—
waiting to pay four & six for
two hours of alleviation.
Let me, then, emerge, start off down
the street in a false burst of faith,
spend two or three hours combing the
streets, parks & shop windows for a cure,
brush past my fellows—displaced persons—
seeing, perhaps, in one or two faces, qualities
that I will not be allowed to know.
Eyes meet, we wonder, but one does not
just go up to a stranger for any good
intention in this best of all possible
worlds.

Returning home & the sun has cooled
off. The threat of warm pavements &
blue skies & all the places you cannot
be at once is receding.
Soon it will be suppertime.
And then there are dishes to wash,

shoes to shine,
baths,
perhaps a little tidying,
and a bedtime paperback.
The malaise is fading fast.
The Home Service goes off the air.
Tomorrow is planned for us, dull as it
may be.

What, then, is the best way of making do?
I am always aware that my days are
numbered. I am always measuring the
quicksilver. Surely, there must be
others like me. Why can't we touch?

I must keep on being light & wide-eyed,
a little kooky, not too much of one thing
or the other.
Am I at home or in exile?
Would I give up all of my wild scratchings
to find a real peace,
to touch another real person?
YES.
But, even as I write this, I know
there is no danger in my decision.
There will never be a real peace,
only false moments.
I will never know another being intimately,
maybe his body, his bookshelves, the
role he has chosen to play for me,
but never him.

So on and on
on and on and on,
scratching and intimating, expounding

& philosophizing, digging & rending.
It is a little diabolic, the thought of it
(the treadmill in Mme. T.'s horror chamber).
But it is all I have and I cling to
the reality of these forty or fifty more
years with a ferocity bordering on insanity.

Fantasies. Coming across a small
bookstore that hadn't been there
before. Walking alone at night
in a strange city with the smell
of the sea. Seeing a face, touching
at first and not being disappointed.
Yet all this happened. It was
not fantasy.

Ah, what now?
I have a feeling of being not here & not there.
Where are all my wonderful people that I
dream about?
What happened to Blowing Rock? Chapel
Hill in the spring? And certain days in
Copenhagen before Niels wore off. And in
Las Palmas.

Now Nat King Cole brings back Ambrose.
I think I shall have Tina say:
"Whenever you're on a dance floor, stay all
by yourself. That's the way to get boys
to ask you to dance."
Part 1: the funeral . . . flashback . . . after the funeral.
What am I going to do with Ben?

The Raleigh program: John Barbour,
"Dancing in the Dark"—

"And the cares that infest the day
Will fold their tents like Arabs
& silently steal away . . ."[20]

The whole teenage world—
late-night necking sessions when
your date tastes of cheeseburger, down by
the lake, groping, caring, loving to
the tune of some sad song by Johnny
Mathis or Nat King Cole.

It's just my book & it doesn't
have to have the problems
of the whole world in it.

---

20. "Dancing in the Dark," a 1941 song by Arthur Schwartz and Howard Dietz, was a favorite of swing bandleader Artie Shaw, and was featured in the film musical *The Band Wagon* (1953), which starred Fred Astaire and Cyd Charisse. The "fold their tents" quote is from Henry Wadsworth Longfellow's poem "The Day Is Done," which also contains the lines:

I see the lights of the village
Gleam through the rain and the mist,
And a feeling of sadness comes o'er me
That my soul cannot resist.

Gail is assembling pieces that evoke her subject and that complement, as it turns out, her experience of a nightwalk.

RESOLUTION

Green Street and back to Old Church Street

MARCH 26–JUNE 22, 1963

On April 17, Doreen, Gail's supervisor and sometimes confidante, questions Gail's integrity. It seems Gail's writer's distance—or is it something else, her need to conform at times?—has disturbed Doreen, who has her own self-images to tender.

Gail treats Doreen's question seriously. First, it's a matter of terminology. What is "integrity"? In her journal, Gail affirms that integrity does not mean one-dimensionality. On May 17 she writes, "One must learn how to measure his own dimensions," and then considers the way that people with a lot of integrity (perhaps because of one-dimensionality) subvert her sense of her self.

It's a natural defense. Gail knows her own goodness. ("In spite of people like Doreen, etc., I believe that I am potentially and innately a good person," she writes on June 22, at the beginning of the next journal part.) People with a striking semblance of integrity may be presenting only a dramatic mask, usually intimidating to a person who considers the human personality an uneasy hybrid.

Robin Challis, a good pal, comes into full flower in this journal part. Fearful of both failure and success, he puts his angst on display, dressed as generosity of spirit. When this admirable quality brings him no return, he grows sour. He is the perfect character for a journal part that dwells on integrity and that needs to present a foil to Gail's new leading man, Gordon.

"I met another one at the party in Lee's Court," Gail jots down on April 7, referring to her latest Mr. Right, at-ease-in-the-world Gordon. Signing off in her journal that night, she wails, "Oh God, I can't stand it. Another god to build up in the absence of anything better to do."

Among the contending selves that Gail directs within herself, two major ones were the woman looking for the man to offer her security, love, and intellectual stimulation (a god), and the writer answering to a calling (God). Many times, the answer seemed to be getting both at once.

In this journal part, though Gordon remains a strong presence, we see the shift toward the lonely calling. Eventually, with the help of a letter sent her by her former priest in Asheville—Father Gale Webbe—she looks ahead to what Webbe calls her "vision."

"You forsake your vision at the peril of your soul," Father Webbe wrote.

The sacrifice in choosing "the search" involves not only making romance and marriage lower priorities, but also splitting one's personality further—into one self that engages passionately with life and another that observes it dispassionately. What is missing in Doreen's view of Gail's integrity is knowledge of her destiny as a writer, since the duality of experience and analysis is integral to being a writer.

The results of Gail's clarity and resolution follow immediately. By the second half of this journal part, Gail Godwin is recording more stories— pure documentation of the life around her—than she had previously. The culmination is the story about the Wests' emblematic pet turtle, Mr. Bedford, which, we know, will inspire and supply her classic novella about her London boardinghouse experience.

[NO DATE]

Fallacies of relevance:

- Their premises are logically irrelevant to their conclusions, therefore incapable of establishing the truth of those conclusions.

- They may be psychologically relevant, evoking attitudes, fear, pity, reverence, disapproval, enthusiasm.

MARCH 26, 1963

I hit bottom again. Anyway, the result was to feel that there was *nothing* at all to continue for—yet to be apathetic about doing anything about ending existence. I am the type that will never commit suicide.[1]

I *need* resolutions to keep me from becoming all squishy.

No alcohol.

Be cool to Doreen.

Get finances worked out the best possible.

Do all the unpleasant things that need being done & I have been putting off.

A temporary regaining of faith. "Ambrose" is worth it. Now do the entire background up to the present—then the funeral—then bring Ben back in just long enough to show that life goes on.

Ben wanted to make her into an image.

"I guess I'm not your Pygmalion."

---

1. Godwin keenly illustrates her interest in and invulnerability to suicide in *Violet Clay*. Violet scares and angers a neighbor who sees her put Uncle Ambrose's gun to her head in an apparent reenactment. Yet the gun was not loaded, and Violet was attempting to understand her uncle. Understanding suicide saves the heroine from feeling suicidal.

MARCH 29

Friday—uninspired. I must wait. I have had an intimation. Loss of faith in some higher being, in some ultimate unifying purpose → loss of faith in oneself → loss of oneself.

I told Jim Jensen[2] in the pub last night: "You will leave to go to your lecture. I will panic. Then I'll walk home & gradually recover pieces of myself. Then I'll get home & crawl in bed, unable to do anything. Then the next morning, I'll wake up & curse myself for not doing anything. I'll get up, full of resolution, thinking it very likely that I will do everything I failed to do last evening *this* evening."

I can't see where I'm going now. But I must go on because there's nowhere else to go.

MARCH 31

—3:10 a.m., now that summer time is on & the time moves one hour ahead. Soon it will be morning, with eggs, coffee, and the newspapers. I went to see *A Taste of Honey*. Walked out of *Oklahoma*. It was just too canned. I kept looking at the ceiling, thinking of Marty.[3] I really loved him. I can't think of anyone I have ever loved like that. It's all in the time and place.

The kinks have come out of "Ambrose" miraculously. I thought I hadn't done any work, but I counted the sheets of yellow paper & *somebody* did six thousand words while I was in despair.

> THIS IS A DIFFICULT BOOK
> BECAUSE ALL THE CHARACTERS ARE
> THEMSELVES—OR TRYING TO BE

It works itself out in the telling.

2. Jensen was a serious writer and lecturer. See the February 16, 1963, entry.

3. Marty was a man whom Gail had known in Miami.

SCENE: a pub.[4] Like the Barley Mow.[5] Music playing in the background. A fireplace. Copper pots hanging from rafters.

CHARACTERS: the barman, other pub characters, a girl, a boy.

> 60 minutes
> Act I (30 minutes)
> The inside monologue
> Act II (30 minutes)
> The outside monologue

In the first act, the characters talk but they say only what they *think*—thus the dialogue sometimes appears to be nothing but a crisscross. However, from their actions (he takes her hand, etc.), you are aware of a conventional progression.

In the second act, the characters talk—the way people usually talk.

—just write it—

As the characters get drunker, the lighting changes.
The music takes on a different effect.
The play will have to be written backwards—that is, the conventional first.
There are other characters who add to the picture. They behave exactly the same in both acts.

APRIL 3

Ruislip[6] medical ordeal undergone (my legs ache as well as my sinuses). The story of Griffith & the drab life unfolds.[7] "Listen . . . tell me, have

4. Gail is sketching out a script that she and Dorothea, the new girl at work, were writing for a BBC production.

5. The Barley Mow is the pub at which Gail had come to know James (Dmitri) Jensen. See the February 16, 1963, entry.

6. Ruislip, a U.S. Air Force base outside of London, was where U.S. government personnel had been required to undergo regular physicals.

7. Griffith, an English psychiatrist, was Dorothea's husband.

you ever felt this?" Hate organization-land more every day. "Now if you'll just go down that corridor." Met a physicist in the office & engineered it so we went to *The Physicists* by Dürrenmatt.[8] He was a good boy. Nice to talk *into* someone for a change instead of *at*. The money problem is critical as hell, but I will not despair. I can live in less luxurious surroundings for a while. It's been a long time since I've ached like this.

APRIL 7

It seems that there are more & more mornings when I wake up with a hangover. And not only that: I met another one at the party in Lee's Court.[9] We did so much talking & I remember so little of it due to my usual tippling. I know his name is Gordon & his great-uncle started Wrigley's Spearmint gum. His father lives in Trinidad, his mother in Scotland. He is a research engineer for a spark plug manufacturer. At the beginning he said, "You're very interesting to talk to," & then I got sidetracked. Finally, we circled the same orbit again & I made a statement about going. He said, "You're not leaving, are you?" And I said, "No, not yet. Let's dance." It was present with us. I can still feel his back through his shirt. Then I got dizzy (*sometime* during the evening he said, "This is very nice," or something to that effect). We stood in a window & discussed camping outdoors. Then I had to go. He took me home & gave me Alka-Seltzer & coffee, which he boiled on the stove. Then we sat on the bed, me leaning back in his arms, & talked. I can't remember this either. He is twenty-five (*twenty-eight*).[10] I told him I was & he said, "Oh, good." I don't know why. His best friend married yesterday & from

8. *The Physicists* was a new play by the nihilist Swiss dramatist Friedrich Dürrenmatt. Dürrenmatt, as a youth, had rejected the orthodoxy of his father, a pastor, and the bourgeois mediocrity of his hometown, Bern. The world of professional art, which he'd hoped to enter, rejected him and his fantastical illustrations. He immersed himself in philosophical studies and wrote stories, including "The Torturer," in which God is the protagonist. At age twenty-six, in 1947, he wrote his first two plays to be produced on stage. They were greeted with audience jeers and critical acclaim. In *The Physicists*, Dürrenmatt turned his attention to the Cold War and nuclear arms. In his worldview, accidents and human nature lead to the worst possible outcomes, and no story is complete until it takes that final step.

9. Lee's Court is an address in Mayfair, near the U.S. Embassy.

10. Gail initially thought Gordon was twenty-five, later learned he was twenty-eight and emended her journal.

what he says, he himself is looking around. Is it because of my present black mood or am I entangled again? He left at two, saying, "Are you on the phone?" And I said no. My office is at USTS, but you'd forget anyway. And he said, "I guess you're right." And that's that.

What he had: an inner calm. An outer calm. Alive eyes. Perception. Height & manliness.

Five hours of the *St. Matthew Passion*. I got to where I dreaded the italics—that meant the verse was sung twice, thrice, etc. Stella in top form pursuing her vision. I think I resent it because she'd kept Lenten resolution re alcohol. I have failed miserably in both of mine. So now I wait for the unknowable, scribbling away in this journal to keep myself under control. What to do for five days & four nights with Henry in Paris?[11] If only he were more adventurous, would not think himself so sound. How sick I am of this monastic life. *Why* can't I learn to live alone & like it? To exist in my own resources, extend my own extensions. But I keep reaching for— Maybe it is because I am a woman & it will always be this way. I have changed my mind fifty-six times about this flat. Some of the things I've seen are so horrible.

Is it the spring?
Is it my black mood
snatching at anything?
It's happened before.
Why do I have to like men so much?
Why can't I take them or leave them?

Oh God, I can't stand it. Another god to build up in the absence of anything better to do.[12]

11. Henry is the intellectually secure music-lover whom Gail had met in January. See the January 20, 1963, entry, in which the anticipated Paris trip bears the wry postscript "ha, ha."

12. After an "Oh God" with a capital *G*, Gail clearly refers to a lowercase god. The building up she has to do is the work of someone who idealizes or fashions her man.

APRIL 9

Here are the things I must do to respect myself:

1. Go to Paris & be nice to Henry. Enjoy it to the fullest. It is not everyone who goes to Paris for Easter. Don't mope or wish for impossibilities.

2. Write a six-thousand-word story entitled "Rush" for *Mademoiselle*.[13] This must be carried through in order to respect my writing & also give a sample of what can be done.

The Southrons came by with their Square Deal. Maxim for future use: Human beings usually respond to other Human beings. So I'm going to Paris & am not broke. Stuart, who is a psychopath, in a way, came by with a frantic tale of woe: his girl besieged by dirty notes (which I'll bet she wrote herself).

Last night, I dreamed of Antonio & a beach somewhere. "You're just a little dreamer," he said. Then he kept changing into other people.

YES. I am hot on the search. That is the triumph. To be hot on the search. To be on the way. I am not sure that this isn't more important than the realization of the goal—which may be impossible. I must learn to be more tolerant of the people around me. Sometimes I feel that I do radiate an aliveness that other people catch & appreciate.

Funny enough. I believe I am "in alleviation," a new term, but a good one. Nothing immediate is that pressing. "Music at Midnight"[14] in Europe & I am very awake. One indication of the degree of the sickness

---

13. "Rush" was a story about a young woman, Janie Lewis, who transfers from a junior college to a university, only to find herself both attracted to and repelled by the elite clubbishness there. Fifteen years later, Gail's rewrite of the story, retitled "The Angry Year," secured publication in *McCall's*. "I went to sorority parties as a rushee," Janie says at the outset, harking back to the earlier title. Gail's new title highlighted the connection between the character's rebellious nature and the spirit of the times. "There were new things . . . to be angry about," she reveals at one point. "The sixties were coming." Ultimately, the protagonist realizes that her anger was also directed at her conformist self.

14. "Music at Midnight" was a program aired on BBC.

is how much sleep I need. Ah, the notes are clear and astringent. *I feel my soul pumping energy from somewhere.* Kierkegaard had a point. To believe, to hope, to have faith in something not yet revealed is not fruitless. I see a network of night watches such as these. I am completely at peace with myself at these times. Not last night when I lay, hot and tumbly in my bed, thinking, What am I but a blob of flesh writhing in the sheets? I know, somehow, although I can't be articulate, who I am. I have faith in my being, I believe in my being, I hope. I must take this unnameable on credit. It is the best I know at present and I believe that a person should be true to the best he knows at that moment.

APRÈS EASTER [APRIL 16]

The comfort of canned music on the "light programme"; a hamburger ("beefburger," she said) in the West London Air Terminal—anything to put off going home. Paris was a huge disappointment. If I had gone there first I would have been tempted to return home. I look forward to tomorrow—an ordinary day of work, full of no fears.

Thoughts over Easter While Hating Henry & Paris:

- If you find yourself losing yourself, or, as "they" put it, approaching a nervous breakdown, make a show of going through the motions both to yourself & to others. Incidentally, I think this is the essence of faith: going through the motions until a glimmer comes.

- Theme from *Romeo & Juliet*[15]—brings back *Romeo & Juliet*—fall of 1958—thinking of Marty, taking it out on Ronnie.[16] Music—*there* is something of the eternal faith. This cannot be all.

- And this faith—it is slippery. You cannot hold it tight. Just go along.

15. Tchaikovsky's fantasy-overture *Romeo and Juliet* uses variations on just a few haunting themes to create drama and pathos, combining the Russian interest in expressive melody with the Western European one in overall design.

16. Ronnie was the Chapel Hill friend who had taken care of Gail's dog when the dean of women evicted the animal from Gail's dorm.

A resolution: Since it seems that these depressions are induced or at least intensified in certain situations, it might be well to stay out of them. One—is the company of certain people. We shall call them "dangerous people" in that they are almost there; they make a good plug for their product; they keep to a straight, well-defined course; they are sure of themselves, their surroundings; they know (think they know) exactly where they are going and what they are to find when they get there. The thing here is to remember no one has ever returned to tell, to verify his expectations. Two—is the lack of concentrated mental effort on something other than myself. This may be writing, or even doing my job as creatively as possible, which I have not been doing. Three—is the lack of physical exercise. This is also bound up in my *will.* I must get up & walk to work. I must play tennis with Dorothea—or something. Walks on Hampstead Heath on Sundays. Anything physical. If I see Gordon again I will ask him to take me camping. The *air* is a good panacea for malaise. Also the sun. Steaks and salad—music. Mental, creative accomplishments.

APRIL 17

THURSDAY

Met Conrad Hilton, went to one of a thousand parties for travel agents, had dinner with the Wests & became regrounded—at least temporarily.[17] The wonder of it all—spinning around Hyde Park in a taxi at 11:00 p.m. Pink skies with the new twenty-seven-story Hilton as part of the blend of old and new.[18] Also met Richard Joseph, travel writer for

---

17. In "Mr. Bedford," Godwin alters actual events substantially to design her drama. The dinner with the Wests, characterized here as a regrounding, does not serve that function in the fictional account. Instead Carrie, the narrator, connects with Mrs. Easton over a beer after Mrs. Easton has tracked her down at the Travel Office. The confidences shared lead Carrie to reflect, "I am still far from 'figuring out' the Eastons." In the fiction, Carrie is loveless and meets a romantic man at a party the night before she goes over to the Eastons' house—in other words, much later than in Godwin's actual life. The concurrence produces in her the feeling of "achieving a true relationship to time." Carrie's fate turns out to be a subtle one—a revelation about the Eastons that enables her to translate life into literature. As a salute to this understanding, Godwin has Carrie lose the manuscript of her precious novel—not the Ambrose story Gail had actually been working on at the time, but a story about a failed marriage in the Florida Keys. Goodbye, "Gull Key"; hello, more evolved self.

18. Conrad Hilton's new hotel in London was an act of evangelism, spreading the gospel of American materialism and security to a world consumed with Cold War bad news. The

Esquire.[19] He wore a salt & pepper beard & had a cute story to tell. Andrew & I give our party next Friday. I have invited the girls connected with Gordon. *Will he come?* If so, will I still like him? My hands still ache when I remember the feel of his shirt. *The summer is coming.* I will write the novel, a novel per summer. I must leave here soon. Find another abode. Mr. Miller asks daily. I say: Consider the lilies of the field—

Last night sitting in the Thistle[20] with Doreen, I let myself get trapped into listening to her tirade on *integrity.* Everybody seems to have *it* but me. I left feeling dejected because it might be thought that I did not have integrity by one Doreen W. But then I began thinking: What is *integrity?* Does she know the meaning of word?

INTEGRITY

State or quality of being complete, undivided, or unbroken.

I am a long way from that, but no one's opinion on how *far* along the way will take me any more or less far—

APRIL 19

SATURDAY

Something about the dignity of feeling love for other people is there in those three color photographs from home. Monie's hand on my sleeve. The incredible roundness & youthfulness of my mother's face. The Horla[21] is passing again. I am reading *Pride and Prejudice.* Longing again for *principles.* Illustration of the lack of them: Stuart dumping my garbage downstairs in the basement. It makes you nauseated when

London Hilton, at a height of 405 feet, became, in 1963, the tallest building in the city, outreaching St. Paul's Cathedral and overlooking Buckingham Palace.

19. Richard Joseph was a well-known author of books and syndicated columns on travel as well as an *Esquire* editor. In Gail's office, he was a celebrity.

20. The Thistle was a cozy pub located at the corner of Sackville and Vigo Streets, next door to the U.S. Travel Service.

21. In the Guy de Maupassant horror tale "The Horla," a madman comes to believe that an invisible demon is tormenting him and that the specter will expand his influence to take over mankind.

someone betrays himself like this. So I think the main thing is for me to develop my stick-to-it-ive-ness, as Father Liston[22] used to say.

Something to explore in story form sometime: the peculiar quality people like Doreen have for draining people like me of all their definiteness. Picking, picking. Don't you find that . . . ? Do you think? Isn't that interesting? *Gail* liked the play very much whereas *you* found it rather a failure.

Qualities I can't quite put my finger on: Doreen's almost parasitic good humor. Henry's self-satisfaction in things like always crossing the street with the traffic light. ("In *my* opinion, I'm just not in that big of a hurry.")

APRIL 23
TUESDAY
Very few writers treat writing (as Mr. Eliot does) as an instrument for living, not as an aim in itself.

G. called. It was as simple as that—I have twenty-four hours to get through. This is the best time. When you are just meeting someone new. (You learn with each one, learn to give yourself away less. I don't know if that's bad or good.) One thing I know: I cannot make any other person like me more intensely than they do . . . The only times I really *touch* earth is when I listen to a certain type of music or when I am just beginning a new romance. Oh God, wouldn't it be awful if he doesn't last one time—if before the evening's over I am dying to get back to my little room & surround myself with books & nightmares.

APRIL 24
WEDNESDAY
This evening there was a cool white haze over London. Before Gordon came, I walked to Grosvenor Square and sat in front of FDR's cloaked

22. Father Liston was the resident priest at St. Genevieve-of-the-Pines.

statue and was conscious of my own well-being. This, I think, is a kind of praying. All the best that was in me was unified with the traffic around me. Today was a day of communication. A healthy eager-to-meet-the-world type named Robin Challis came in to see Mr. Miller & a look was exchanged & he took me to lunch. Dorothea & Doreen asked me what I did to "convey" myself to men. ("It's something I wish I had. You say things to them I wouldn't dare say.")

Gordon. We start down the dusty trail. Only this time . . . or did I say that before? Gordon sits and watches or stands and watches. He says things to people that they expect him to say. He puffs on his pipe. He has a large, pure, sculptured face and a sensitive, generous mouth. He puts metals together in a laboratory for a living ("They pay me once in a while") and sails & camps. He owns a cottage, which he rents. He wants to fix himself so that he has a ceramics plant, a restaurant & can write. Is not this craving to write simply a crying need to communicate?! I told Gordon how I'd watched him all evening talking to the South African couple, yet never really entering into them. He said, "You're the only one of my friends that notices. I was afraid you'd think: What a nasty social bore. But you do see things."

He kept saying, "I like the way you get around & live in different countries." The queers upstairs were flooding the bathtub & the deluge outside my window broke the tension.

I said, "Yes, you like me & I like you, but give us two more go-rounds & we'll be finding flaws."

"Ah, no, don't say that. That's horrible." And then: "Give me a tinkle."

I explained I didn't "call men."

"But you're not calling them to ask them to marry you." (He blushes here.) "After all, I feel the same way about calling you." So he takes down my number.

APRIL 27

Crosscurrents & adjoining doors—so much done, said, & thought by connecting human beings & it all has relevance if I can only fit it in.

Keynotes to the discovery of G.: Score one point for the conversation while dancing (at last, after being a good hostess for hours—all of which he noticed). "Do you drive to work every morning?" "Yes." "I'll bet you do a lot of thinking on those drives." He looked as if I'd caught him naked and clasped me to him and said, "Shut up. You make me talk too much."

Doreen on the subject of G.: "Gail, now is the time to remember everything you learned in Sunday school." She likes him. They danced together much of the evening. What I think he does is insert himself painlessly into any number of roles to accommodate as many people as possible while keeping himself apart & untouched & uninfluenced. I must beware of complimenting him too much. He thought I was insincere at the beginning, I think. Numela[23] came with Andrew & went home with David, G.'s roommate—a very blond, David-like type, slightly aware of his blessings in the looks department. This morning, David called at 21 Old Church Street to pick up £2 Numela had given Andrew for safekeeping. Andrew was magnificently composed, wrote her a short note itemizing the money he had spent on her during the evening while she was his date. Taxis, dinner & cigarettes came to £2. Said David, respectfully, "Oh, I never would have thought of that."

Temporary alleviation arrives in the pleasant springtime form of lacquer & bath salts, new clothes and a new man to explore.

Warning signals about G., so I can play "I told you so" with myself later:

1. The way he liked Alden for his quaint Americanisms. "I snuck up the aisle." Said: "He's just the type we want." It smacked of something that has displeased me before.

2. When he was tight: "Get tight, woman, so I can take you to bed." And he actually asked me to come back to his flat before my party was over.

23. Andrew had been dating Numela since as early as September 27, 1962.

3.   I don't know if this is good or bad. It is a trait that points either
to sluggishness or to sublime indifference. The way he stands
against a wall, making himself part of the wall. The way he
tells a story—slow, unhurried, pausing, not at all concerned
whether anyone is listening or not. Doreen, whose summations
of people have been known to be grossly wrong, said, "He's
thought about you a lot." At the moment, I think I know what
he feels: I am a novelty to be with. I have all sorts of potential-
ities, but he's not sure which ones relate to him.

His conversation is meaningful—*or is it just the slow, unconcerned
manner in which he speaks?*

His style is not my favorite. James's, I think, came nearer the mark.
It was a studied one, but permitted because I do not hold it against someone for wanting to make their envelope as easy to read as possible. James's
Chelsea boots of brown suede, pipe-stem trousers, car coats & plaid weave
suits presented James to the world as James saw himself. And he knew
how to make the most of it. G., on the other hand, wears atrociously fit-
ting casual clothes, the seat of his pants is baggy, his socks are off-shades
of green, and his leather shoes of that mud color that ruins any suit.

To be remembered: While in "alleviation," keep on friendly, intimate terms with yourself, so that when the other period returns, you
will not have the discomfort of getting acquainted all over again.

Tonight we embark on Round 3. Will it dim or brighten?

That's the way it was—before the beginning last night, I projected
myself into the end. It seemed so awful that, as I sat on the bed in my
green dress, waiting for the doorbell to start the motions again, I had a
fleeting despair: Why do anything at all if it is already over before
you've begun? But this is the mystery of the time cycle. T. S. Eliot is trying to express it.[24] God, how incredibly gentle this mutual probing is.

---

24. Gail is referring to T. S. Eliot's *Four Quartets*, an expository poem about timelessness
and art.

Except for the moments when we sat on the floor getting tight & shooting darts at each other's vulnerabilities.

Gordon & me by the Thames: "London's bridges are good, aren't they?" A chorus of "Onward Christian Soldiers" throbbing over the shortwave radio. This is another type of alleviation.

The bridge. The black waters. Gordon talking, a hand on my shoulder. He said, "I've never been as happy as I am now." "We deserve it," I said. "Yes, you're right." The lights. The Thames has always held a fascination for me. Last fall, I walked there at night alone or with James and suspended time for a moment at least.

Then we came back here, went through the pretexts, making coffee. (How many romances have been forwarded by the excuses of coffee? "Let's have a cup." "Stay for a cup." "Come in for a cup," etc.) I told him some more about Copenhagen & about my trip to Berlin and writing in my journal about the horrible Hansen boy[25] while he was in the same room in the other bed.

APRIL 30

Here I am with tried-and-true company: the radio (Chopin). A glass of Rémy Martin (so smooth it slides down your throat) and aids to the next plateau: T. S. Eliot & a book called *The Outsider*.[26] I have fed Alden a mushroom omelet and sent him off to Jill,[27] secure in the knowledge he'd rather have stayed with me. A man from the London County Council Architects came in to see us today, has invited us over to inspect the human models, quiet chaps from MIT, & go sailing, etc. He retires next year & sculpts again. He is good. We are all trying to say something. I was just thinking: I'd rather spend an hour with a man of sixty-five who

---

25. The Hansen boy had shared a room in a hostel with Gail and had tried continually to sponge off of her.

26. *The Outsider* was the title of the English edition of Albert Camus's *L'Étranger*, translated as *The Stranger* in the American edition.

27. Jill was the friend who had gone with Gail to Paris in October 1962. (See the footnote for the October 31, 1962, entry, and also see May 7 in this journal part.)

has been hot on the search than six weeks with a man my own age who is navel-gazing.

> *There is a time for the evening under the starlight . . .*
> *(The evening with the photograph album).*
> *Love is most nearly itself*
> *When here and now cease to matter.*[28]

This, for some reason, is comforting.

Also the lesson B. taught me: "When you love someone you should have enough confidence in them to know that whatever they are doing, they should be doing. That is, if they are worthy of confidence."

Eliot: "For us, there is only the trying. The rest is not our business."[29]

MAY 1

I am fed up. But at least I have reached the point where I know it is only part of the cycle. I have only to flip back through the pages for proof of the ups & downs, in and outs.

Robin came by in his white raincoat. There is definitely something in an uncomplicated soul with a *buena cara.* "If I ever have children, I shall teach them not to think."

Dorothea & I discussed Gordon & the ways of men. They compartmentalize their lies so logically. The central thread of work is flanked by women, sports, and, *perhaps* some intellectual pursuit—unless that is included in the work they do. So my Gordon drives to Putney, invents his little ceramics, drives home in the still of the afternoon, sails, reads, plays baseball, eats or cooks in the little community circle (depending on whether or not it's his week), then retires to read or lets himself be pursued by some girl. Or—who knows what he does or thinks.

Had three gins with the sleepy-eyed man from Washington. Some

28. From T. S. Eliot's *Four Quartets,* "East Coker," section 5, stanza 2, lines 8–12.
29. T. S. Eliot, *Four Quartets,* "Burnt Norton," section 5, stanza 1, line 18.

people are perfectly genuine but there's just not enough of them—of their nature, I mean.

I said: "Dorothea, what do you do when a man doesn't call?"

"I have hysterics, I go back over what I have said, I know it is ended, & I am in hell."

MAY 5

SUNDAY

The retreat at Peace College—the fine preacher—take a problem to him—no communication. "His name was the Reverend Michael Briggs and he had come all the way from Edinburgh, Scotland, to lead the spring retreat at Juniper College."[30]

MAY 6

"Gee, it's hard to do away with these Sundays." Two full days in anybody's company is too much. Alden & Robin got along so well they didn't miss my contribution. With tales of the Yukon & good men's talk (Robin gave Alden a pipe), I was content to sit and watch. Sitting in one of Robin's big overstuffed chairs, listening to de Falla[31] & watching them, blond heads bent, facial construction so different, I loved both of them. Robin is more than a body, after all, & I wish he weren't. He writes & writes a lot. It is unpolished, but has something. Said Robin: "I could, or can, straighten you out." He's a saint, says Alden.

MAY 7

Even rewriting two pages of "Ambrose" gets me back on the track. Dinner with Jill. She was in the Royal Ballet & had her appendix out & suddenly got fat & depressed. (She tells it with great guffaws. She does give good value for an evening.) Robin crucified himself last night & this

---

30. This story would find published form, as "An Intermediate Stop," in *North American Review*. Gail finished the first draft of it on March 18, 1965, calling it "The Illumined Moment—and Consequences."

31. With Alden and Robin, Gail is listening to *The Three-Cornered Hat*, a ballet created by Manuel de Falla at the urging of Sergey Diaghilev and staged in 1919 with sets by Pablo Picasso. Even in 1963, it would be considered exotic with its takes on the fandango, seguidilla, and Gypsy *jota;* and with its combination of fanfare, melody, sound effects, classical allusions, and French impressionism.

morning.[32] Dorothea sums people up too well. "He's not integrated. He makes me feel unquiet." How we take everything to pieces.

MAY 8

Said Jim Jensen in his never-hackneyed, pleasantly pedantic English: "Even if you get 98 percent of the way with someone, there's always the other 2 percent. And if he's so good, then you can get up to 98 percent contact. The corollary is usually that the 2 percent is an extremely vital part." He has a good lectureship at McGill University next fall. Of all the people I know, he certainly rates among the most perceptive and the most tender—once you get through his protective coating. Alden & Robin, blond & alive, came in "to have an audience" about their sour party. ("The Sour Hour," Alden says.) Robin has bundled up his entire typewritten soul & handed it to me in a folder to read and tell him what I "really think." The mistakes he makes make me tired because I can remember when I made them & how oblivious I was to them; thus they make me wonder just how bad are the ones I'm making now.

MAY 12

Mother's Day, and no red rose for me. But I carry one mentally anyway. This brings me around to thinking about my mother. She did what I think is the right thing. It looks as if we (meaning women) have a choice: free woman or man's woman. I do not hesitate. I know the beginning of that long road—Sunday afternoons with tea and walks and the papers and a good book. The stylish clothes, the carton of eggs bought at the last possible minute after no one has asked you out to dinner. I do not want to be like Marie A.,[33] like Doreen, like all those women who deny the Big Threat. As yet, I don't know how to resolve the problems of the second way: that of with one man. There are the temptations of other men with their other ways. I love a change. And there are the times when he is away or alone willingly in his own growth.

32. Robin had engaged in a bout of drinking in the basement bar of the American Embassy along with Gail, Alden, and Dorothea. Gail reflects, "Nobody was at their best, but Robin got particularly sour and earned Dorothea's harsh comment, 'He makes me feel unquiet.' "

33. Marie Anderson was the women's page editor at the *Miami Herald.* She and Gail corresponded about "bachelorhood vs. commitment" while Gail was in London.

I don't like limited people, small tight people. I don't want to be a cynic or a career woman. If I ever get my writing will back, I know what I want to write. I want to extract the moments in life when man behaves like the human being he is supposed to be; when people make the whole business better for one another—like the moment when Boo Radley emerges in *To Kill a Mockingbird*. The moment in *Anna Karenina* with Kitty and her father, & in *Lear* when Cordelia awakens her father, & in *Zooey* when Zooey tries to reach Franny.

I am tired of cold, determined, calculated people who make it a code to appear disdainful & sophisticated. (All overused words. They have lost their meaning; they convey too much & nothing at all.)

Later in this interminable Sunday. I am in a kind of limbo where even newspapers & eggs leave me cold. I am depressed with the thought of going back to 21 Old Church Street, yet it seems practical and I still enjoy the Wests. "You must always make your choice & pay the price"— Frank Cole. What frustrates me is that I've thrown away £60 several times over. But it will not be this monk's cell, this absolute retreat from the world where I can do as I damn please.

According to statistics, I should be remarried by June.[34] I don't see the slightest possibility of such a thing. My own determination scares me because I know just what I'm capable of. Yet, reading Doris Lessing's *The Golden Notebook*,[35] I shivered and vowed, "I promise myself to marry as soon as possible." Anything is better than the life of the lonely girl.

MAY 13

All of life is a series of shifts—of infallibility to utter helplessness; elation to depression; creativity to apathy. Finished Doris Lessing's *Golden Notebook*. It is supposed to describe "the sickness of our times, the prob-

34. A magazine article stated that if women didn't remarry within their first three years after a divorce, statistically their chances of remarriage declined greatly.

35. *The Golden Notebook*, published in 1962, was Doris Lessing's thirteenth book in as many years. Lessing chose to represent a woman with writer's block, and one who uses writing to achieve wholeness; yet the overall tone is disappointing, for wholeness involves an adaptation to an ordinary and lonely life.

lems of living in the modern world." But when you finish, you feel let down. Here is this woman who has done & seen so much & who writes so well, but she has let you down. Or am I being an ostrich? A "romanticist"? No. I think it is possible to do more. I see the book I want to write—rather I hear it—as Glenn Miller "heard" his band long before they achieved the Miller sound. I do not think I will prove anything, but I want to say something about human beings who try to be human. I do not want to write "minor stuff." I do not want to be "new" or "original." I think it is possible to combine discipline with vitality—

I must go back and rescue "Ambrose."

At 9:30, I was beginning to go back & get "Ambrose." I was at the point (and this is important) of willing withdrawal from the world, I *wanted* to be back with my project. The doorbell rang and there was Gordon. "Am I welcome?" he said. It was as simple as that. And all the time in between hadn't counted. All the worrying, all the emotionalizing. It would have happened anyway.

I became nervous in that Dexedrine way & spilled instant coffee all over the kitchen. Apologized, of course (what else could I do?). He said, "I like it." Notices everything. The envelopes, neatly labeled for packing. "Ambrose." He said six or seven times, "I've been thinking about you a lot." And I knew he had & I knew a lot more with it. He saw my clippings & read a few & was impressed. Kept asking: "Why did you give it all up—you could have been . . ." I said, "If you'd been me, you would have done the same thing. But you weren't me & you wouldn't understand, therefore." "But why are you living the way you do now? Why were you living in all those countries?" "Looking for my soul," I said, to make him think I was getting him off the track. "No, you're too sensible. You'd never lose your soul." He was awed when I said "Did she tell you to press the spinach between the plates?" (he had called up Cordon Bleu to find out about his spinach) & he said, "Why, yes! Yes. It must have been the same girl who teaches you." "You're a romantic," I said. "That's what's printed in the CB cookbooks." "But she didn't *have* to say two plates," he said.

· · ·

He has just perfected a ceramic that has been accepted for production & I said, "What are you going to invent next?" "Oh, I think I'll make something for you. I'll make you a man." "That would make a good story," I said. "The scientist loves a girl so much, he makes her the man she wants & then she marries what he's made & leaves the scientist alone & unhappy." "Oh, no. She marries the man & then finds out she's looking for just the opposite qualities & then she marries the scientist."

We spoke of the Merry Days of 1660 when Charles II returned to the throne. I quoted that passage from the Duke of York.[36] "Women make two mistakes in love: one, they give in too easily; two, they are never really convinced that when a man says he is through with them, he really means it." And then I asked him what he would have been in that era & he said, "A cavalier."

"I would have been a woman who was just a woman & who waited. Simple days."

"That's the trouble with the modern world . . . ," he said, & continued as I'd predicted.

"I'd like to be honest twenty-four hours a day with one person," I said.

"Be honest with me. Tell me about your writing." I told him about the "sound" I heard—the same thing I wrote earlier in this book. About the human element.

"At least that would be a contribution," he agreed. He admitted that the hermit life was not on his list & neither was a future of four flatmates. He wants a woman badly, but by God his standards are high.

He said several times, "You're a good girl. Your mother would be proud if she saw how you are living in London. Not living on hot air like Sheila & those girls. I like that about you. You keep separate."

36. Gail had read Kathleen Windsor's steamy historical romance *Forever Amber* in 1952, when she was fifteen. The novel, praised for its historical detail and banned in Boston for its references to sexual acts, illegitimate pregnancies, and abortions, was the number-one fiction best seller in 1945. Its heroine, Amber St. Claire, rises from pregnant street person to favorite mistress of Charles II in Restoration England, reminding one of Nell Gwynn, cited by Gordon in the same conversation.

MAY 17

Every so often, some friend's remark, some event makes me aware that I am not the person I ought to be (or want to be) or have in mind for myself. Last night it began. Robin & I in a huff, all the way down Wigmore Street. We were so angry, so entranced with each other's duplicity, that we walked all the way to Soho. Then when he called the waiter & said, "I want a coarse, hard red wine," sanity returned. Ravello's Gran Caruso = a memory of reconciliation. Although Robin hates people who think in labels. But, anyway, all this talk last night. "You have to put the marker somewhere," he said. "With you, one has reason to wonder just how much is phony & just how much is real."

Where *do* I put the marker in?

Some old collector in me makes me want to list the moments I have known when someone I care about cares about me. Gordon, on the morning of my move from no. 5 back to no. 21: "You seem to have so much energy. That's what I like about you." (Helping me lift the tweed coat from the closet.) "You are the kind of person one hopes to know all his lifetime" (down the beginning of King's Road) & always his "You're looking good, woman." And after the boxes had been put away & we went to the Black Lion for a drink: "I think you'll be spending another winter in England." Also, he is going to take me to his cottage near Rugby one weekend. He described the people, the ones whose families had lived there for centuries. "You'd like them." I told him I was impatient. "So am I," he said. "When I know I'm going to do something, I can't concentrate on anything else." He also said, "I have a bad habit of treating people like subjects. I want to get to know all about them and then when I do, I think, 'Well, now I know all there is to know about *him.*'" He specified that I was excluded from this data processing. "Like Robin," he said, & what followed was, I am sure, a very deft, subtle advertisement for himself. He had read about Robin's Kayak Journey through the Barren Lands . . . He had said earlier, "I started to call you & ask you to bring him round to my place for a drink." Nobody else I know would have had the impersonal touch needed for that remark. Now, in the Black Lion, he said: "Someone like Robin. I'd like to get to know him, find out everything about him, & then I'm pretty sure there'd be not much else to know." He looked me straight in the eye & I read a challenge. Also, about the Ronald Searle picture,[37] he said the bloated Roman god on the pedestal could be Robin if he didn't watch his weight. The Wests liked Gordon immediately & Mr. W. walked all the way back to the pub to invite him to lunch, which wasn't lost on G. even though he couldn't accept.

I like the way he takes the initiative in pubs. He always orders me brandy, without saying "What do you want?" Or, if I specify Scotch, he says, "Bell's Scotch, please."

Walked the Old Walk up the Embankment & recaptured time. I don't know what there is about those two walks—along the Thames & up Kimberly[38] beside the golf course. Those two times, things are almost unbearably real—in a noble sense, in the sense that "Just this is enough." Just that I have existed up to this point.

Thoughts while walking: One must learn how to measure his own dimensions. This is the difference between people who make you quiet & those who make you unquiet. It has something to do with being acutely conscious of one dimension, one proportion to the exclusion of others. Therefore, when I am with Melanie Miller, I become unquiet about my physical envelope. I look at her nails, her hair, her fashion, & I sum up the hours spent to achieve this end. When I am with Robin, I feel as if I must justify myself in *his* terms. Many people achieve the effect of seeming well-rounded. This can be deadly because if I do not recognize it, I become caught up in the longing for "a dab of everything"— a small compact box with twelve sample perfumes—"Yes, I play rugby, write a bit, and make money in town during the week."

37. See the April 14, 1962, entry in Part 5.

38. Kimberly Avenue in Asheville passed through Gail's childhood neighborhood. The street is as wide as a boulevard, with sidewalks and trees on either side. Fine, architecturally various homes grace the west side, while the east side is occupied, in large part, by the Grove Park Inn golf course. The greens rise to the inn itself and Sunset Mountain.

£32.0   May 9

‾7.7   Uncle William's birthday card
_____

24.30

‾2.10   Evansky[39]
_____

22.20

‾5.0   cash
_____

17.20

‾0.7
_____

16.5

‾5.0   anything I may have forgotten
_____

11.5

‾10.00   Wests till May 26
_____

bra from M & S[40]

pair of walking shoes

£42.00   May 24

‾19.4   Wests
_____

22.60

‾3.0   Transportation
_____

19.60

‾7.0   Glasses
_____

39. Evansky was a hair stylist near the U.S. Embassy.

40. Marks & Spencer, a pioneering clothing retailer with department stores all over the world.

12.60

−2.6
─────

£10.0   to spend/save

MAY 19

Bertrand Russell, in a book entitled *The Conquest of Happiness,* says
that a person is happy in direct proportion to his outside interests. He
goes on for some time about introspective people & urges us to seek outside interests, hobbies, people we love. Sitting in the sun, enclosed by the
garden wall, a Caravelle slicing the afternoon sky, I thought, "That man
is exactly right." And pitied the unaccomplished in other-directedness.
But night falls, I walk along the river and begin wondering. What do
these other-directed people think about when they walk along river
banks? How does one get outside himself? And yet how I admire them.
These people. What can I do to achieve this?

Went back & cleaned out the remnants of 5 Green Street. Already
the disintegration process had started. "How drab it all looks. I like my
high window in Chelsea much better." And so one becomes "adaptable,"
as they say.

G. wore his kilt on Saturday because he had sent his trousers to the
cleaners. He sat on the arm of my chair in a roomful of people & I read
RLS's *Travels with a Donkey,*[41] while he played with my hair & neck &
watched the Manchester register cup finals in soccer. I remember thinking that this was the nearest I'd ever come to being in perfect balance (or
conjunction) with a man. There were several enlightening passages in
the book. I am glad he likes RLS because of the passage about life under
the stars not being complete unless you shared a camp cot with the
woman you loved.

RLS says that there is something narrow about people who throw
over a friend because he has displayed a fault. I mentioned this to Gor-

41. Robert Louis Stevenson's *Travels with a Donkey* exemplifies turn-of-the-twentieth-
century travel writing with its outdoorsmanship, good humor, and clean, muscular prose.

don & he said: "The girl I fall in love with will have faults but I will like them, too. However, I think you're perfect."

JUNE 4

My cobalt blue night sky, the chimney tops. All is now. I am suspended here reflecting upon the past & shaping the future. There is so much to get down. Events branch off into introspecting. I walked past the river tonight and wished for G., but knew that he was in his own time; he could come when he chose; that the outcome of ourselves is yet undefinable. And the Fun Fair lights shone in the amusement park across the river and I thought of Ambrose and unfulfilled pleasures.

The Wests were coming out as I was coming in & we went to Phene's Garden for a drink.[42] The Chelsea pubs in summer are magic places with their colored lanterns & overhanging greenery. Mrs. W. had an iced crème de menthe & the color of it made the evening for me. We all three conspired & discussed our marriages. She was with her first husband at a sanitarium in Europe when she met a couple named Adams. Then later, when she was married to her second, they entertained the female Adams (whose father—Davis—had run for the presidency and later was ambassador to the Court of St. James's),[43] who was divorced from Adams & married to Mr. West. Thus it started. The plots & counterplots. If I had not married Doug Kennedy, I would not have met Gordon W. If Gordon negates that marriage, then he is in effect negating our meeting. He is saying, "It shouldn't have taken place."

Weekend camping in the country—Alden & Robin. Alden playing his pipe (flute) under the trees. Robin waging continual war against himself—tossing the knife in the air and catching it until he cut himself to the bone. Then putting on a handkerchief bandage & throwing some more. He, out of his hurt, attacked me. It kills him because he cannot get

42. Phene's Garden was, Gail recalls, "a magical Chelsea pub located deep within a mews and having a fairy-lit back garden." Leaving her boardinghouse, she'd head up Justice Walk, turn right, then left, and "it seemed to grow out of nowhere."

43. John William Davis, West Virginia congressman from 1911 to 1913, was ambassador to the Court of St. James's from 1918 to 1921 (under Woodrow Wilson), and was the Democratic candidate for president in 1924, losing to Calvin Coolidge in a landslide.

to me where I live, he cannot destroy one iota of what I have. I cried bitterly out of frustration, but most of all because I wished I were back here away from the wastefulness of it all. Alden got very drunk & lost control. Both of them came in today with tails between their legs.

Mr. West: ". . . and Peggy went up to the Chelsea pensioner & he wanted twenty-five shillings for that postcard."

Peggy West: "No darling. Four shillings."

And it goes on, foibles and diatribes. But it is all moving and seeking toward something.

We discussed my copybook blot[44] & they advised. I liked asking it & they liked giving it.

"Be quick about it," says Paul. "It all makes you, equals you, my dear. I don't feel like a hard roué for having had those first two go-rounds."

"I only wish I had met Paul first," says Peggy.

Gordon must know. Mr. West: "Tell him when you're crossing the street in heavy traffic."

JUNE 6

Staying up all night at gunpoint is what I deserve. Calmness. Get it all down. I am twenty-six years old (almost), I am going to learn to put good things in writing. I am going to play it straight from the shoulder, only never give myself away at bargain again.

Robin returned Alden's briefcase today. I went rummaging through it though it was none of my business (I must have inherited this from Monie) and found: (1) a flute, (2) *Le Petit Prince*, (3) philosophy notes & a paperback of Hume, (4) a wallet with a student ID card, membership to Ronnie Scott's Jazz, (5) a small journal-like entry on either side of an

---

44. "Copybook blot" is a term for a divorce that Gail had picked up from an Englishman.

index card, reading: "I went around tonight all primed to see her. She said she was sick. *Was* she? Maybe she was. But then again, maybe she wasn't. Oh damn. Ah, shit. My life revolves around this weakness. Always hoping to reach—what? That happy little prize. That one chance."

And then, at the bottom in small letters: "Still, after all, I will go on playing it straight from the shoulder."

—All this for Jill, a girl who isn't worth him. So, at least I know there is a male in the world who goes through the same agonies as I do. But he is twenty-three. They'll knock it out of him in ten years. At thirty-three, he'll be a B.

"Has Gordon mentioned me?" I asked Alden, hating myself.

"Yes." He laughed. "But the context doesn't exactly suit your frame of mind now."

"No, tell me. I've got to know. You must tell me."

"Well, we were all discussing how expensive booze was at the dinner table and I thought this was a good time to get you into the conversation so I mentioned as how you could get it cheap at the PX, and he said, 'Gosh! I wish I'd remembered that. I would have asked her to dinner tonight.' "

"Oh God, Alden, I'm going to die right here on the spot. Oh God, I can't take it. Ah, he'll pay for that."

"No, no. You can't do that. You've got no evidence of anything at the moment so you're putting interpretations on minute details. You don't know anything."

JUNE 9

SUNDAY

I am almost twenty-six and have only a stamped passport, a photostatted copy of a divorce decree, an envelope full of *Miami Herald* clippings, a rejected novel, and a bill from Internal Revenue for $200 in back taxes to show for it.

·　·　·

The pigeons' throaty ode; George the bartender at the Black Lion wiping off the counter with a dishcloth, dreaming of his two-eyed football days.

Andrew & I went up the street to the Essoldo to see *Mondo Cane*, a documentary film of all the unpleasant things going on all over the world—native women suckling pigs; cars being destroyed & smashed into scrap metal; a turtle dazed by radiation, crawling away from the sea & then, in a final hallucination, thinking she is again swimming in the sea; Vic Tanney's reducing salon; fleshpots. Came home to find Stella looking ghostly & high-strung. The Wests apparently confronted Peter & told him it was an unhealthy relationship, etc., and—with the fumes of gin still on his breath from pre-supper sizzling—forbade Peter to enter Stella's room again & told him he must be in bed by twelve every night. Said Stella, looking like a painted ghost in a white starched blouse with a Queen Anne collar, deep in eye shadow: "It makes one lose faith in people even though I accepted their oddness at first." They still owe her £50. She has told them it must be paid when she leaves at the week.

Grieg—coming over the radio—each piano note evoking the idealism-spangled days when I could recite the whole of the death of King Arthur—The old order changeth, yielding place to new—& when I walked up to the hill & out in front of the hospital & watched the tower at Saint Genevieve's grow dark against the sky & I wish I were there with Mother Winters & all the nuns, going soundlessly down corridors, moving in a world of incense & regular times for everything and living side by side with God.

JUNE 11

It is a beautiful summer's day and will also be a beautiful summer's night with late blue sky & dark stretches of buildings, the drone of airplanes & the river, flowing on & on. It has been a hot day in London town. Going into the Piccadilly subway, I thought: I won't be the first to go down these stairs and I won't be the last.

The office is endured. Dorothea is upstairs on the switchboard and

Doreen floats quietly in a haze of too much Patou,[45] caught in the act of being late by Herr Miller.

PAIN ENDS WHERE ART BEGINS
Motto for June.

Battersea Pleasure Gardens[46] were achieved and within the hour I know that Robin will be writing a poem about it.

And tonight—the orange & lemon lanterns, the sighing trees. Purple sky in a puddle of water fountains (like Bazaar International at West Palm Beach) and periwinkle blues, hollyhocks, parrots & fortune-tellers. Popular tunes blaring from an amusement ride (and I think of Ambrose—no longer the Mose of Carolina Beach, but the much better Ambrose in white suit & fictional reality). A bench painted pink and a tree house. Robin made me go on the Roto: you are plastered against a wall by centrifugal force. (The thing is to keep your eyes closed.) The moment when I knew I couldn't do it—the moment when I did do it. And afterwards the triumph was so good, it made my mouth dry.

These long, light summer nights. Soon the Equinox. Then the slow subtle fading away. Funny I didn't notice the skies last year. I want to be a good person, to have a strong will but not be inflexible; to court joy; to develop humor and loyalty and patience; to learn to say less when no words improve the situation.

Robin (flexing his muscles, presenting himself): "Made in England."

· · ·

45. The perfume Joy was introduced in 1930 by Jean Patou to dispel Depression blues and uplift American women who could no longer afford his clothes.

46. The Festival of Britain, created in 1951 to celebrate the centennial of the Great Exhibition in Hyde Park, included a scientific and cultural exposition as well as the Battersea Pleasure Gardens, which survived as Battersea Fun Fair. The Fun Fair was located across the Thames from Chelsea and featured the Big Dipper roller coaster and the Water Chute, among other rides. It was an immensely popular holiday destination. After a fatal accident on the Big Dipper in 1972, the rides were dismantled.

"What do you do, Mr. Challis?"[47]

"I'm a try-er."

"Oh. Ha, ha. No, I mean, what do you *really* do?"

JUNE 14

"Ambrose." Can't be as tender as *Death in the Family*.[48] I have to work out my own breakthrough.

Alden told me about how (this is the last indulgence in subjectivism) they discussed me on the Rifle Range at Bisley. They discussed my writing and Gordon said—when he got home—"I think I'll call Gail & ask her if she wants to go out." Then Bobbie[49] called & invited him to dinner, so he went.

JUNE 15

Last night (or early this morning) I dreamed that B. & I were playing golf on a new and excellent golf course that I had discovered as a result of working for the Travel Service. I had gotten away from work after some argument with Doreen & Dorothea.

I woke up because someone was knocking at my door & it was Stella saying cheerily, "I've got bad news." It was a letter from her lawyer in Asheville saying that B. "committed matrimony" sometime in May. Thus fell one of my most solidly built houses. *Nothing*, absolutely nothing, can surprise me now. Gordon could be eloping with his Bobbie this

47. Robin Challis, Gail says, "was larger than life, like a Roman centurion. He had a job in PR or travel, but his main love was playing rugby for the London Scottish team, and collecting antiques. He hadn't gone to university. From the first, we were cohorts. We behaved toward each other as though we knew the worst about the other, yet he could be extremely insightful as well as kind, and he came up with amazing turns of phrase. He also taught me to be physically braver—such as the time he talked me into riding the whirlabout at the Battersea Amusement Park. He is the first and last person with whom I ever went camping."

48. James Agee's *A Death in the Family,* which Gail had read a few years earlier, reveals the effect that a father's death has on a family through the narrations of each of its members.

49. Bobbie was Gordon's young girlfriend, who called him frequently. They went on camping trips.

very minute. I could be fired Monday. The Travel Service could be shut down. My family could die in a fire. I realize now that there is no person in this world that I can absolutely count on.

I went over to Battersea Pleasure Gardens and heard the pipe organ on the Wonder Boat, watched the people on the rides, the gray river lapping against the rocks . . . Now, I am very tired. I want to rest, to get out of this body & into another. I cannot kill myself over B. or anyone else. I cannot stop going if any of my family dies. I cannot confide my innermost beliefs & emotions to casual people. I cannot let this introspective dervish go one step farther. I am tired of speaking & telling & giving myself away. I am tired of letting people know what counts with me. I am tired of basing my minutes & hours on the faint chance that someone may want to see me.

Somewhere I took a choice between utter & complete commitment to knowledge & truth and limited (but secure) happiness. And I must have chosen the search, for here I am with a million memories, a little wisdom & a soul that still—somehow—says yes. I may be in a room of my own & have absolutely nobody in the world to share this search with. But I just cannot be bothered anymore.

JUNE 16

Reread Father Webbe's letter. "You forsake your vision at the peril of your soul." And I know this to be true as well as I know I have seen a glimpse of the better way. I cannot afford to end my stories with the death. They must:

1. hit home enough to communicate to the reader, "I've been through this, too";

2. suggest a way of human action to lift one out of the many temporary ruts into which we fall.

JUNE 17

I need, about now, to be put away in a TB sanitarium or sent to jail (like O. Henry).[50] This, I am afraid, is the drastic measure it will take to get it all down. Tomorrow will be number 26 for number one. Gordon doesn't know what day he will be spending with me.

Isabel[51] frowns: "I should nebber ha' come to London. Now I see so much. The people are so free in the government. I cannot 'splain it to my husband. He will not understand. I was different before I left. But now I am more different."

JUNE 18

Before dinner the ring of the bell
I love my life

JUNE 20

Bought two new notebooks today & one will be used purely impersonally. I have a dull-thud headache. Remind me to write of the slow, steady, painstaking ways Doreen wins her points.

JUNE 21

It is June 21, the longest day of the year, & I am lying in a semilight room listening to a sad French song. I do not understand the words, but I know it is about striving and being let down, & striving. I am looking out upon a pair of chimney tops and thinking, "I should walk by the river, because it is the longest day," but whether I will or won't doesn't really matter. Or does it? I hear children calling (after their supper) and the birds and another French song. I have been out drinking with Robin & Dorothea & Griffith even, and came home lying in a taxi. Everyone ate silently because it was Friday night (hark, an airplane) & we were all slowly becoming accustomed to our separate reliefs. The planes, the

50. O. Henry—William Sydney Porter, the famed short-story writer—was particularly familiar to Gail because he was born and raised in Greensboro, North Carolina.

51. Isabel was the Spanish boarder at 21 Church Street. Her husband was a policeman.

planes, I should go out and walk. If I do, I will be celebrating, marking the turning point.

JUNE 22

I feel better already. The Wests at the beginning of their third respective marriages—finally to each other—found a turtle one day while walking in the fields of Bedford, New York. They named him Mr. Bedford and took him back to their rooftop flat on Sixty-sixth Street in New York City. Mr. Bedford slept in the rooftop garden and at night would come clunking down the stairs—a kind of combined crawl-fall—and into their bedroom, where he slept. It took him hours to follow them from room to room, and sometimes, by the time he had gotten to one room, they had already left for another. One day, Mr. W. found Mr. Bedford half buried in the hot tar on the roof. It took three hours of concentrated effort, using a bottle of turpentine, fingers, and a spoon. When the Wests had parties, sometimes Mr. W. would fix a lighted candle on the top of Mr. Bedford's shell and he would come marching in all aglow, making the ladies scream. He ate flies, lettuce leaves, and meat. When the Wests went to Elba on a Greek boat, taking Mr. Bedford—in a hatbox—the bartender on board tried to interest the turtle in whiskey, but Mr. Bedford was not the drinking sort. The family flourished in Elba until, one day, Mr. Bedford fell from a second-story window during one of his prowlings & cracked his shell. Mr. W. was again to the rescue with iodine and adhesive tape. The shell grew back but Mr. B.'s legs remained slightly paralyzed despite Mr. W.'s faithful massages.

One day, some friends came to take the Wests' picture for the front of a Christmas card. The Wests & their dog and Mr. B. all were posed looking out of a window. Afterward, Mr. B. was left to lie in the sun. But when he didn't come in by nighttime, Mrs. W. got worried & went to look. But he was nowhere to be found, though they both looked under every leaf & vine & rock. It was agreed that a dog had probably carried him away and dropped him somewhere too far from home for his paralyzed legs to return him. Mrs. West cried for several days because Mr. B., besides being an unusually faithful, intelligent character, also had been the last link with another era, the days when they had gone walking in the fields of Bedford, New York.

Sensitive to pitfalls and false leads in life, Godwin was, at an early age, aware that she was the protagonist in her own psychological odyssey. Her first efforts at journal keeping were, she tells, "to trace every recordable thing about a certain eighth-grade teacher." Idealists must often go on instinct in their quests. The recognition of a role model is a valuable instinct.

In the next journal part, titled "The Illumined Moment," Gail encounters Carl Jung, whose self-examining, well-informed, and courageous life provides an inspiring example. In a similar spirit of inquiry, Gail has kept journals regularly for five and a half decades and counting, through periods of self-doubt and exhaustion. The effort represents a faith in the outcome—personal and professional—and a lack of faith in one's defensive ego's ability to embrace the mystery of its own existence unaided.

Gail's journals were a way for her both to record her adventure— from the job at Mayview Manor and her transatlantic journey through Klampenborg, Las Palmas, and London—and to survive it. "Be your own savior, confidante, best friend," Gail advises journal keepers.

Journal keeping as Gail practices it is a method of living a religious life, conceived nondoctrinally. "Eventually," she continues with her advice, "it becomes a ritual." The second voice that the journal keeper establishes is not only a cheerleading friend, but also a trusted truth seeker. "To be a true journal keeper," Gail says, "you have to have a confidential relation to yourself. A diarist divides herself into two. One confides to the other. One strengthens the other. One questions, challenges, taunts, and comforts the other."

She quotes George Herbert, "Dresse and undresse thy soul."[52]

One of the beauties of this "religious" ritual is that it is sympathetic

52. From "The Temple": "Summe up at night, what thou hast done by day / And in the morning, what thou hast to do. / Dresse and undresse thy soul: mark the decay / And growth of it."

as well as encouraging. Thus, Gail strikes the following chords in her advice:

- *You do not have to give a blow-by-blow account.*

- *Chronology, consistency, and accountability are not required.*

- *You do not need to write complete sentences.*

- *Put down what you can—a phrase, a picture; later, it will connect to related memories.*

- *For every phrase, try writing a companion phrase, packed with specific details.*

- *Don't make anything into an assignment.*

- *Realize you have seasons. (There are times when I fill up a three-hundred-page journal in a month and a half—after Robert died— and times when a three-hundred-page journal lasts more than a year.)*

- *Assess yourself—where you've been straight and where crooked.*

- *Write at least a line or two every day—or not—but when you do write again, comment on the "not" day.*

Gail is not only using her journals for personal reasons, she is using them to further her creative writing. Consequently, reflections and observations alternate with professional judgments about books and drafts of stories. Put on the page, the parts interact and produce answers that had not originally been in the author's mind.

The test of this theory is not only the published stories we see gestating in Gail's journals—in the spring of 1963 alone, "An Intermediate Stop," "The Angry Year," and "Mr. Bedford"—but also the not-yet-published stories that gaze up at us from Gail's journal pages. Robin and Alden, tormented pals, do quite a dance. The Ambrose story, which found some expression in Violet Clay *and in manuscript form in the 1966 unpublished* novel-as-journal *"The Possibilitarian,"*[53] *contains unresolved tensions. The Gordon phenomenon sits like a cat on a tree limb.*

When writers sit down to tell a story, do they rely on memories and chronological narration, on descriptions and character sketches? Or do they depend upon something more syncretic, something more chemical and quickening—an idea nourished by passion and by deeply felt understanding, something life-giving?

53. Gail's unpublished novel "The Possibilitarian," also titled "The Ruptured Link," is one week's worth of journals kept by "a semialcoholic" named Ambrose during a holiday visit by his daughter. The 142-page manuscript is part of the Gail Godwin Papers, Manuscripts Department, Library of the University of North Carolina at Chapel Hill.

Part eleven

THE ILLUMINED MOMENT

Old Church Street, London

JUNE 22–JULY 19, 1963

A lot has been said about the experience that Gail has gained in her quest to be a masterful writer. After a nearly two-year foray into an alien environment and writer's laboratory, she finds herself, following her twenty-sixth birthday: hooked into the concept that her era is suffering an epochal loss of purpose; ornery about workplace pettiness; unsure about her own instinct that her personal material might serve to enlighten others; insomniac; and attuned to how one's biases and ideals limit one's vision.

It is time for an illumined moment. What we find in this journal part are some of young Gail Godwin's clearest articulations about her own purpose.

"What is incredible," Gail writes on June 22, "is how one can, through the process of memory, imperfect as it is, conjure up lost days, and then, by writing, reshape them so that they are more meaningful than at the time when one is experiencing them." She is sure that her "selfish motive" provides a model for others walled in by fears and passions.

"The inner motive might just be this," *she writes,* "to go back and examine the past, remove the pain by changing it into form and thus free ourselves for the next battle. *For how can we be expected to distill the significance from every day if we are living that day passionately?"*

Freeing oneself for the next battle is such a key concept that it deserves reemphasis. There are no final solutions, only solutions that allow one to proceed to the next—what?—challenge, engagement, rite of passage, transformation. In fictional terms, this means: Plots should never be pat. Godwin's generous recognition of ever-branching themes leads to resolutions that are musical, but not pat.

Anyway, what is the meaning of a literature of despair? Despair is silent. After all, silence itself is sense if the eyes speak. True despair is agony, tomb or abyss. If it speaks, analyzes, especially if it writes, immediately a brother stretches forth his hand to us, the tree is justified, love is born. A literature of despair is a contradiction in terms.

—ALBERT CAMUS[1]

TERGIVERSATION

Desertion of a cause—a shift, subterfuge (L. *tergum*, back + *versare*, to turn).

For at the bottom of the tergiversation of the present age is vis inertiae. *And everyone without passion congratulates himself upon being the first to discover it, and so become cleverer still.*

—KIERKEGAARD[2]

JUNE 22, 1963

Three thousand words from ten till eleven. It comes so fast when it does come, but I cannot sustain it for long. What is incredible is how one can, through the process of memory, imperfect as it is, conjure up lost days, and then, by writing, reshape them so that they are more meaningful than at the time when one is experiencing them. What a thought. Is this the selfish motive for art? The outward motive is to reach a hand across to the less articulate to guide them in defining their various alleviations. For only if they are recognized as being alleviations and not ends in

1. From Albert Camus's *Notebooks, 1935–1942,* published by Alfred Knopf in 1963.

2. From Kierkegaard's *The Present Age, and Of the Difference between a Genius and an Apostle,* translated by Alexander Dru (Harper & Row, 1962).

themselves can we continue on toward the real purpose and pursue the main search. *But the inner motive might just be this: to go back and examine the past, remove the pain by changing it into form and thus free ourselves for the next battle.* For how can we be expected to distill the significance from every day if we are living that day passionately? Passion must have an object & often the object is not what will remain significant in time. *I really do believe that passionately is the only way to spend a good day* . . . and I am further justified if I can go back later, retracing my steps and picking up the scattered significances like dropped coins and, without the impediment of that same passion, weave them into a continuation, a form, a bridge of learning between then and now.

At least this has not been a wasted Saturday—read Robert Nathan's *The Wilderness Stone*[3] & James's *Daisy Miller.*[4] Just shows how the mores of one culture can be tragically misinterpreted by one who has been brought up to observe the mores of another culture. There was just a time, right before dinner and after dinner, when the light was fading on summer day number two and the couples were making their plans on how to buy time for another Saturday night. Old Church Street came alive with people on their way to somewhere else and I looked out over the window box of geraniums and up at the chimney pots against a fading sky . . . And I almost succumbed when Andrew's friend wanted me to come with them for drinks. "Why not," said Andrew. "You can get drunk. Then time will pass quicker." But the old formulas don't work anymore, not when I know the bitter taste of an ennui-brewed mixture. It never fails to catch in your throat the next morning.

Before I began to write tonight, I experienced an almost overwhelming loathing for my project. It took sheer will to throw me into that "once upon a time." I think one main drawback is that I never think it's going to be good enough, but ours is only the trying & you for-

3. *The Wilderness Stone,* published in 1961, portrays a young woman who flees back in time to escape the new world order, which includes the threat of nuclear holocaust.

4. Henry James's *Daisy Miller* immediately became a sensation when it was published in 1878. The protagonist had been a fresh invention—an innocent, enthusiastic American young woman delighting and dismaying Europeans with her mores.

sake your vision at the peril of your soul. So, as long as I feel the need to write down things, I must go on using up paper & ballpoint pens.

In spite of people like Doreen, etc., I believe that I am potentially and innately a good person. I believe that I will go far in my search. I believe I will be given the chance to prove my capacity for love to some man who can comprehend it all. The thing is to fill up the silences and the spaces with my unflagging belief in my own purpose on this earth.

JUNE 23

Jung says in his autobiography[5] that each of us has two sides, which play against each other until the end. There is the number one side, which is what we are in the eyes of the world, our parents' product, successful in studies, profession, or marriage, or unsuccessful, judged wholly by this. The number two side is how we see ourselves in relation to God, the universe, flowers, mountains, and ideas. Sometimes in moments of exceptional serenity, like four o'clock this afternoon, when I came upstairs and went guiltlessly to sleep, I glimpse the eternity of the number two side. I know that I am never alone because in my highest moments I am thinking thoughts that others of my kind have thought in the past or will think in the future. And I see myself as part of a link in a chain. I know that these people once did, or will, take me into consideration—just as I have taken them.

But then the American pragmatism takes over and makes the number two side seem as unreal and as unsubstantial as smoke dreams. I awake and I think no longer of time eternal but of the unforgiving minute; I think not of my relationship to the great try-ers but of those around me *in my immediate sphere*. I think of my age, twenty-six, and I become afraid that I will never marry again. I feel sometimes—indeed in my true moments—that I was never married anyway. I don't feel that any part of me was left down there in Key Biscayne. I never felt like

5. *Memories, Dreams, Reflections*, by C. G. Jung, recorded and edited by Aniela Jaffé, translated from the German by Richard and Clara Winston (Pantheon, 1963). Gail must have read a review of the Jung autobiography, or glanced at a copy at a bookstore, for it isn't until July 8 that she purchases the volume.

Mrs. Anybody and I sometimes think I am perpetuating a great big lie when I tell someone I have been married. Because, at times, it is a reassurance. It was done once & it can—feasibly—be done again.

So it is six o'clock. Soon the supper hour. Then the hours that tax my number two self out of shape. The attempt at writing to assert my independence. And then the fading of the sky to the short night. And the prospect of a day at work and homecoming and supper and waiting. Sometimes I see such a great gap between me and all the people I know. I fool myself that they understand something of what I am saying. The Wests. Andrew. Robin. Gordon. But I am aware even when I attribute to them this understanding that I am fooling myself. I *see*, for instance. What Gordon is and all he can be. He can never, never even begin to understand. Remember Doug. Remember Doug. He just couldn't listen. I began to talk to him in his terms. *And then, of course, they win, because number two language cannot be translated into number one talk. I am tired of giving out samples of my soul for people to examine at their leisure and return to me slightly handled, and none the wiser.* The old anger is coming back.

Another weekend dying fast and tomorrow the ritual of killing eight hours at work in order to get back to Chelsea and kill five or six more. There are always all sorts of hopes. A new person. Oh, hell, I am absolutely fed up with my everlasting laziness, my vacillation of purpose . . .

JUNE 24

Robin said: I haven't seen you in such a spirit since your party. Alden is back from a two-week sojourn in Dublin pubs.

While visiting travel agents today, I suddenly "switched sides." Instead of thinking, What are they thinking of me? I started thinking, What do I *really* think of them? Quick way to eradicate a neurosis.

JUNE 25

Rain, and I like it. All day the wind whistled in the office (faulty construction; steel & glass at the corner of Sackville & Vigo). Now it has stopped as suddenly as it started. Today the debit pile was heaped high. One of those mornings when the egg is runny, some shopper picks your stocking with her go-to-market basket. BH wrote Doreen a letter (they all write her after they leave in spite of the names they call her when they are there). Jill called, bringing with her that indescribable, corrupt feeling, that splayed, disintegrated sensation. She has moved back to Charles's flat in Lowndes Square & thinks (hopes) she is going to have a baby.

So, on the day went & I remained detached and undemolished. Except for the sick feeling in the pit of my stomach & I cannot really wish my future to be free of *that*. If I can just learn to hold myself together in the very bad times when the world encroaches, when I pick up a magazine & see an article entitled "What to Do if You're 25 and Still Single," etc., then the good times will take care of themselves. Letter from Frank today, which I will have to keep. Several very striking observations. It's hard to believe that soon he will be forty. I met him almost twenty years ago. Good lord. My mother's second marriage has lasted sixteen years! He said I had gained a peace within myself, he could tell from the letters, and again lauded patience. Patience, it is true, is a virtue. But so is action. What a hell of an assignment: Learn to balance patience with action.

There may be something to writing *around* the thing you want to say, thus leaving more to the powers of imagination.

> Smell of charcoal steak. Sun on the chimney tops.
> Water glistening on leaves. Sound of traffic down
> on the Embankment and the airplane. My
> friend the airplane.

Embrace these moments when you don't particularly want to be anywhere else. I suppose it is a sort of prayer. It is good to be calm inside

& know it has not been caused by *any outside influence*. And today's calm is produced by only one thing.

MY UNCONQUERABLE SOUL[6]

jocosely—

marplot—

moral obliquities—

I dreamed last night of hailing a taxi to
go I don't know where & then going to sleep &
then waking and having to pay an enormous bill.[7]
Why, why don't I overcome this? It's nothing
but a neurosis.
I could have gotten up & walked at four in the morning &
redeemed myself.
But I lay there under the bedcovers & didn't
do anything at all.

JUNE 26

Was haunted all day by the taxi dream. (So symbolic! A warning against wasting time.) I've had warning dreams before. They are peculiarly lucid. Also the "dawn chorus" this morning, chiding me, urging me to redeem myself by getting up & dressing, but I didn't. Crises change from day to day, yet in the end it's only one person who is responsible: me. As I exchange & discard Maxims for Better Living, a few keep cropping up.

6. This goes back to Gail's reflections at the beginning of the journal, when she was absorbing the advice of B. He wrote about the "indestructible pyramid." On January 2, 1963, the advice still carried weight, for Gail wrote, "Now I am here again, working toward that unconquerable soul B. preaches."

7. In *Violet Clay*, the heroine, Violet, recalls her arrival in New York City and how she "began having variations on a nightmare about a taxi." She'd give the driver her destination—"art"—and would find herself driven into an urban hell by a driverless vehicle; or let off, having forgotten her portfolio; or awakening from a long sleep and being sexually assaulted by the driver in lieu of the $800 fare she doesn't have.

1.   Do what can be done; be silent about the rest.

2.   Preserve an implacably calm exterior. Show this to world. They aren't listening anyway. If, by chance, an exception comes along who wants to listen, then he will make it known.

3.   Don't get overwhelmed by otherworldliness. One can think so much and then certainty wavers, inner calm turns to disquietude.

I think if there must be a choice in any matter whatsoever, the guiding light should be TO KNOW as opposed to not knowing.

Saw a plane coming down, landing lights on red tail blinking. Heading toward the landing strip at London airport.

Hastings[8] & I went to see Jack Lemmon & Lee Remick in *Wine & Roses*[9]—about alcoholics & nothing spared. Came home & Mr. West was sitting alone in the dark room facing a blaring TV. There was an empty cider bottle on top of the phone pad.

JUNE 27

Robin: "All I can say is this: It's like buying antiques. Name your price and then walk out. If they want to sell, they'll call after you. If they don't call after you, keep walking."

JUNE 28

A long week over which hung a cloud of "floating anxiety"—it was everywhere, nameless, ambiguous. In the high-ceilinged panels of the P & Orient passenger office on Cockspur Street, in the watery sunshine up & down Pall Mall, in the tone of a receptionist's voice, in the wicker chairs of the ladies' room at the Ceylon Tea Center, in the too-light-and-

---

8. Hastings was a young boarder at 21 Old Church Street who was preparing for Sandhurst.

9. *Days of Wine and Roses* is an emotionally wrenching movie about a couple destroyed by alcoholism.

airy, perfume-and-salad dining room populated by female lunchers. In some cases I could name it. The wicker chairs brought back the afternoons at the Grove Street YWCA where Monie worked in her first job to accrue some social security. I would sit in the lounge overlooking trees & a weedy garden & thumb through magazines, gnawed by the vague restlessness that comes from wishing you were somewhere else. The dining room at the Ceylon Tea Center had the same trivial and fastidious odor of the Jordan Marsh Rooftop Restaurant in Miami where Eleanor Sherman and I would eat, glad to be away from our husbands. But other twinges of the week I cannot name. It is all so tied up, one with the other. The honeysuckle smell in Paultons Square, strong and nostalgic, after the daylong rain, and I was six years old again in Asheville and walking up that short street, Bond Street, behind Emily Osborne's vine-covered house. Sometimes you could hear her mother playing the piano, defiant quick tunes; this was before she started parachute jumping.[10] We are the sum of all our summers.

JUNE 30

Tomorrow July begins & I am better equipped to deal with life than I was in June. Stella has been up in the room. We have been discussing writer's blocks & the Wests. Came to several conclusions today after unearthing some of my writing. I overwork things. For instance, the short story on Ambrose was much better than the entire fifteen-hundred-word novel-beginning. It is important to know just when a story rates novel form & when it would be better as a short story.

My biggest drawbacks are lack of faith in myself & laziness. There is also something else which might be called a neurosis—that is, I feel positively repelled by the thought of writing at certain times. This could be that the material has not "jelled" in the subconscious & that I am pushing things. There are several things—ideas, subjects, problems—I would like to get down sooner or later. One of them is, I was thinking

10. Martha Osborne, Emily's mother, worked as one of Thomas Wolfe's secretaries when he rented a cabin in Chunn's Cove. She was the inspiration for Taggart McCord in Godwin's novel *A Mother and Two Daughters.*

tonight, the problem (and solution) of resolving reality with our pre-conceived image of it. This can be shown over & over again in the case of people & places: i.e., going to a new country to find yourself—and not finding the dream—and, most of all (my biggest groan), fashioning your man & then watching one after another fall short. WHO, WHO have I ever really known well whom I didn't lose faith in? One was B., but he's not there anymore. What about all the rest on whom I spent eons of tears & time?

Last night I dreamed of ostracism by Stuart Pegram (a recurrent dream—she must represent society to me).[11] She was saying she had ten invitations to graduation parties & I was so hurt because I didn't have any. Then I saw Captain Carlson and I went up to him and said: Look, please marry me. I think we could make a go of it because you're away all the time (being a sea captain) and I wouldn't get tired of you.

JULY 1

One comes back again & again to the last fortress—oneself. I am weary of love games & I am weary of the intricacies of myself. To kill this writer's block, I shall begin with short stories (really short & then on from there). Also, I will only write, *not* think about them before or after I write. Don't mention the name of the story in these notebooks or discuss what I am trying to do. Robin brought me Le De perfume from France.

JULY 3

Lately I have been feeling guilty about keeping a journal. Nobody I know keeps one. I look over my shoulder and think: Who is that crazy girl sitting in her window and putting down versions of things that are happening to her? Here I sit, putting down little pieces of people. But nevertheless: I must. I must. Have been thinking a lot lately about "ideal people"—what makes a good person—and about action vs. reflection.

11. Stuart Pegram had been a classmate of Gail's at St. Genevieve's. She was the inspiration for the character of Freddy Stratton in *A Southern Family*.

Results of this thinking follow presently. Tomorrow is a holiday for us Americans & how glad I am of it.

Being alone more & more dominates the texture of my life. Who can understand, if I tell them, the *completeness* of sitting in the open window looking at the darkening evening sky over the chimney tops (all odd assorted shapes pointing crooked fingers into the sky) and listening to a sad, powerful, exultant symphony all the better because I do not know what it is and therefore know that I like it because I like it & not because I have been conditioned to like it. And, in that brief segment of time, when the jet streaked upward into my sky, the takeoff light in its belly blinking every five seconds, I saw the whole sum of my life and was glad for it. But I did not begin to write of this.

JULY 5

It is a thought that perhaps I am neurotic & have resolved my neuroses by using these notebooks. I want to say so much. Like right now, sitting in the window, having walked pokily to & from buses & changed into slacks & cleaned my face with witch hazel, I am very much resolved. The garden below is full of flowers & I am for a minute full of the same promise that I felt at Blowing Rock the summer of '61. Yes, there are still barriers, but I am learning; oh, brother, am I learning. At 4:00 p.m. today, I temporarily "cracked" under the strain of trying to diet & having to be in talking distance of Doreen W. for six hours at least. What does matter is that I've decided to make a small assessment of every-thing as it stands and then work from that. Incidentally, part of this as-sessment will be to record that some things cannot, will not be assessed by pen & paper & that these same things make up most of the magic so it's just as well.

JULY 6

RAIN   RAIN   RAIN   RAIN
RAIN   RAIN   RAIN   RAIN
RAIN   RAIN   RAIN   RAIN

Finished "Wesley Phipps"![12] My writer's block is gone. And I am free for one & a half more days. Tonight—Pirandello's *Six Characters in Search of an Author*,[13] with Ralph Richardson. Going with Stella.

JULY 7

The Wests have gone to the Connaught Hotel for dinner with old friends.[14] Andrew & Anna Rosa are together in her room. Stella is reading or writing. Isabella is visiting her friend Mercedes. Hastings & little Robert have gone to a pub, hoping they can slip through the age barrier and get a drink. Leonardo[15] has gone to see *Boccaccio '70*,[16] which the cousin of his father helped to produce. I am filled with that tight impotent rage which comes from depending for my happiness upon the actions of another.

This is indeed a time of sustained rage and I will fight like hell not to let it break out & expose its ugly face to the world. It is tension, tension everywhere I turn. Tension at work. My lungs actually fill with loathing when I unlock that blue door every morning. Then Doreen enters and Dorothea enters and the tug-of-war begins. I imagine a lot of it. I probably imagine most of it. I see in every word Doreen addresses to me a kind of moral reproach. And whenever they go out to lunch together, I am positive they are in league against me. If only I could not see them at all & just work steadily through the day, but the job involves constant shifting so that each of us can attend to all her extracurriculars. Then, I waste away all of my energy on defenses, hate-waves, etc. What could I not do if these stops were removed!

I believe very strongly in building up powers of various sorts (not

---

12. "Wesley Phipps" was a short story that Gail wrote about a man who dreams for a year and then returns to his family's business. The story is lost.

13. Luigi Pirandello's *Six Characters in Search of an Author* shatters and plays with the line between fiction and reality.

14. The Connaught Hotel, located in the Mayfair district, is a late nineteenth-century hotel that retains the atmosphere of a refined English country house. It has been a favorite lodging and eating place of statesmen and celebrities.

15. Leonardo was an Italian boarder, heir to a sparkling-wine fortune.

16. Four of Italy's leading filmmakers—Vittorio De Sica, Federico Fellini, Mario Monicelli, and Luchino Visconti—collaborated to produce *Boccaccio '70*, a quartet of modern tales inspired by Giovanni Boccaccio's *Decameron*.

the least of which is self-discipline). What the hell was that last clause for? "Not the least of which"—MY GOD. So: for the thousandth and ninety-millionth time I will try to reshape the material of my existence so it will be satisfactory. I can only use what I know of myself, some of what I have read, & what I have observed about other people.

The stalemates are these: On one hand, there is what I want; on the other, there is what I have. How much can I resolve of what I want with what I have?

I want to write what I have seen & felt in such a way that it can help other people "name" their own perceptions & feelings. I want to marry again, I do not like the life of a boarder, a celibate, a single girl. I want a man in bed with me at night. I want to share meaningful & pleasant experiences with a man.

Now: In my present circumstances, I am working away eight hours of energy and frustration over a job I do not like & people I do not like. I am wasting countless hours on a man who is not sure of his own feelings & who does not see me as much as I think is enough.

Added factor: I have no desire to leave London.

As I am an alien in this country, it will be difficult to find another job. But: I must try every possibility. If UPI says no, *the AP, and so on down the line.*

Then there is the man situation. Robin will not do, in spite of the fact I sometimes like to delude myself into thinking he would. The problem is to meet other men. But how? Thought: Attend night school—hope for a face across the room at the next party—just forget the hurry and don't panic.

Meanwhile, here are the toothpick resolutions upon which I will base my existence this week. Just to get out of the rut.

1. Look good every day this week (even if it means ironing & washing & polishing shoes at night).

2. *Make it a point of honor to work* unceasingly at the office until every little letter has been answered, every letter filed; perhaps rewrite some sheets on American cities or offer to. Be as unof-

fending as possible & as impersonally pleasant. This will also be a good test to see if I am imagining things in people's attitudes towards me. The worst part of this job is the segment of time in which I am completely and utterly bored & feel guilty because I know there is something to be done.

3. Retype "Wesley," doing it the best I can & then starting on something else. What? Since I have decided from now on to write only what I feel & how I feel it, why not write the story of Gordon & myself? Condensed, of course. Only this afternoon, I was reading a story in the *New Yorker* which was a simple (but intricate & clever) account of a young girl's unhappy affair with her older cousin's husband.

Stereotyped plots told with new insight are not bad. In fact, the reason things are stereotyped is because they are such common human situations.

So, briefly, here is the story of a woman who is very much the acter, the do-er—and a man who is a reflector, a wait-er. It is further complicated by the fact that she is American and he is English & that neither of them know for certain whether traits are personal or nationalistic. But where does it all lead, anyway? The spaces between meetings contain the bulk of the story; as soon as they separate they continue refashioning each other.

All that's needed in the Wesley scene is to rewrite the description of the room—tighten it up—& take the picture off the wall—describe the look he gave me—*the acknowledgment of a shared exhilaration.*

11:00 P.M.

Monday Monday'll soon be here
Then we'll put away our fear,
For, for eight consecutive hours,
We'll misuse our latent powers
And when evensong is heard
We return to wait for word.

—refrain—
Happy Happy Ennui
Sailing down the River Me
Please pour me a glass of wine
Please be handsome; say you're mine.
(How I love to be afloat
Just so you will steer the boat.)
When we reach the other bank
You will get your word of thanks—
Thanks.
Splash.
Soon it's time to go to bed
Thank you! Thank you now I'm dead.

JULY 8

Got the core of Wesley's room. Bought Jung's *Memories, Dreams, Reflections.* Thought about Gordon and thought up things to say when I see him again. Came to blows with Doreen. ("Why can't we have Detroit Hotels?" "Because I haven't got around to doing them yet.") Etc. I could do a stage performance on her mannerisms. My God, how she repeats herself. Wrote to Franchelle at camp.[17] Wrote to Kathleen an SOS about the job & about Gordon's indifference. Going out with Jim Jensen tonight. How good to be able to talk the way I like to talk for a change. His mind fascinates me. Gordon will not seem so *central* as long as there are other diversions.

I have:

party Friday night

rewrite "Wesley"—mail

wash clothes

Saturday—Evansky's for hair

17. Franchelle is Gail's half sister.

JULY 9

So it is once again ten o'clock. Now the hours outstrip themselves. They fly! All hope of the outside world sending word is gone. These are my hours, the hours when Brother Loneliness steals softly around my bed, turns the pages of my book, crouches beside me and whispers, "Nothing's so bad after all, is it? You can read and think about all tomorrow's possibilities. After all, tomorrow anything is possible. Soon it will be eleven, then twelve—then we are justified in going to sleep. And in sleep we meet our other friends, the shadows of what we have been, the mirrors of people we once thought we knew, the threats of those who have become symbols to us, the comfort of the merged ones who offer, in one lump sum, all the love of which we dream."

There is something not quite aboveboard about swearing off Gordon while he fails to call & clinging to myself, then accepting him without question when he does call & relegating myself to second place—forgetting my pride, my independence, all the things that make me the way I am. This is tantamount to denying all that I am & I won't have it—I just won't.

TRY TO LAUGH AT IT

JULY 13

The retreat at Peace College—Dr. Michael Gordon:

> "His name was Dr. —— & he
> had come all the way from
> Edinburgh, Scotland, to
> lead the spring retreat
> at Juniper College . . ."[18]

18. Gail has produced the seed of her story "The Illumined Moment—and Consequences" here.

JULY 16

Where do I think all this scratch-scratching in journals will get me? Everywhere, somewhere, or nowhere? Will I learn to put words together? Will I learn to confide to sheets of paper, more harmless than confiding in people? Will I accomplish the desired goal of winning a husband? And—having won him—will I then pour out my disillusionments about him in a later journal? I think so much & a lot of it goes around in circles, eating itself. It is so frustrating to go back & salvage such small rewards. I have only vestiges of what seemed at the time monumental thoughts, but I must keep going.

Last night Isabel & I went to eat at Gordon's. The boys were all charming, cooking, cleaning up, plying us with conversation, sherry & coffee. I even liked Harry the Australian. He was almost tender with Isabel. Her classic remark of the evening, referring to the freedom in which Anglo-Saxon men lived & traveled in bachelor states: "In Es-pain, the man, he come out from his mother & go under his wife."

Gordon showed three films of his holidays for the past five years. I think that makes the epitome of all the things he's done the essence of which I deplore. Yet I accept his shambling, absentminded ways, his smelly socks, his baggy pants, his terrible shoes, his boring habits—*Who presumes to show homemade films to guests except the characters in humorous novels?!*

Isabel's feminine Latin deduction was: I think you are more okay than he. I think he wants to make sure you love him.

Come to some terms re the writing. I think the answer is writing about something outside myself.

Tomorrow I buy something interesting to wear.

Saturday (stick to skirts)—must look my best, even though he doesn't.

JULY 19

FRIDAY

I have lost sight of my eternal bearings and am suffering the inevitable results. When you forsake the highest point you have ever reached, in the still hours, in the times of truth, then you also forsake the sublime indifference the post offers. I owe it to myself to continue the search. Writing for me is the only way I know to express what I have found on my search. But I won't be shaken down. I do waver, but I must keep faith. All things have come in the past. Therefore, is there any reason I shouldn't expect them to come in the future? True, they might *NOT* come, but is it logical to deduce that because I have won in the past I will lose in the future? Ah! As I sit in the window and look out on the flowers over the fence, wild untampered-with hollyhocks, out of the range of Peter Rhododendron's clippety-clippety confines,[19] I feel myself coming back, saying, Gail, Gail. Why did you panic? Why did you clutch at straws? Do you not remember: *I'm* here?

19. Blue Peter rhododendron is a large-leaf rhododendron with light lavender-blue flowers that bloom in the late spring.

AFTERWORD

The narrative of Part 11 breaks off on a note of reassertion and resolve. So what happens next to the twenty-six-year-old diarist (I sometimes think of my young self in the third person) admiring the hollyhocks from her upstairs window at 21 Old Church Street?

Robin brought a fellow rugby player, Andy Hurst, to Gail's 1963 Christmas party at 21 Old Church Street and Gail and Andy got engaged in the spring of 1964 and unengaged in the winter of 1964. Gordon married Barbara, a South African girl who had charmed Gail and Gordon with her reading of D. H. Lawrence's poem "Snake" when they visited her in her bed-sitter.

Gail continued to work at the U.S. Travel Service until July 1965, when she married the English psychiatrist Ian Marshall, whom she'd met in an evening writing class at the City Literary Institute. In 1966, she went back to the States to visit her family and decided not to return. A divorce followed.

After a brief stint in New York as a fact-checker for the *Saturday Evening Post*, she applied to the Iowa Writers' Workshop, in which her friend Lorraine was enrolled with her new husband, Chap Freeman. In January 1967, at age twenty-nine, still an unpublished writer, Gail flew to Iowa in a snowstorm (the airline lost her luggage).

The work that had gained her admittance to the workshop was "The Illumined Moment—and Consequences." It is the story begun in July 1963 in London. It is about an English vicar who has a vision of God and loses it in the United States while promoting his best-selling book about the experience. Retitled "An Intermediate Stop," the story went through many more drafts in Iowa and was at last published in the *North American Review*, several months before the publication of her novel *The Perfectionists* by Harper & Row in May 1970. *The Perfectionists* was drafted under the tutelage of Kurt Vonnegut Jr. in the spring of 1967, and went through several rewritings.

Gail Godwin

APPENDIX 1

Note: Gail began writing "Halcyone and the Lighthouse" in an outpouring of memory and fantasy as she embarked on her inaugural ocean voyage to Europe. She based it, in part, on a romance she had had with a sea captain whom she'd met while on assignment for the Miami Herald *a year earlier. The first name of her heroine, Halcyone Harper, was derived from that of a daughter of Aeolus, Greek god of the winds. This mythical mariner's widow has come to symbolize calmness after a storm. Gail's novel went through many title and plot changes over several months. Eventually, shedding the sea captain romance, its heroine and setting were transferred to another novel, "Gull Key."*

By eight o'clock, the morning of July 6 in Fort Lauderdale promised to be unbearable. In the bureau office of the *Star,* Keith Landridge swirled about in his chair and began typing out the assignment sheet. He knew that most of the stories stacked on the spindle that afternoon would have to be done as vicariously as possible. Reporters had become very attached to their telephones since the bureau had gotten air conditioning, he reflected wryly.

He pecked out the usuals first, habitually, without having to think.

CITY HALL—REDFERN

POLICE COURT—HANGER

COMMISSION MEETING—SMITH

PORT AUTHORITY—GRAY

No, Gray was on vacation, he'd have to send Halcyone. Halcyone, the young problem, headache of the bureau, fresh from journalism school, full of delusions of Hemingway, blond and naive. Oh God, deliver one, muttered Landridge, and pecked out HALCYONE next to PORT AUTHORITY. Well, we'll try her. Do her good to get buried in with those dullards one afternoon a week till Gray got back. When she started trying to verbally decorate subjects like cargo and tonnage and ILA grievances, she'd lose her illusions fast.

Captain Carl Wanderer stirred in his narrow bunk aboard the SS *Tempest* and listened with a congealed throat. Something was wrong. The sound that he had come to know as he did his own heartbeat, the pound which spoke to him with its monotonous soothing night and day for fifteen years, had stopped. The engine was not running and he heard the voices of his men unsure and hesitant and scared. When the first mate knocked and entered without waiting, he knew before he was told. He knew they were not due into Port Everglades for another two hours.

A year later, in October, Halcyone took a freighter to Copenhagen. On the third day out she connected the look of the decks and the engine room and the smell of salt and fuel and fresh paint with memories of Captain Wanderer. She saw him hurtling down the ladders, those magnificent brown legs rippling with motion. She smelled the good male scent of pipe tobacco and took in the crisp sturdiness of his khaki bermudas and shirt. She could hear the harsh bass sounds he uttered: "D'ya have Tuborg beer?" and "Brinkly. Let's have the men clean the decks today while it's still nice." Even: "He was a *tak*-iturn man, Haly, if y'know what I mean."

She remembered the scene in the New Orleans restaurant and felt violently ill like a girl who has had too much to drink and too much to eat and too much to say. She wanted him with her now more than anything in the whole world, here now to share with her these thoughts, to feel the life she felt, to explain the sea to her, to give her the confidence she knew was his when no land was in sight. Never had she felt so terrified, so frustrated, and so ashamed. Never had she felt so blocked from her purpose. Because he was gone now and gone a year and you can't just take out twelve months and push the ends together and make it whole and tidy. No, he was gone and she was angry mostly with herself and secondly with . . . with the way things always seemed to come out, crooked and mismatched.

Finally, about two hours later, she got out some paper and her ballpoint pen and poured out her heart to Captain Wanderer. The letter affected her so much that she cried herself to sleep as the ship pursued its northward course.

When the ship docked for a day of unloading at Oslo she mailed it. She put her return address: Halcyone Harper, American Express, Paris, France, for she calculated it would take him that much time to receive it and answer it.[1]

All during her travels in Scandinavia and down through the wine-festival country of the Rhine, into Florence where she had some shoes made for herself, into Milan where she heard *Il Trovatore* for the first time, through Rome's pinnacles and illusions, down through Spain's poverty and fantasy, back to Paris, she kept with her at the back of her mind the knowledge that she had something to look forward to.

· · ·

1. As Halcyone had made the fateful decision not to stay with the sea captain, she now makes the fateful decision to send her impulsive letter. Story logic dictates that she'll have to pay in some way for her idolizing passion, and what follows indicates that Godwin was aware of the drama that was to be born of Halcyone's abdication of self.

The letter was there, sure enough, at the Express office in Paris. How could she have doubted it? He never broke a promise. It was five and a half pages long, written on both sides of the thin tissue, which made it very hard to read.

He was so delighted to hear from her, it said, and so glad she had a pleasant voyage. He himself felt there was nothing like the sea. He thought of her often and remembered her saying she wanted to travel. "See, Haly, if a person really wants something bad enough, he or she can make things work out." (Then she found herself skipping, and she blushed, furious with herself, and forced her eyes to reread the skipped passages.) He was back home in Michigan, he said, and that's why it had taken him so long to answer her letter, the steamship company had just forwarded it to him, but he answered as soon as he received it. He was kind of "retired" from the sea, now, he explained, as the *Tempest*'s company had put all their ships under foreign flags to cut down costs. He had a little house and was dabbling a little in real estate now. He wondered if it would be at all possible if, when she finished "exploring the far corners of the earth," she might come and visit him. He would, of course, send her a round-trip ticket by airplane. "I always cared for you, Haly, and thought you were a little different from the ordinary run of pretty girls. At my time of life, the adventure kind of wears out and a man starts thinking about the pleasures of a home. I don't know how you feel now, but apparently you must have something in your heart for me or you couldn't have written a letter like that."

The letter continued for two more pages and was signed, "With all my love."

Haly crumpled the letter and stuffed it in her pocketbook and concentrated very hard on a travel poster for Air France. A jet plane was imprinted over the Eiffel tower. She decided she would go find one of those clever little Parisian bars that everybody talked about when they came home, and have herself a good, stiff drink.

The call of the sea was very far away, something that happened to someone else. Nothing seemed very magic, or really very urgent. But in all her dispassion, Haly was aware of one thing she had known before: She had missed it again. Or had it missed her?[2]

For three days, Halcyone and the photographer went out in the pilot boat morning and evening and sat and waited for a glimpse of Captain Wanderer.[3] For the photographer, this elusive mariner represented an insult. He did not like people who would not pose for him. At first, Halcyone simply wondered what the captain of a ship looked like . . . her only acquaintance with such men had been in *Anthony Adverse*[4] and a few movies starring Errol Flynn. But when Wanderer failed to appear after the third day, he became a personal affront to her, also.

Keith had said blithely, "Go on board and talk to the Captain. Find out what it feels like to be stuck. Get personal impressions, reader interest, you know. This could make a good color story for page one." Oh, how easy it was to sit in offices and give orders! Ask him how it feels to be stuck.

By the second week, the *Tempest* had become a local attraction. Swimmers paddled out on rafts and yelled up to the crew. Children stood in the sand and tirelessly watched the big boat sitting helplessly on the reef, unbudged by the tugs that appeared twice a day to pull her free. A giant boat in a bathtub, she was utterly misplaced and out of her element, all dignity gone.

She watched him appear from the cabin and hurl himself effortlessly down the ladder, his bare brown legs rippling with muscle, his heavy sandals twanging against the metal rungs. He wore khaki shorts and shirt, and a pipe hung from the corner of his mouth. His face was a combination of angles and bones and thought-lines and strength.

·   ·   ·

2. At this point, Gail took a short break from writing, and noted about the sea captain's fate, "No, I just cannot have him ending up selling real estate. But I may have to."

3. Gail is rewriting the story, starting with Haly's initial contact with the sea captain.

4. *Anthony Adverse* was a twelve-hundred-page, best-selling novel by Hervey Allen, depicting an orphan's rise to fortune as a merchant seaman.

During the Coast Guard hearings, she did not dare to speak to him. But she was aware of every move he made and she was aware that he was aware of her. That delicious suspense of sitting there and wondering if he would ever speak to her. Her first shock had been seeing him dressed up and noting happily that he knew how to slip that outdoor form into a well-cut suit. His feet looked enormous in cordovans and he wore a black pearl ring on the little finger of his right hand.

On the last day before she went on vacation, she was sitting outside the Port Authority building, waiting to meet the photographer for lunch, when Captain Wanderer approached her, bowed deeply, and, with otherworldly courtesy, said: "Miss Harper, under more happy circumstances, I would consider it my pleasure to take you to lunch. I'm sure you understand."

When she returned to the bureau, she wrote her story, ran it over the Teletype to the main office, and sat down at her typewriter and wrote a very honest note, which she mailed.

7/20/60

Dear Captain Wanderer:

Please excuse my brashness, but I am leaving for my vacation and will not see you again—therefore I do not have to worry about what you will think. I regret more than anything not being able to know you well. You are the kind of man I've always wanted to meet, but seemed to find only in books. (Trite.) Also you have the strongest hands, the most powerful face, and the most beautiful hair that I have ever seen. There. I've said it. I just wanted you to know.

Sincerely yours,
Halcyone Harper
(the eager beaver)

During her entire drive up the coast of Florida, Halcyone kept herself occupied by imagining the most intimate scenes between herself and Captain Carl Wanderer. By the time she stopped at a motel to spend the night, she had worked herself into a frenzy of imaginative sensations. She was sure that this man would have been the answer to all of her romantic wishes. And now she would never know.

But she was wrong. When she returned to the bureau two weeks later, she found a message to call the dockmaster at Port Everglades. Before she could call, Keith slouched over to her desk and said, "Well, back from the hills, ha! Want to go back to your old beat? The SS *Tempest*! Ha."

"You mean . . . you mean he's . . . I mean, it's still stuck?"

"No, they brought her in but she's being dry-docked. The Captain called you several times while you were away. You better get in touch with 'im. Might be something for us."

She never tired of him. He admitted her into his quarters and they sat across his writing table for hours, listening to a symphony on the huge shortwave radio, drinking pots of black coffee, which he told her had to be made just right with a pinch of salt and dry mustard among the grounds. He told her about India and measured her foot with a pencil, promising he would send her a pair of sandals the next time he went to Bombay. He spoke of Alexandria and Hong Kong and San Francisco in the same breath. His face, a study in mobility, fascinated her, and once again she was absolutely positive. She was in love. He regarded her with respect and called her "Miss" until she finally grew angry.

Finally, on the last dark night when there was no moon, she kissed him while they stood on the bridge. (He had been explaining to her how the first mate had mistaken the port for Fowey's Rock.) After that, they went below and drank half a bottle of brandy and he put her to bed in his bunk and made love to her with the hunger of a man who has been at sea for a long time.

She never should have come to New Orleans. And the rest of it all boils down to this: Is it better to leave something unfinished?

The way he first looked when he walked in that room in New Orleans. Like a fish out of water, too tall for the door, too loud for such a small room.

The way he added up the check with his finger.

The way she grew sleepy and just wanted to sleep.

The night in Brennan's when he mispronounced a word.

And when she got back to Miami International. Walking down the ramp to the parking lot, still tasting too many oysters, still smelling a surfeit of his tobacco mixture, still recoiling at those homely phrases. "God," she said aloud to the whining jet overhead, "I'm glad that's over."

He wrote her many letters from New Orleans. And from Galveston and once from Hong Kong, long troubled introspective letters, letters that can only be written by a lonely man, surrounded on all sides by water. At first, she read parts of them and felt guilty and embarrassed. Finally the time came when she could, quite quickly and without any feeling at all, slip the unopened bulk into the garbage can and forget the whole episode.[5]

"My name's Halcyone Harper," she screamed, teetering in her spectators in the stern of the pilot boat, cursing the *Tempest* for being so high. "From the *Star*." She paused to let the name sink in, but Wanderer was simply looking at her patiently, legs poised for retreat up that ladder and into the cabin.

"Yes, Miss." His voice was unbelievably deep.

"Do you have any comment on . . . on what has happened, Captain?"

"*No, Miss.*"

"Well, you'll at least admit you're stuck, won't you?" she yelled up angrily.

"Can't deny that." He sucked on his pipe. "Now, if you'll excuse me,

---

5. Gail stops again and advises herself to rewrite her story. "Correct narrative," she says, "leave out parts which you found boring, don't worry about other stories and how they are written. The idea is here. It just has to be smoothed and loved and pampered. The dirty work is over."

Miss, I know you're a real eager beaver and all that . . ." His words stung her, but before she had a retort framed, he was agilely taking the ladder rungs two at a time, and finally disappeared around the bridge.[6]

Later, as the pilot boat plowed back to shore, transporting her and the representative from Lloyd's (they regarded each other sullenly, enemies on purpose), she saw the Captain peering through binoculars, his elbows resting on the rail of the bridge.

Deliberately she hoisted her skirt up, so the lens could take in a nice firm calf, caramel colored, and getting farther and farther away every minute.

Note: In January 1962, while housed in Denmark, Gail began writing a story titled "Halcyone and the Lighthouse" that had little to do with the Captain Wanderer story. It featured a young woman trapped in a marriage in the Florida Keys. Her salvation seemed connected to painting a picture of the historic local lighthouse. Renamed "The Gall Crab" and then "Gull Key," the novel was completed, but not published.

"It'll keep you busy till you get pregnant"—and she sets out to paint.

Every day she goes down there and paints and has uplifting thoughts. When she finishes it (in the middle of May, when it is getting hot), she hangs it in the living room at Evan's insistence and he invites Thelma and Bunny over for a drink. Thelma praises her, comparing it to her own attempt, and suggests she enter it in the island art show.

Sometimes, late in the night, she would go into the kitchen to get a glass of water and stand by the dark window listening to the sounds of the crickets, and sometimes she would hear the distant blast of a steamship

6. Gail has removed the description "those magnificent brown legs rippling with motion," included in the first gush of writing.

passing around the key and she would experience a feeling which she could not put into words . . . it was something like the feeling of missing a friend or a train by five minutes . . . or like feeling the silent walls of the brain coral[7] closing slowly above her head.

She had married Evan because she thought she should be married by twenty-three. He was the type of man one picks for a husband: gentle, hard-working, healthy; only later did she have intimations that he was unimaginative and . . .

But some nights in August and September of that year, when the still heat made her restless, she would lie awake for some minutes, hearing the dry clacking of the palm fronds, which sounded so much like rain. Then she would climb out of bed and walk barefooted over the cool terrazzo floors to the kitchen to get a drink of water. Standing by the window, a crepuscular square sketched with shadows of her trailing arbutus, she would listen to the chirring of the cicadas and press her palms gently, inquisitively against her swollen belly. Sometimes she would hear the single blast of a steamship rounding the tip of Gull Key and she would experience a feeling she could never put into words. It was something like missing a friend or a train by five minutes . . . or like feeling the silent walls of the brain coral closing slowly above her head.

The trip up the Florida coast she would always remember as the most memorable of her life, plodding through interminable stoplights, heat, and Howard Johnsons until she reached the turnpike.[8] Then three solid hours of letting go, feeling the small car whipped by the wind, urging it on, 65, 70, 80, guiding it over rims, around curves, past slower cars.

She stopped at four in the afternoon in Daytona Beach, her father's

7. Brain coral closes around a female gall crab after she lays her eggs in the coral, trapping her forever.

8. "Gull Key" shared the south Florida environment with "Halcyone and the Lighthouse."

old haunt. She could still hear him saying in the resonant lazy voice, "Think I'll take a couple of weeks off and drive down to Daytona." It was his answer to the unsolvable problems, his escape hatch. Then when he got to Daytona and became properly browned and soaked in sun and in whiskey, he would announce: "Think I'll get back to Carolina. That's what I need, the good clean air. I've had enough of all this falseness." Perhaps he found his answers somewhere between Florida and home, on a flat, narrow road through the unexciting territory of Georgia, where an unmarked patrol car hid behind every bush, or in some drowsy small South Carolina town while he was waiting for a red light. God only knew. God would have to know. No one else did.

She bought a book (a hardcover novel she paid too much for) and ordered tea in a small elegant "tea shoppe" with an antique showroom in the rear. She made a conscious effort to sip the tea, to make a ritual of it as the English did, to read some pages in her book. But her new awareness made her nervous in a good sort of way—not the nervousness of a woman waiting alone in a dark house, but the nervousness of a diver about to spring. She kept thinking, "I'm free, dammit, I'm free.

"I got to do both: I looked behind the curtain and still escaped."

Hurriedly, she scraped back her chair and walked over to the waitress to pay the check. She wanted to be out on the open highways again, to open all the windows and let her hair fly wild as she drove, to stop at gas stations and slouch around the Coke machine, drinking a Coke and smelling the wonderful raw, chemical smell of gas being pumped into her car, to flex her bare toes in her sandals and make small talk with the garage men.

"Sure is getting hot again for April . . ."

"Sure is . . ."

"Fine little automobile you got here, Miss. Tell me, how many miles does she really do on a gallon?"

"Well, you know the advertisements. If it says 30, you can count on 20 . . . if you're lucky."

"Ha! Ain't nobody gonna fool a clever girl like you, eh?"

"Well, I bought it, though, didn't I?"

"Well . . . still, it's a great little car, fine little automobile. Like to have one myself . . . Check the oil and water?"

"No, that's okay. How much do I owe you?"

"Stop in on your way back down."

"I won't be back down."

"Oh . . ."

"But thanks anyway. Have a good summer."

"Right you are. Same to you. And . . . good luck."[9]

She drove out onto the road again and managed for the first time to get through Jacksonville without missing any turns. The sun was going down when she reached the outskirts of the city. She would stop at the motel in Clayton, right over the line. That is, if she felt like it. That was the whole thing. She was free to stop wherever and whenever it suited her.

"And it's going to stay that way," she said aloud to nobody, pressing her toes on the accelerator to underscore her vow.

Note: On March 10, 1962, Gail was still calling her heroine Halcyone. By July, the name had changed to Bentley. At this point, she places Bentley in danger of having an affair, and she inserts a Florida traffic scene into Bentley's unconsummated rendezvous with her seducer. In the next scene, Gail applies a frequently rewritten drive up the Florida coast to her new ending. Bentley takes flight from her husband, Evan, who, after bouts of disillusionment and rage, has recommended that she visit her mother in the mountains. Gail had advised herself to make Evan as sympathetic as possible. She places that softening into Bentley's mind by having her telephone him just before crossing the Florida state line.

She drove faster when she came in sight of the Miami River Bridge. But this just wasn't her day. When she was almost within fifty yards of it, the

---

9. This conversation went as is into the final manuscript of "Gull Key."

warning bells started clanging and the barriers went down. "Oh God!" she cried, exasperated. "Oh God, how can it . . . how can everything be so filthy all at once!"

The drawbridge raised slowly, creaking and groaning, and she looked down at the brackish river to see her enemy. A smooth, expensive yacht waving a little American flag with four people wearing shorts sitting under a deck umbrella sipping drinks. "I hope you all four rot in hell," Bentley said through clenched teeth. It was almost eleven.

After the bridge, she was caught by virtually every red light between the Dupont Plaza Hotel and the Miami Beach street on which he lived. She did not have the right change when she drove into the pay-yourself toll stall on the beach causeway and had to back out (to the accompaniment of more horn blowing by disgruntled drivers behind) and drive into the second stall from the end, marked "Change" and manned by a uniformed nonentity who mechanically gave her back a quarter and a dime, saying, "Y'all come back soon."

She hung up on him, staring a minute at her own hand on the impersonal black instrument. Then, automatically, she felt in the refund box just in case her coins had been returned by mistake. She hastened out into the evening and got back into her car and drove back onto the highway. She could reach Waycross by dark if she hurried, and stop there for the night in a friendly little motor court near to the road where she could lie in bed and hear the trucks purring by all night long. Waycross wasn't very far into Georgia from Florida, really, but at least it was a new state and that would be the start.

Note: Gail let Bentley find some solace in her stepfather, who echoes what Gail's friend B. had written to Gail. "Gull Key" concludes, in fact, with one of B.'s lines that Gail had taken to heart: "So rises the indestructible pyramid." It refers to the process by which the heroine slowly builds a personal foundation that will not weaken as she fulfills herself in life.

Dear Bentley:

When I received your letter, I had a kind of a split reaction. I was sorry that you and Evan aren't getting on (naturally), but on the other hand I must confess that my pride was considerably restored when I realized that you had, for the first time since we've known each other, actually come to me for advice. It almost scares me. This is what I've waited for for years. I used to have it all bottled up and packaged for you, but you just never seemed to be in the market.

If I tell you what I would do, it might not work and you'd blame me, or it might work and then you'd feel shortchanged because you couldn't claim all the credit and you'd blame me . . .

Are you sure that you didn't make one mistake? The mistake of saying to yourself, "I do means I quit. You take over and entertain me for the next years." . . .[10]

It's kind of like building a pyramid. The only difficulty about pyramids is (shades of my old Tech days!) that the higher it gets, the steeper the slope becomes. (Is this true?) . . .

So, all this runaround and I can see you sitting there reading this letter, saying, "But he hasn't told me the answer yet." I've gone on and must confess I've enjoyed writing this letter. Why do people write letters anyway? True, this one was ordered, but one does love seeing oneself on paper. But back to the so-called purpose of this letter. You ask: what to do. And I must answer, the *one time you've come to me* for an answer, neither I nor anyone else can help you.

10. Here, and in the next quote, Gail gives her friend B.'s words to Bentley's stepfather.

APPENDIX 2

LITERARY INFLUENCES IN THE WORK OF GAIL GODWIN

In addition to responding to the ways that books resonate with their lives, aspiring writers register suggestions about how they might fashion their own work and be part of a literary tradition. Gail's journals reveal the following influences:

PRE-1961	Classic poems: Alfred, Lord Tennyson, *Idylls of the King;* John Keats, "Ode on a Grecian Urn"; Edwin Arlington Robinson, "Richard Cory"
	Thomas Wolfe, *Look Homeward, Angel*
	Jane Austen, *Pride and Prejudice* and *Emma*
	George Eliot, *Middlemarch*
	Gustave Flaubert, *Madame Bovary*
AUGUST 1961	Stories in leading literary magazines—*Esquire, Atlantic, Mademoiselle, New Yorker*
SEPTEMBER 1961	J. D. Salinger, *Franny and Zooey*
OCTOBER 1961	Søren Kierkegaard, *Either/Or*
NOVEMBER 1961	Isak Dinesen (Karen Blixen), *Winter's Tales*

DECEMBER 1961   Lawrence Durrell, *The Alexandria Quartet*

                       Thomas Wolfe, *The Web and the Rock* and *Of Time and the River*

JANUARY 1962   Ray Bradbury, *The Golden Apples of the Sun*

MARCH 1962   Aldous Huxley, *Point Counter Point*

MARCH 1962   Philip Roth, short stories; and later, *Letting Go*

NOVEMBER 1962   D. H. Lawrence, *Women in Love*

FEBRUARY 1963   Henry James, *The Portrait of a Lady* and *The Golden Bowl.*

APRIL 1963   T. S. Eliot, *Four Quartets* and *The Sacred Wood*

JULY 1963   C. G. Jung, *Memories, Dreams, Reflections*

Writers and works that have provided a counterpoint:

PRE-1961   James Joyce, *Ulysses*

SEPTEMBER 1962   Franz Kafka, *Diaries*

JANUARY 1962   Hortense Calisher, *False Entry*

MARCH 1962   Reynolds Price, *A Long and Happy Life*

SEPTEMBER 1962   Marcel Proust, *Swann's Way*

NOVEMBER 1962   Samuel Beckett, *Happy Days*

APRIL 1963   Albert Camus, *The Outsider* (*The Stranger*)

MAY 1963   Doris Lessing, *The Golden Notebook*

JUNE 1963   James Agee, *A Death in the Family*

APPENDIX 3

Important Dates in the Life of Gail Godwin, 1937–1963

Born in Birmingham, Alabama, June 18, 1937, to Mose Winston Godwin and Kathleen Krahenbuhl Godwin. Parents divorce after a short period.

With mother, moves in with widowed grandmother, Edna Rogers Krahenbuhl, in Weaverville, North Carolina, 1939; and then Asheville, North Carolina, 1941.

Kathleen Godwin marries Frank Cole, 1948; they have three children, Franchelle, Tommy, and Rebel.

Attends St. Genevieve-of-the-Pines, in Asheville, 1944–1952.

Attends Peace College, in Raleigh, North Carolina, 1955–1957.

Attains B.A. in journalism from University of North Carolina at Chapel Hill, 1959.

Works as reporter for the *Miami Herald*, 1959–1960.

Marries *Herald* photographer Douglas Kennedy, December 10, 1960; divorces in May 1961.

Boards SS *Oklahoma* for trip to Europe, October 6, 1961.

Arrives in Copenhagen, October 22, 1961; takes up lodging with the Høiaas family, November 9.

Receives letter of employment from U.S. Travel Service, London office, January 18, 1962.

Travels to Spain, January 24, 1962; and to Las Palmas, January 31.

Begins work on the novel that will become "Gull Key" (unpublished), March 14, 1962.

Arrives in London March 20, 1962; rents room from the Wests at 31 Tregunter Road in South Kensington.

Begins work at U.S. Travel Service, April 11, 1962.

Moves to 21 Old Church Street in Chelsea with Wests and fellow boarders, August 1, 1962.

Stella Anderson arrives in London to stay at Wests', September 12, 1962.

The Cuban Missile Crisis begins with President John F. Kennedy's blockade of Cuba, October 23, 1962.

Begins reading D. H. Lawrence, October 30, 1962.

Moves to own apartment at 5 Green Street in Mayfair, November 14, 1962.

Begins story "Father Flynn" (later incorporated into "Mourning"), February 9, 1963, on the fifth anniversary of father's death by suicide.

Moves out of 5 Green Street apartment to move back in with Wests at 21 Old Church Street, May 19, 1963.

The Wests relate the story of Mr. Bedford, June 22, 1963.

Begins "The Illumined Moment—and Consequences," the story that will become "An Intermediate Stop," July 13, 1963.

Books by Gail Godwin

The Perfectionists. New York: Harper & Row, 1970.

Glass People. New York: Knopf, 1972.

The Odd Woman. New York: Knopf, 1974.

Dream Children: Stories. New York: Knopf, 1976.

Violet Clay. New York: Knopf, 1978.

A Mother and Two Daughters. New York: Viking, 1982.

Mr. Bedford and the Muses. New York: Viking, 1983. A novella and five stories.

The Finishing School. New York: Viking, 1984.

A Southern Family. New York: Morrow, 1987.

Father Melancholy's Daughter. New York: Morrow, 1991.

The Good Husband. New York: Ballantine, 1994.

Evensong. New York: Ballantine, 1999.

Heart: A Personal Journey Through Its Myths and Meanings. New York: Morrow, 2001.

Evenings at Five. New York: Ballantine, 2003.

Queen of the Underworld. New York: Random House, 2006.

INDEX

GAIL GODWIN is a three-time National Book Award finalist and the bestselling author of twelve critically acclaimed novels, including *A Mother and Two Daughters, The Odd Woman, Violet Clay,* and *Father Melancholy's Daughter.*

She has received a Guggenheim Fellowship, a National Endowment for the Arts grant for both fiction and libretto writing, and the Award in Literature from the American Academy of Arts and Letters.

She has written libretti for ten musical works with the composer Robert Starer. Currently she is writing her next novel, *The Red Nun,* and preparing *The Making of a Writer,* volume II, with Rob Neufeld.

ROB NEUFELD is a librarian and a book reviewer for the *Asheville Citizen-Times.* He directs the Together We Read program for western North Carolina.

ABOUT THE TYPE

This book was set in Walbaum, a typeface designed in 1810 by German punch cutter J. E. Walbaum. Walbaum's type is more French than German in appearance. Like Bodoni, it is a classical typeface, yet its openness and slight irregularities give it a human, romantic quality.